CANTONESE
PHRASEBOOK

Kam Y Lau

Cantonese phrasebook
3rd edition – August 1999

Published by
Lonely Planet Publications Pty Ltd, ABN 36 005 607 983
90 Maribyrnong St, Footscray, Victoria 3011, Australia

Lonely Planet Offices
Australia Locked Bag 1, Footscray, Victoria 3011
USA 150 Linden St, Oakland CA 94607
UK 10a Spring Place, London NW5 3BH
France 1 rue du Dahomey, 75011 Paris

Cover illustration
Dragon Me Down by Mic Looby

ISBN 0 86442 645 3

text © Lonely Planet Publications Pty Ltd 1999
cover illustration © Mic Looby

Printed by The Bookmaker International Ltd
Printed in China

ABOUT THE AUTHOR

Kam Lau was born and educated in Hong Kong. After obtaining his degree from the Chinese department at the Chinese University of Hong Kong, he went on to further studies in Japan. There, he obtained his Masters degree, and a PhD candidature from Waseda University. He has worked in both the electronics field and the tourism industry for many years. Kam has also taught Japanese and Cantonese for more than two decades. He is multilingual, speaking Cantonese, English, Mandarin, Japanese and Teo-Chew (a Chinese dialect). He is also the author of Lonely Planet's Cantonese Phrasebook editions 1 and 2, and Lonely Planet's Japanese Phrasebook edition 2.

FROM THE AUTHOR

I would like to thank all of my family, Grace, Sally, Sophia and Honoria, for their love and support. Thank you also to HKTA, Mr K H Wong and Ms Sheila Chan for supplying useful material for this phrasebook. Thanks also to Mr S L Yeung for providing much invaluable information regarding travelling for disabled people.

FROM THE PUBLISHER

This book was put together in an atmosphere of harmonious and loving cooperation. Those involved have all had their lives changed by the experience. They include Joanne Adams who laid out the book and cover; Olivier Breton, editor; Peter D'Onghia and Sally Steward who proofed and oversaw the whole beautiful process; Mic Looby who did illustrations and cover art. Patrick Marris helped with layout. Finally thanks to Dan Levin the fontmaster and Danny Tedeschi for his technical support.

CONTENTS

INTRODUCTION

Cantonese is one of the five major dialects of the Chinese language (the mother tongue often referred to as *hanyu* by the Chinese) although it is spoken by only 6% of the *hanyu*-speaking population worldwide. The five dialects are putonghua (Mandarin, the official language of China), *yue* (Cantonese), *wu*, *min* and *kejia*. These dialects are, however, sufficiently different from each other to be more commonly referred to as individual languages.

Although *putonghua* is the official Chinese language, it has a history of only around 700 to 800 years, compared to Cantonese which has a history of over 2000 years. Cantonese has retained most of the characteristics of the classic *hanyu*, such as the clipped sound of words ending with -p, -t and -k, and the -m. It is also the only dialect in *hanyu* to have retained its complete series of tones.

The major Cantonese-speaking areas include most of Guangdong (Canton), the southern part of Guangxi, Hong Kong and Macau. It is the language of most overseas Chinese.

Cantonese has been enriched over time by the addition of many words from other languages, resulting from centuries of contact with many European and South-East Asian countries. Canton, known to the Chinese as Guangzhou, used to be the place where Cantonese was considered to be at its purest, but due to the influence of Hong Kong's media and pop music throughout the Cantonese-speaking areas, Hong Kong Cantonese has become the more acceptable, or even official, standard of speaking. Basically now, Cantonese can be described as an old language with a new life.

It's hard to write every word spoken because Cantonese is an oral dialect. Many of the words used are slang and cannot be written. However the language that is written is written in the same script as Mandarin.

This phrasebook is based on contemporary Hong Kong Cantonese, although vocabulary specific to mainland China is included, and all words and phrases included are polite and colloquial – the sort of words you'll encounter as you travel.

INTRODUCTION

The word 'Chinese' used in this book means all things Chinese, including Cantonese, while the word 'Cantonese' means specifically all things Cantonese, or from a Cantonese-speaking background.

ABBREVIATIONS USED IN THIS BOOK

col   colloquial
gen   general
for   formal
adj   adjective

PRONUNCIATION 發音

The pronunciation described in this chapter is based on the Cantonese spoken in Hong Kong, as this is increasingly the most commonly heard. Some tones, vowels, consonants and vocabulary vary within the different Cantonese-speaking regions however, most Cantonese-speaking people are able to understand Hong Kong Cantonese.

If you're unsure of the pronunciation, ask a local to pronounce the words for you. Even if they don't understand the phonetic system used in this book, most will be able to read the Chinese characters. Hearing the correct sounds and relating them to the characters is obviously the best way to learn. If you have difficulty getting your message across, you can try pointing to the appropriate Chinese characters.

Younger people nowadays tend not to pronounce certain consonants, or they change one consonant to another. For example, ng- is often ignored or not pronounced at all. Thus ngō jàu (Australia) becomes ō jàu and ngóh (I) becomes óh Another common practice is the dropping of the consonant win kw- and gw; as in gwóng dùng wá (Cantonese language) which becomes góng dùng wá and kwōng (a mine) becoming kōng Finally, young people often mix the n- and the l; as in núi (female) which becomes lúi (travel), and ngóh ngòi néi (I love you), becoming óh òi léi

TONES 聲調

Tone is the decisive factor when judging whether your Cantonese is good or not. It's also the most difficult aspect of the language to learn – which will probably come as no surprise.

In total, there are more than 10 different tones in Cantonese, including the variations. However, they may be simplified into six basic tones.

This phrasebook adopts a tonic sign system in which the six basic tones are described in terms of a pitch scale of one to five.

PRONUNCIATION

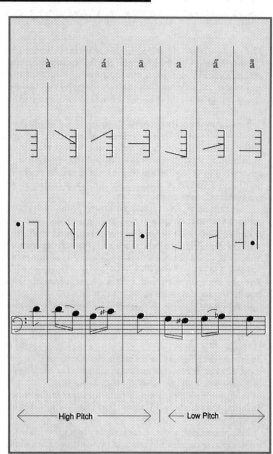

Level five on the pitch scale is the highest and level one the lowest. The basic tones are divided into two groups: high pitch and low pitch. The symbols used in this phrasebook are similar to the existing pinyin system, where the symbol represents the tone. (see box page 12)

High Pitch Group 陰聲調

Tone number one has the highest pitch and is given a five on the pitch scale. Words with the first tone have either a clipped sound see page 14), a long, lingering pitch or a sound that drops slightly. These words are indicated by the symbol (`) on the first vowel.

The second tone starts on three on the pitch scale, and rises to five. Words with the second tone are marked by a rising symbol (´) on the first vowel.

The third is a levelled tone and has a clipped sound, or it could have a lingering sound. Words with the third tone are shown by the sign (˜) on the first vowel.

fòo	fóo	fõo
husband	tiger	wealthy

Low Pitch Group 陽聲調

The fourth tone starts on two on the pitch scale and drops to one, the lowest tone. Words with the fourth tone have no symbols. The fifth tone also starts on two, but rises to three on the pitch level. Words with the fifth tone are marked by the sign (ˇ) on the first vowel.

The sixth tone is a levelled tone. It has a clipped sound, or it may stay on level two on the pitch scale. Words with the sixth tone are shown by the symbol (¨) over the first vowel.

foo	fŏo	föo
to lean	woman	owe

PRONUNCIATION

Clipped Pitch 入聲

Cantonese words ending with the consonants -p -t and -k have a clipped sound, similar to words with a silent letter in English, such as the word 'climb'. The silent letter is on the verge of being pronounced but is stopped intentionally before a sound is made.

For example, although màt(what) and màn(mosquito) start on the same pitch, the endings are different. The màt has a higher but short, clipped sound, whereas màn has the same pitch but the sound is sustained for a longer period of time. Words ending with -p -t or -k normally only belong to the first, third and sixth tones.

Although the ending -m isn't a clipped sound – because it prompts a mouth-closing action and is stopped intentionally before the -m sound is made – it behaves like one.

CONSONANTS   聲母

The following is a list of consonants you will come across in phonetic Cantonese; most you are already familiar with.

b, ch, d, f, g, gw, h, j, k, kw, l, m, n, ng, p, s, t, w, y

VOWELS   韻母

Different text books adopt different systems when dealing with vowels in Cantonese. In the author's view, the system used in Sidney Lau's textbook, *Elementary Cantonese* (Government Printer, Hong Kong), is the most appropriate system for this phrasebook.

There are many variations when pronouncing English. The sounds described here are based on standard British English in order to provide some uniformity. In the following list, a is a short sound and the aa is long.

Vowel Combination	Sound in English	Example		Meaning
a	rather	fà	花	flower
aai	find	gàai	街	street
ai	lie	gài	雞	chicken
aau	loud	bàau	包	bun
au	now	chàu	秋	autumn
aam	farm	sàam	三	three
am	come	sàm	心	heart
aan	aunt	sàan	山	mountain
an	fun	fàn	分	minute
aang	arn+ng	sàang	生	birth
ang	sung	dàng	燈	lamp
aap	carp	tāap	塔	tower
ap	cup	sàp	濕	wet
aat	art	bāat	八	eight
at	cut	yàt	一	one
aak	ark	bāak	百	hundred
ak	luck	bàk	北	north
e	let	chè	車	car
ek	neck	tēk	踢	to kick
eng	length	gēng	鏡	mirror
ei	pay	fèi	飛	to fly
euh	fur	hèuh	靴	boot
eung	'urn'+'ng'	hèung	香	fragrance
euk	jerk	gēuk	腳	leg
i	me	sì	獅	lion
iu	'ee'+'ew'	sìu	燒	to burn
im	him	tìm	添	to add
in	in	tìn	天	sky
ing	king	sìng	星	star

PRONUNCIATION

Vowel Combination	Sound in English	Example		Meaning
ip	lip	jĭp	接	to receive
it	it	jĭt	節	festival
ik	sick	sìk	識	to know
o	go	dò	刀	knife
oh	or	sòh	梳	comb
oi	toy	hòi	開	to open
ok	lock	gwōk	國	country
on	on	gòn	干	dry
ong	long	fòng	方	square
oo	food	fòo	夫	husband
ooi	'oo'+'ee'	bòoi	杯	cup
oon	moon	bòon	搬	to move
oot	foot	fōot	闊	wide
ot	hot	gōt	割	to cut
ue	like 'ew'	yúe	魚	fish
uen	like 'ewn'	jùen	磚	brick
uet	flute	sūet	雪	snow
ui	'oy'+'ee'	kùi	區	area
un	very short 'oo' + 'n'	chùn	春	spring
ut	put	chùt	出	out
ung	very short 'oo' + 'ng'	jùng	鐘	bell
uk	cook	jùk	竹	bamboo
m	mmm	m	唔	not
ng	rang	nǧ	五	five

Here are some sayings which use all the tones.

tèng góng fōh; chai séung hōk   聽講課齊上學

'to listen, to lecture, lessons; together, to attend, school' – this literally means 'going to school together and listen to the lectures'.

jùng góng ngō; cham mǎai mǎai   中港澳尋買賣

China, Hong Kong, Macau; to seek, to buy, to sell – this literally means China, Hong Kong and Macau joining forces to attract businesses.

gùng héi! gùng héi!   恭喜! 恭喜!

Congratulations! Congratulations! You should now have no trouble speaking Cantonese.

As mentioned above the consonant and vowel system used here is seen to be the most appropriate for this book. Compared to other systems this system can be seen as the most comprehensive. Following are the comparison tables for those who were familiar with others Cantonese phonetics systems.

PRONUNCIATION

CPH	*Cantonese Phrasebook*
HUN	*Cantonese Sounds and Tones*, Parker Huang, Yale University
LAM	*Functional Cantonese*, Martha Lam & Stanley Po
LAU	*Elementary Cantonese*, Sidney Lau
NKM	*Cantonese Dictionary*, Nakamura
RAO	*Cantonese Dictionary*, Rao Bing Cai
IPA	*International Phonetic Alphabet*

	CPH	HUN*	LAM	LAU	NKM	RAO
High, High Falling, High Clipped	à	āà	å	1	ā à	1
High Rising	á	á	á	2	á	2
Level, Level Clipped	ā	a	ā	3	a	3
Low Falling	a	àh	à	4	à	4
Low Rising	ǎ	áh	ǎ	5	á	5
Low Level, Low Clipped	ã	ah	ā	6	a	6

HUN* Words beginning with m, n, ng in the upper-tone group are indentified by underlining _ to differentiate m, n, and ng from m, n, ng in the lower-tone group.

PRONUNCIATION

IPA	CPH	HUN	LAM	LAU	NKM	RAO
p	b	b	b	b	b	b
ts', tʃʻ	ch	ch	ch	ch	ch	c,q
t	d	d	d	d	d	d
f	f	f	f	f	f	f
k	g	g	g	g	g	g
kw	gw	gw	gw	gw	gw	gu
h	h	h	h	h	h	h
ts, tʃ	j	j	j	j	j	z,j
k	k	k	k	k	k	k
kw	kw	kw	kw	kw	kw	ku
l	l	l	l	l	l	l
m	m	m	m	m	m	m
n	n	n	n	n	n	n
ŋ	ng	ng	ng	ng	ng	ng
p	p	p	p	p	p	p
s, ʃ	s	s	s	s	s	s,x
t	t	t	t	t	t	t
w	w	w	w	w	w	w
j	y		y	y	y	y

CPH	HUN	LAM	LAU	NKM	RAO
a	a	a	a	a	a
aai	aai	aai	aai	aai	ai
ai	ai	ai	ai	ai	ei
aau	aau	aau	aau	ao	ao
au	au	au	au	au	eo
aam	aam	aam	aam	arm	am
am	am	am	am	am	em
aan	aan	aan	aan	arn	an
an	an	an	an	an	en

CPH	HUN	LAM	LAU	NKM	RAO
aang	aang	aang	aang	arng	ang
ang	ang	ang	ang	ang	eng
aap	aap	aap	aap	arp	ab
ap	ap	ap	ap	ap	eb
aat	aat	aat	aat	art	ad
at	at	at	at	at	ed
aak	aak	aak	aak	ark	ag
ak	ak	ak	ak	ak	eg
e	e	e	e	e	é
ek	ek	ek	ek	ek	ég
eng	eng	eng	eng	eng	éng
ei	ei	ei	ei	ei	éi
euh	eu	euh	euh	eo	ê
eung	eung	eung	eung	eong	êng
euk	euk	euk	euk	eok	êg
i	i	i	i	i	i
iu	iu	iu	iu	iu	iu
im	im	im	im	im	im
in	in	in	in	in	in
ing	ing	ing	ing	ing	ing
ip	ip	ip	ip	ip	ib
it	it	it	it	it	it
ik	ik	ik	ik	ik	ig
o	ou	o	o	ou	ou
oh	o	oh	oh	o	o
oi	oi	oi	oi	oi	oi
ok	ok	ok	ok	ok	og
on	on	on	on	on	on
ong	ong	ong	ong	ong	ong
oo	u	oo	oo	u	u
ooi	ui	ooi	ooi	ui	ui

CPH	HUN	LAM	LAU	NKM	RAO
oon	un	oon	oon	un	un
oot	ut	oot	oot	ut	ut
ot	ot	ot	ot	ot	od
ue	yu	ue	ue	yu	u
uen	yun	uen	uen	yun	ün
uet	yut	uet	uet	uet	üd
ui	eui	ui	ui	eui	êi
un	eun	un	un	eun	ên
ut	eut	ut	ut	ut	êd
ung	ung	ung	ung	ung	ung
uk	uk	uk	uk	uk	ug
m	m	m	m	m	m
ng	ng	ng	ng	ng	ng

GRAMMAR

語法

The Chinese script (including Cantonese) is fundamentally different from many other scripts. Every character bears its own meaning as well as its own sound.

SENTENCE STRUCTURE

句式

The word order in sentences is very similar to the English order of subject-verb-object. The function of words relies on their position in a sentence. For example, the simple sentence 'I love you' follows exactly the same order in Cantonese, ngőh ngői néi and, like English, would take on a different meaning if the position of the words was changed.

ARTICLES

冠詞

Cantonese has no equivalent to the English articles, 'a', 'an' and 'the'. Words meaning 'one' and 'this/that' are used, and often a classifier word, such as bóon is required (see page 255). For example,

I want a book.	ngőh yīu yàt bóon súe (lit: I want one [classifier] book)
I want the book.	ngőh yīu nì/góh bóon sùe (lit: I want this/that [classifier] book)

NOUNS

名詞

Nouns do not have gender or numerical values. Usually nouns exist as single characters, though they may also exist as two or more characters. A single character noun, made up of two words, is the most common.

ADJECTIVES   形容詞

Adjectives in Cantonese are normally placed in front of the noun, with some exceptions. Sometimes, the possessive word gēmay be placed between the adjective and the noun; however, the meaning doesn't change.

good	hó
good book	hó sùe
good book	hó gē sùe

Comparisons 比較

good	hó
better	hó dì; gāng hó
the best	jūi hó
cheap	peng
cheaper	peng dì; gāng peng
the cheapest	jūi peng

PRONOUNS   代名詞

I/me	ngőh	we/us	ngőh dēi
you	néi	you(plural)	néi dēi
he/she/him/her	kűi	they/them	kűi dēi
this	nì gōh	that	góh gōh
these	nì dì	those	góh dì

VERBS   動詞

The usage of verbs in Cantonese isn't nearly as complicated and confusing as it can be in English. The verb remains the same regardless of tense; it doesn't change with past, present or future. It also stays the same regardless of the pronoun used (see page 23).

I drank tea (yesterday).	ngőh (kam yăt) yám cha
I drink tea.	ngőh yám cha

GRAMMAR

To Be 確定式

The verb 'to be' is simply hāi It's normally used when two nouns are linked.

I am American.   ngőh hāi méi gwōk yan
                            (lit: I hāiAmerica person)

To Have 有無

The words yáuand mődenote 'have' and 'not have' respectively. They are placed in front of the object.

I have a pen.   ngőh yáu yàt jì bàt
                            (lit: I have one [classifier] pen)

I don't have a cup.   ngőh mő bòoi

TENSE   時態

Tense is not indicated by the verb as it is in English. Additional time words such as 'yesterday', 'tomorrow', 'last year' and so on, are needed to indicate time/tense.

I drink tea.   ngőh yám cha
I drank tea (just now).   ngőh (tau sìn) yám cha
I drank tea (yesterday).   ngőh (kam yàt) yám cha

GRAMMAR

USEFUL VERBS

to call	ngāai	嗌	to look for	wán	搵
to carry	nìng	擰	to press	gǎm	撳
to do	jǒ	做	to see	tái	睇
to drink	yám	飲	to speak	góng	講
to eat	sĭk	食	to stand	kéi	企
to give	béi	俾	to trick	ngàak	呃

The word jóh, placed straight after a verb, indicates that the action is completed.

I have drunk tea.	ngőh yám jóh cha
	(lit: I drink jóh tea)
I went.	ngőh hūi jóh
	(lit: I go jóh)

The word wóoi, placed immediately in front of the verb, denotes intention as expressed in English by the words 'am going to' or 'will'.

| I will go. | ngőh wóoi hūi |

Placed after a verb, the word gán means that the action of the verb is being carried out.

| I'm going. | ngőh hūi gán |

COMMANDS   命令式

In a positive command, you simply have to emphasise the verb:

Go!	hūi!
Sit!	chóh!
Look!	tái!
Come here!	gwōh lei!

You may also add chéng, which means 'please', in front of the verb to make it a more polite and gentle command.

| Please sit down. | chéng chóh |
| Please come in. | chéng yắp lei |

For a negative command, you have to add m jún, meaning 'not allow to', in front of the verb.

| Don't go! | m jún hūi! |
| Don't sit! | m jún chóh! |

Sometimes, instead of m jún, you will often hear the colloquial word mắi, which means 'don't'.

| Don't move! | mắi yùk! |

NEGATIVES 否定式

Simply put m in front of the verb or adjective to make them negative.

| (I'm) not buying. | (ngőh) m mǎai |
| Not pretty | m lēng |

YES & NO 正反式

'Yes' is indicated by the word hǎi and 'No'(not+yes) by m hǎi.

Sometimes you might use hó, which means, 'okay', 'yes' or 'good', and m hó, meaning the opposite. The word ngàam means 'correct' or 'right', while m ngàam means 'incorrect' or 'wrong'.

QUESTIONS 發問

There are basically three types of questions in Cantonese:

• The first type is a positive/negative or a yes/no question. These can be used with verbs or adjectives. The word ā is usually found at the end of the question.

Are you going to ...?	něi hūi m hūi ... ā?
	(lit: you go not go ... ā)
Are you buying?	něi mǎai m mǎai ā?
	(lit: you buy not buy ā)
Are you a student?	něi hǎi m hǎi hǒk sàng ā?
	(lit: you be not be student ā)
Is it pretty?	lēng m lēng ā?
	(lit: pretty not pretty ā)

• The second type concerns what are known in English as 'question words': 'what', 'when', 'why' etc. These questions need specific answers. They are formed by simply adding the question word to the front of the sentence or at the end. For beginners, the simplest way is to say the topic, then add the question word at the end.

GRAMMAR

| Where is the library? | to sùe gwóon! bìn dõ ā?; |
| | to sùe gwóon hái bìn dõ ā? |

How?	dím yéung ā?	點樣呀?
What?	màt yế ā?	乜嘢呀?
When?	géi si ā?	幾時呀?
Where?	bìn dõ ā?	邊度呀?
Who?	bìn gõh ā?	邊個呀?
Who(polite)?	bìn wái ā?	邊位呀?
Why?	dím gáai ā?	點解呀?

- The third type are the questions with the word mā. In English, the position of the verb and subject is often swapped to make a question, 'She is going' becomes 'Is she going?' For these types of questions in Cantonese, you only have to add the word mā after your sentence to make it a question.

| He/She is a student. | kűi hãi hõk sàng |
| Is he/she a student? | kűi hãi hõk sàng mā? |

GRAMMAR

POSSESSION 所屬

To indicate possession, the word gē is put after the noun and before the object.

my book	ngőh gē sùe
mine	ngőh gē
yours	néi gē

MODALS 情態助動詞
Obligation 必要

Obligation or duty is shown by the verb, yīu, which is similar to the English 'have to' or 'must'.

| You have to pay. | néi yīu béi chín |

Want & Need 需要

A want or a need is expressed by the word yīu

I want.	ngőh yīu
I don't want.	ngőh m yīu
I want to go.	ngőh yīu hūi
I want to go to yum cha.	ngőh yīu hūi yám cha

A wish or hope is expressed by séung or hèi mőng respectively.

Can 可能

The word 'can' is expressed by the words hóh yí. It is placed in front of the verb to indicate the ability to do something.

I can sing.	ngőh hóh yí chēung
I cannot go.	ngőh m hóh yí hūi

CLASSIFIERS   數量詞

When you talk about quantities of any noun in Cantonese, you need to use a classifier, or 'measure word' as they're better described. The measure word goes between the number and the noun. There are many words which may be used used, depending on the noun. (see page 255)

Some Useful Words 應用詞匯

after	jì hău	之後
also	dò hăi	都係
and	tung maai	同埋
at	hái	喺
because	yàn wāi	因為
before	jì chin	之前
but	bàt gwőh	不過
if	yue gwőh	如果
from	yau	由
just now	tau sìn; jìng wă	頭先; 正話

GRAMMAR

now	yi gà	而家
or	dīng hãi	定係
to	dō	到
with	lin maai	連埋
without	m lin maai	唔連埋

MEETING PEOPLE 人際交往

Even if you don't read the rest of this chapter, it's important to memorise a few basic magic words. They are:

(I wish) you well.	néi hó	你好

which is similar to 'How are you?' in English.

Excuse me.	m gòi	唔該
Please.	chéng	請
Sorry.	dūi m jūe	對唔住
Thank you.	dòh jē	多謝

Although the common Cantonese phrases wāi or wēi, meaning 'Hi' or 'Hey', are used to draw someone's attention, it is not suitable to use them for first encounters.

VISITING 拜會

It is common courtesy to take a gift when visiting someone in their home. Fruits, biscuits and other foods are usually given, while flowers and wine are becoming increasingly popular. In the Chinese New Year period, when visiting an elderly person or someone for the first time, it is essential to take something. The Cantonese are very hospitable people. You may be asked to stay for tea or a meal, or to go to a restaurant.

GREETINGS 問候

The all-purpose phrases in Cantonese are '(I wish) you well', néi hó and 'Good morning', jó san, which obviously can only be used in the morning.

Between friends, you may ask each other, 'Have you eaten?' and 'Have you yum-cha'ed?', which aren't expressions of curiosity, but are typical forms of greeting.

How are you?	néi hó mā?	你好嗎?
Are you well?	néi hó mā?	你好嗎?
Good morning.	jó san	早晨

| Have you eaten? | | |
| sīk jóh fāan měi ā? | | 食咗飯未呀? |

| Have you yum cha'ed? | | |
| yám jóh cha měi ā? | | 飲咗茶未呀? |

Although 'good afternoon' and 'good evening' do exist, these terms are rarely used nowadays, except perhaps at formal occasions, or during TV/radio broadcasting.

| Good afternoon. | | |
| ńg ngòn | | 午安 |

| Good evening, everyone. | | |
| gōk wái mǎan ngòn | | 各位晚安 |

Here are some more useful greetings that could be used to greet someone you know or someone you have met before.

| (Mr Chan), how are you? | | |
| (chan sìn sàang), néi hó mā? | | (陳先生), 你好嗎? |

| What are you doing? | | |
| néi jó gán dì màt yé ā? | | 你做緊啲乜嘢呀? |

| Where are you going? | | |
| néi hūi bìn dõ ā? | | 你去邊度呀? |

| How are you? | | |
| néi gān lói dím ā? | | 你近來點呀? |

Replies 回應

Reply to 'good morning' with the same jó san. Some useful replies include:

| I am fine. | ngőh géi hó | 我幾好 |
| Fine. | géi hó | 幾好 |

Fine, and you?	géi hó, néi nè?	幾好, 你呢?
Not too bad.	m chōh	唔錯
Very busy.	hó mong	好忙
As usual.	yáu hãi gám yéung	又係咁樣
So so.	ma má	麻麻

I am fine, thank you. And you?
ngőh géi hó, dòh jē néi yáu
sàm néi nè?

我幾好,多謝你有
心.你呢?

In reply to 'Where are you going?',

I'm/We're going ...	(ngőh/ngőh dēi) hūi ...	(我/我 哋)去 ...
to the cinema	tái hēi	睇戲
to school	fàan hŏk	番學
to shopping	haang gùng sì	行公司
to work	fàan gùng	番工
to yum cha	yám cha	飲茶

We're taking a walk.
ngőh dēi hūi sāan bō

我哋去散步

GOODBYES   告辭

The easiest way is to say 'goodbye' or 'bye' in English. The most common phrase bàai bāai has been adapted from English.

Bye.		
bàai bāai		拜拜

Come again please.
dàk haan chéng jōi lei

得閑請再嚟

Good night.
jó táu

早唞

See you!
jōi wŏoi!

再會!

See you! (col)
jōi gĭn!

再見!

See you another time.
　dǎi yǐ sí gīn　　　　　　第二時見
See you soon.
　chi dì jōi gīn　　　　　　遲啲再見
See you tomorrow.
　tìng yǎt jōi gīn　　　　　聽日再見

[wish you ...]	jùk néi ...	祝你 ...
Bon voyage	yàt faan fùng sǔn	一帆風順
Have a safe trip	yàt lǒ ping ngòn	一路平安

BODY LANGUAGE　　　　　　　　身體語言

The Cantonese people have been in contact with and influenced by Western culture for a long time, most notably since the Ming Dynasty. Although generally frowned upon by the more reserved and conservative Cantonese people, it's not surprising to see some signs of affection between people in public, such as holding hands. The younger generation is more willing to walk arm in arm with friends of the same sex or otherwise, or even hug in public! Avoid showing too much affection with friends when in public, however, as some people may be offended by it.

Although pointing isn't offensive, it's more polite to point with your hand, with the palm facing up.

FORMS OF ADDRESS　　　　　　　稱呼
Surnames 姓氏

There are thousands of surnames, most consisting of just one character, although there a few with two or more.

Au-Yeung	ngàu yeung	歐陽
Chan	chan	陳
Chang/Cheung	jèung	張
Ho	hoh	何
Lau	lau	劉
Lee/Li	léi	李
Ma	mǎ	馬

Tang	dǎng	鄧
Tsang	jàng	曾
Tse	jē	謝
Wong	wong	王/黃
Yang/Yeung/Young	yeung	楊

Traditionally, a married woman would adopt her husband's surname which then becomes a prefix to her maiden (full) name, thus creating her legal name. It may become a little confusing when she marries as it would still be acceptable to call her by her christian name, maiden name (Miss Ma Lei-Lei), married surname (Mrs Chan) or even her legal name (Madam Chan Ma Lei-Lei).

BOSS

Some people prefer to be addressed bòh sí, lố sāi, lố báan, sǐ táu (or sǐ tau poh for women), meaning 'boss'.

Titles 稱謂

Mr ...	... sìn sàang	... 先生
Miss ...	... síu jé	... 小姐
Mrs ...	... tāai táai	... 太太
Mrs (formal) ...	... fòo yan	... 夫人
Madam ...	... nűi sǐ	... 女士
Ms ...	... nűi sǐ	... 女士
Ladies and	nűi sǐ moon	女士們
Gentlemen!	sìn sàang moon	先生們
Kids(children)	síu pang yấu	小朋友
Friends	pang yấu	朋友

Term of endearment:

| My old friend. | lố yấu gēi | 老友記 |

In Cantonese the surname is said first, then the first and second names, and finally, the title. The title always comes last. For example, Miss Suk-Ling Lau becomes lau sŭk ling síu jé.

The beauty of this language is, if you can't remember or if you don't know the surname, addressing him/her by his/her title only – 'Dr', 'Teacher', and so on – is fairly acceptable.

The following words may be applied with or without a surname.

Chairman ...	... júe jīk	... 主席
Dr ...	... bōk sī	... 博士
Doctor(medical) ...	... yì sàng	... 醫生
Father(Catholic) ...	... san fōo	... 神父
General Manager	... júng gìng léi	... 總經理
Inspector(police) ...	... bòng báan	... 幫板
Manager	... gìng léi	... 經理
Master(skilled person) ...	... sì fóo	... 師父
Pastor(Christian) ...	... mŭk sì	... 牧師
Professor ...	... gāau sŭu	... 教授
Supervisor	... júe yǎm	... 主任
Teacher	... lŏ sì	... 老師

DID YOU KNOW ...

There are various meanings to the title sìn sàang.

Firstly, it's a respectful title to call a man, being similar to 'Sir'. By putting the surname (say Lau) in front of it, you obtain lau sìn sàang, meaning 'Mr Lau'. Sìn sàang is also the word for husband, as in ngőh sìn sàang meaning 'my husband'. Finally, sìn sàang can also be another word for 'Teacher', regardless of gender.

MEETING PEOPLE

Mr ...	... sìn sàang	... 先生
Miss ...	... síu jé	... 小姐
Mrs ...	... tāai táai	... 太太
Mrs(formal) ...	... fòo yan	... 夫人

More often than not, when asked what their names are, Cantonese people will give you their surnames. After establishing the surname, you should add a title (Dr, Mr, Miss, Mrs).

Mr Wong	wong sìn sàang	王先生
Dr Lung	lung bōk sǐ	龍博士
Mrs (Smith)	(sí mǎt fòo)	(史密夫)
	fòo yan	夫人

It's best not to address the Cantonese by their first name(s), even if you know what they are. Only schoolmates and close friends call each other by their first names. Decades of Western influences have resulted in most young Cantonese people having an English given name, as well as a Chinese name.

Typically, men address each other by their surnames, however, good friends show their affection or informality by adding the prefix ā to the surname, for example, ā láu. Remember, this is normally used between close friends or people whose relationship is fairly informal.

For the younger generation, some relatives' titles may be used when meeting people for the first time. The terms are aunty, ā yì or ā sám, and uncle, ā sùk, or ā bāak, which is normally addressed to a female/male who is roughly their parents' age.

May I ask your (family) name?
    chéng mǎn gwài sīng ā?   請問貴姓呀?
    (lit: may I ask your honorable surname)

My surname is (Lau).
    síu sīng (lau)   小姓(劉)
    (lit: my humble surname is Lau)

MEETING PEOPLE

How should I address you?
  dím chìng fòo néi ā?

點稱呼你呀?

You may just call me (Ah-Lau).
  néi gīu ngőh (ā láu) dàk lā

你叫我(亞劉)得喇

FIRST ENCOUNTERS

幸會

My name is ...
  ngőh gīu jő ...

我叫做 ...

I'm a friend of ...
  ngőh hǎi ... gē pang yấu

我係 ... 嘅朋友

(Mr Chan) referred me to you.
  (chan sìn sàang) gāai sīu
  ngőh lei gīn néi

(陳先生)介紹我
  嚟見你

His/Her name is ...
  kűi gē méng gīu jő ...

佢嘅名叫做 ...

I'd like to introduce you to my ...
  ngőh séung gāai sīu ngőh
  gē ... béi néi sìk

我想介紹我嘅 ...
  俾你識

(Annie/David)	(ngòn nei; dãai wǎi)	(安妮; 大衛)
is my ...	hǎi ngőh gē ...	係我嘅 ...
boss	bòh sí	波士
colleague	tung sī	同事
daughter	nűi	女
fiancé	mẽi fan fòo	未婚夫
fiancée	mẽi fan chài	未婚妻
friend	pang yấu	朋友
husband	sìn sàang	先生
partner	pāak dōng	拍檔
relative	chàn chìk	親戚
secretary	bēi sùe	秘書
son	jái	仔
subordinate	sáu hǎ	手下
superior	sẽung sì	上司
wife	tāai táai	太太

I'm pleased to meet you.
ngőh hó gò hīng tung
néi gīn mĭn

我好高興同
你見面

Have we met before?
ngőh děi yǐ chin yấu mố gīn
gwōh mĭn ā ?

我哋以前有冇
見過面呀?

We like China/Hong Kong very much.
ngőh děi hó jùng yī
(jùng gwōk/hèung góng)

我哋好中意
(中國/香港)

Which hotel are you staying at?
néi děi hái bìn yàt gàan
jáu dím jŭe ā?

你哋喺邊一
間酒店住呀?

I'm/We're staying at (the Peninsula) hotel.
(ngőh/ngőh děi) jŭe
hái (bōon dó) jáu dím

(我/我哋)住喺
(半島)酒店

SIDE-KICK

Someone may address you as, lő yấu gēi, lő yấu or séi dóng.
These mean 'faithful partner' or 'side-kick'.

NATIONALITIES   國籍

Which country are you from?
néi hái bìn yàt gōh gwōk
gà lei gā?

你喺邊一個國
家嚟㗎?

What nationality are you?
néi hăi bìn yàt gwōk yan ā?

你係邊一國人呀?

I love (Hong Kong/my homeland).
ngőh jùng yī (hèung góng/
ngőh gē jó gwōk)

我中意(香港/
我嘅祖國)

To show your nationality, simply add the word 'person', yan,
after the name of the country. Unfortunately, we can't list all
countries here.

I come from (Canada).
ngőh hái (gà na dăai) lei

我喺(加拿大)嚟

I am (Canadian).	ngőh hãi	我係
	(gà na dãai yan)	(加拿大人)
America	měi gwōk	美國
Australia	ngō jàu	澳洲
Belgium	béi lěi si	比利時
Bangladesh*	mãang gà làai	孟加拉
Cambodia*	gáan po jãi	柬埔寨
Canada	gà na dãai	加拿大
China	jùng gwōk	中國
Denmark*	dàan mãk	丹麥
Egypt	ngài kãp	埃及
Europe	ngàu jàu	歐洲
Finland*	fàn laan	芬蘭
France*	fãat gwōk	法國
Germany*	dàk gwōk	德國
Holland*	hoh làan	荷蘭
Hong Kong	hèung góng	香港
India*	yān dõ	印度
Indonesia*	yān nei	印尼
Ireland	ngõi yĩ laan	愛爾蘭

DID YOU KNOW ...

The words fàan gwái and gwái ló, literally mean 'foreign devils' and are often used in the region; gwái poh, gwái mòoi and gwái jái, respectively, refer to women, girls and boys. These used to have a negative connotation, but nowadays people use them as a substitute for the word 'Westerners' without a second thought.

MEETING PEOPLE

Israel*	yí sìk lìt	以色列
Italy*	yì dāai lēi	意大利
Japan*	yāt bóon	日本
Korea*	hon gwōk	韓國
Laos*	liu gwōk	寮國
Malaysia	má loi sài ā	馬來西亞
New Zealand	náu sài laan	紐西蘭

Norway*	noh wài	挪威
Philippines*	fèi lūt bàn	菲律賓
Russia*	ngoh loh sì	俄羅斯
Singapore	sìng gā bòh	星加坡
Spain*	sài bàan nga	西班牙
Sweden*	sūi dín	瑞典
Switzerland	sūi sī	瑞士
Thailand*	tāai gwōk	泰國
UK	yìng gwōk	英國
USA	méi gwōk	美國
Vietnam*	yūet naam	越南

MEETING PEOPLE

*You may also add the word 'language', wá, after the name of these countries.

Are you (Vietnamese)?
neí haĩ m haĩ
(yŭet naam yan) ā?

你係唔係
(越南人)呀?

I am not (Vietnamese), I am (Indonesian).
ngőh m haĩ (yŭet naam yan),
ngőh haĩ (yān nei yan)

我唔係(越南人),
我係(印尼人)

I speak (Spanish) and (Italian).
ngőh sìk (sài bàan nga wá)
tung maai (yī daãi lēi wá)

我識(西班牙話)
同埋(意大利話)

Have you ever been to (France)?
neí yaŭ mő hūi gwōh
(fàat gwōk) ā?

你有冇去過
(法國)呀?

I live in a/the ...   ngőh jŭe hái ...   我住喺 ...
   city   sí kùi   市區
   countryside   gàau kùi   郊區
   village   hèung chùen   鄉村
   mountains   sàan kùi   山區
   suburbs of ...   ... kùi   ... 區
   seaside   hói bìn   海邊

AGE   年歲

How old are you?
   chéng maãn neí géi dòh sūi ā?   請問你幾多歲呀?

The above is the most common question when asking one's age.
The following would be better when asking the age of elderly people.

   chéng maãn gwāi gàng ā?   請問貴庚呀?

SUPERIOR

The phrases daãi ló, ā gòh, daãi gòh and daãi gòh daãi
(lit: elder brother), mean 'superior male'; for females
use ā jè.

chéng mǎn nếi géi dāai	請問你幾大
nin géi lā?	年紀喇?

When asking children, you may use:

| géi dòh sūi lā? | 幾多歲喇? |

Most Chinese people like you to guess their age. Usually, the older person would be happy if your guess was younger than their real age. The opposite is the case with the teenagers or young adults.

Guess how old I am?
| nếi góo há ngổh géi dòh sūi? | 你估吓我幾多歲? |

I think you are (20) years old.
| ngổh góo nếi (yǐ sǎp) sūi | 我估你(二十)歲 |

I'm (21) years old.
| ngổh gàm nín (yǐ sǎp yàt) sūi | 我今年(二十一)歲 |

(See page 255 for more information on numbers.)

ZODIAC　　　　　　　　　　　　　　　　　　生肖

Unlike the Western zodiac, where 12 signs exist within each calendar year and your sign is determined by the day and month you were born, the Chinese zodiac consists of yearly signs, each based on an animal, and your sign depends on your birth year. The first zodiac is the rat, the second the ox, and so on. The Chinese base their zodiac on the lunar calendar, so each sign

ZODIAC SIGNS					
rat	súe	鼠	horse	mǎ	馬
ox	ngau	牛	sheep	yeung	羊
tiger	fóo	虎	monkey	hau	猴
rabbit	tō	兔	rooster	gài	雞
dragon	lung	龍	dog	gáu	狗
snake	se	蛇	pig	jùe	豬

MEETING PEOPLE

recurs once every 12 years: 2000 is the Year of the Dragon, as will be 2012. 2001 is the Year of the Snake, as will be 2013.

Very often, instead of asking people how old they are, Chinese people might ask what Year (of the Zodiac) a person belongs to, and subsequently they can work out the age. Traditionally, Cantonese people believe that some zodiac signs are not compatible. For example, a person born in the Year of the Tiger and a person born in the Year of the Rat shouldn't get married.

What Year (of the zodiac) were you born in?
néi hái màt yé nin chùt sāi gā?　你喺乜嘢年出世㗎?

Which zodiac do you belong to?
néi sǔk yùe bìn yàt gōh
sàng chīu ā?　你屬於邊一個
生肖呀?

I was born in the Year of (Pig).
ngőh hái (jùe) nin chùt sāi　我係(豬)年出世

I belong to the Year of (Dragon).
ngőh sǔk (lung)　我屬(龍)

OCCUPATIONS　　　　　　　　　　　職務

What is your occupation?
néi gē jìk yìp hái màt yé ā?　你嘅職業係乜嘢呀?

This may be the most direct question when asking one's occupation. There are other ways: jō sǐng hong ā? or jō bìn yàt hong ā? literally meaning, 'Which honourable business do you belong to?', and hái bìn dǒ fāat choi ā? literally meaning, 'From where do you make your money?' (used for 'where do you work?')

I am a/an ...	ngőh hái ...	我係 ...
accountant	wǒoi gāi sì	會計師
actor	yín yuen	演員
architect	gīn jùk sì	建築師
athlete	wǎn dǔng yuen	運動員
businessperson	sèung yan	商人
chef	chue sì	廚師

chemist	yĕuk jài sì	藥劑師
clerk	man yuen	文員
dentist	nga yì	牙醫
doctor	yì sàng	醫生
driver	sì gèi	司機
engineer	gùng ching sì	工程師
farmer	nung fòo	農夫
fisher	yue fòo	漁夫
hawker	síu fáan	小販
homemaker	júe főo	主婦
interpreter	fàan yĩk	翻譯
journalist	gēi jé	記者
labourer	gùng yan	工人
lawyer	lŭt sì	律師
lecturer	góng sì	講師
manager	gìng léi	經理
musician	yàm ngõk gà	音樂家
nurse	wŏo sĩ	護士

office worker	jìk yuen	職員
pastor/priest	mŭk sì	牧師
poet	sì yan	詩人
politician	jīng jĭ gà	政治家
professor	gāau sŭu	教授
public servant	gùng mŏ yuen	公務員
receptionist	jīp dòi yuen	接待員
salesperson	sŭu fōh yuen	售貨員
sales rep	ying yĭp dòi bíu	營業代表
scientist	fòh hŏk gà	科學家
secretary	bēi sùe	秘書
soldier	gwàn yan	軍人
student	hŏk sàng	學生
teacher	gāau sì	教師
technician	gĕi gùng	技工
tourist	yau hāak	遊客
waiter	fóh gēi;	伙記;
	fŭk mŏ yuen	服務員
writer	jōk gà	作家

Some Useful Words & Phrases 應用詞句

amateur	yĭp yue	業餘
casual	sáan gùng	散工
full time job	chuen jìk	全職

HUMILITY

The humble way to address oneself is hìng dăi, or sāi ló which means 'little brother'. It is the opposite of the dàai ló (see page 40).

The informal term for children is síu pang yău, which has the same meaning as sāi lŏ gòh, sāi lŏ jái, and sāi màn jái, the latter few being less formal.

MEETING PEOPLE

looking for a job	wán gán gùng	搵緊工
part time job	bōon jìk	半職
profession	jùen yĭp	專業
retired	tūi yàu	退休
side job	gìm jìk	兼職
specialist	jùen gà	專家
unemployed(in China)	dōi yĭp	待業
unemployed (in Hong Kong)	sàt yĭp	失業

STUDYING   進修

What is your major/minor subject?

| nĕi (júe sàu/fōo sàu) mảt yế fòh ā? | 你(主修/副修) 乜嘢科呀? |

My major is ...	ngŏh júe sàu ...	我主修 ...
I'm studying ...	ngŏh dŭk gán ...	我讀緊 ...
administration	hang jīng hŏk	行政學
art	ngãi sũt	藝術
arts/humanities	man fòh	文科
business	sèung fòh	商科
Cantonese	gwóng dùng wá	廣東話
computer	dĭn nő	電腦
education	gāau yŭk	教育
engineering	gùng fòh	工科
foreign language	ngŏi gwòk yŭe	外國語
history	lĭk sí hŏk	歷史學
journalism	sàn man hŏk	新聞學
law	fàat lũt	法律
management	gwóon léi hŏk	管理學
Mandarin	pó tùng wá	普通話
medicine	yì fòh	醫科
music	yàm ngŏk	音樂
science	léi fòh	理科

MEETING PEOPLE

social work	sé wóoi gùng jòk	社會工作
sociology	sé wóoi hŏk	社會學
tourism	lúi yau	旅遊

FEELINGS   感覺

How are you feeling?
néi gōk dàk dím yéung ā?   你覺得點樣呀?

Are you (feeling) ...?	néi gōk m gōk dàk ... ā?	你覺唔覺得 ... 呀?
angry	nàu	嬲
ashamed	cháu	醜
cold	dūng	凍
comfortable	sùe fŭk	舒服
happy	hòi sàm	開心
hot	yīt	熱
hungry	ngŏh	餓
sad	sèung sàm	傷心
scared	gèng	驚
sick	m sùe fŭk	唔舒服

DID YOU KNOW ...

The phrase dím ā?, or dím yéung ā? meaning 'How?' is an alternative way to ask how someone is feeling.
Another colloquial Cantonese word dím means 'capable', 'job well done', and 'success'; kúi hó dím means 'He's had great success'.
dím sāai means 'It has all been perfectly settled'.
The difference between dím and dīm is in the tones.

sleepy	ngǎan fān	眼瞓
thirsty	háu hōt	口渴
tired	gwǒoi	癐
well	hó	好
worried	dàam sàm	擔心

Replies 回應

When answering, add the appropriate adjective from above to the following stems.

| I feel (very) ... | ngǒh gōk dàk (hó) ... | 我覺得(好) ... |
| I don't feel (very) ... | ngǒh m gōk dàk (hò) ... | 我唔覺得(好) ... |

CULTURAL DIFFERENCES 異俗

How do you do this in your country?
    hái něi děi gwōk gà hǎi
    dím jǒ gā?
喺你哋國家係
點做㗎?

Is this a local or national custom?
    nì gōh hǎi bóon děi dīng hǎi
    chuen gwōk gē fùng jǔk ā?
呢個係本地定係
全國嘅風俗呀?

I am sorry, it is not the custom in my country.
    hó dùi m jǔe, ngǒh mǒ
    gám gē jāap gwāan
好對唔住,我冇
咁嘅習慣

I don't want to offend you.
    ngǒh m séung dàk jǔi něi
我唔想得罪你

I am not accustomed to this.
    ngǒh m jāap gwāan
    gám yéung
我唔習慣
咁樣

I don't mind watching, but I'd prefer not to participate.
    ngǒh m gāai yī hùi tái, dǎan
    hǎi ngǒh m séung chàam yúe
我唔介意去睇,但
係我唔想參預

LANGUAGE DIFFICULTIES 語言溝通

Do you speak English?
    něi sìk m sìk góng yìng mán ā?
你識唔識講英文呀?

MEETING PEOPLE

I (don't) speak Cantonese.

ngőh (m) sìk góng gwóng
dùng wá   我(唔)識講廣東話

He/She speaks (a little) Putunghua.

kűi sìk góng (síu síu) pó
tùng wá   佢識講(少少)普
通話

Do you have an interpreter?

néi yáu mő fàan yĩk ā?   你有冇翻譯呀?

I need an interpreter.

ngőh yĩu wán fàan yĩk   我要搵翻譯

How do you say this in Cantonese/English?

nì gōh hái (gwóng dùng
wá/yìng mán) dím góng ā?   呢個喺(廣東
話/英文)點講呀?

Can you repeat that please?

chéng néi jōi góng dòh yàt chī   請你再講多一次

Could you speak louder/slower please?

chéng néi góng (dāai sèng/
mãan) dì   請你講(大聲/
慢)啲

Could you write that down please?

m gòi chéng néi sé dài   唔該請你寫低

Please point to the phrase in this book.

chéng hái nì bóon sùe dõ
wán chùt néi góh yàt gūi   請喺呢本書度
搵出你嗰一句

Let me see if I can find it in this book.

dáng ngőh wán nì bóon sùe
tái yáu mő nì yàt gūi   等我搵呢本書
睇有冇呢一句

Do you understand?

néi mìng m mìng bãak ā?   你明唔明白呀?

I (don't) understand.

ngőh (m) mìng bãak   我(唔)明白

What does (it) mean?

(nì gōh) hãi màt yế yī sì ā?   (呢個)係乜嘢意思呀?

FAMILY

家庭

Are you married?
 néi gīt jóh fàn mēi ā?

你結咗婚未呀?

I'm ...	ngóh hãi ...	我係 ...
single	dàan sàn	單身
married	gīt jóh fàn	結咗婚
divorced	lei jóh fàn	離咗婚
separated	fàn jóh gùi	分咗居
a sole parent	dàan chàn	單親
a widow	gwá főo	寡婦

How many children do you have?
 néi yáu géi dòh gōh jái núi ā?

你有幾多個仔女呀?

I don't have any children.
 ngőh jŭng mēi yáu jái núi

我重未有仔女

I have ...	ngőh yáu ...	我有 ...
(and ...)	(tung maai ...)	(同埋 ...)
a son	yàt gōh jái	一個仔
two sons	léung gōh jái	兩個仔
a daughter	yàt gōh núi	一個女
(three) daughters	(sàam) gōh núi	(三)個女

Do you have a boyfriend/girlfriend?
 néi yáu mő (naam/núi)
 pang yáu ā?

你有冇(男/女)
朋友呀?

Yes (I have).	yáu	有
No (I don't have).	mő	冇

I don't want to tell you.
 ngőh m wã béi néi jì

我唔話俾你知

How many brothers (and sisters) do you have?
 néi yáu géi dòh hìng dãi
 (jí mőoi) ā?

你有幾多兄弟
(姊妹)呀?

I don't have any brothers or sisters.
ngőh mő hīng dāi jí mőoi   我有兄弟姊妹

I have ...	ngőh yáu ...	我有 ...
(and ...)	(tung maai ...)	(同埋 ...)
a brother	yàt gōh hìng dāi	一個兄弟
a sister	yàt gōh jí mőoi	一個姊妹
two brothers	léung gōh hìng dāi	兩個兄弟
three sisters	sàam gōh jí mőoi	三個姊妹

Family Members 家族

Formally, the Chinese use different words when talking about
their own family members, as opposed to others' family members.
Here are some examples of the traditional or formal terms.

This is ...	nì gōh hāi ...	呢個係 ...
my father	gà főo	家父
my husband	ngői jí	外子
my mother	gà mő	家母
my wife	női jí	內子

Is this ...?	nì wái hāi m hāi ... ā?	呢位係唔係 ... 呀?
your daughter	lìng chìn gàm	令千金
your elder brother	lìng hìng	令兄
your father	lìng jùen	令尊
your husband	jùen fòo	尊夫
your mother	lìng sáu tóng	令壽堂
your son	lìng lóng	令郎
your wife	jùen fòo yán	尊夫人
your younger brother	lìng dái	令弟

For casual usage, simply apply the following words to the sentence.

He/She is my ...
kűi hāi ngőh gē ...   佢係我嘅 ...

Is he/she your ...	kűi hāi m hāi néi gē ... ā ?	佢係唔係你嘅 ... 呀?
aunt	ā yì	亞姨
boyfriend	naam pang yắu	男朋友
child	sāi lõ gòh	細路哥
Daddy	ba bà	爸爸
daughter	nűi	女
elder brother	goh gòh	哥哥
elder sister	je jè	姐姐
eldest brother	dāai ló	大佬

father	fõo chàn	父親
friend	pang yắu	朋友
girlfriend	nűi pang yắu	女朋友
grandfather	jó fõo	祖父
grandmother	jó mõ	祖母
husband(col)	lõ gùng	老公
husband	jēung fòo	丈夫
mother	mõ chàn	母親
Mummy	ma mà	媽媽
old friend	lõ yắu	老友
relative	chàn chìk	親戚
son	jái	仔
uncle	sùk sùk	叔叔
wife	tāai táai	太太
wife(col)	lõ poh	老婆
younger brother	dai dái	弟弟
younger brother(col)	sāi ló	細佬
younger sister	mooi móoi	妹妹
younger sister(col)	sāi móoi	細妹

Useful Words 應用詞匯

de facto	tung gùi	同居
partner	bŏon lŭi	伴侶
spouse	poōi ngău	配偶
fiancé	mĕi fàn fòo	未婚夫
fiancée	mĕi fàn chài	未婚妻

USEFUL PHRASES 應用句式

Sure.	mŏ mǎn tai	冇問題
Just a minute.	dáng yàt jǎn	等一陣
OK.	hó ā	好呀

GETTING AROUND 週遊

Public transport in Hong Kong is convenient, clean, cheap, extensive and frequent. It is available from early morning until midnight. If you have a detailed and accurate map of the transport routes, you shouldn't have to ask anyone for directions. Everything normally runs on time. Taxis are also abundant so there shouldn't be any trouble getting around in Hong Kong. Being so close to mainland China, Hong Kong also offers direct bus/train/ferry services to most of the nearby major cities.

The transport situation in Macau is very similar to that found in Hong Kong. However, there are fewer modes of transport to choose from, and they run less frequently.

Local transport in Guangdong and Guangxi is much cheaper than Hong Kong and Macau. Getting around in China could be a little more troublesome and complicated. The main problem is the language barrier because hardly anyone speaks English. There are few signs and fewer timetables (if any) available to visitors. Buses, trains and local ferries are always crowded, and may not run on time.

You have to be very careful of pickpockets, especially in Hong Kong and Guangzhou, when visiting crowded markets, travelling in a full bus or walking on busy streets.

I'd like to go to ...
  ngóh séung hūi ...   我想去 ...

How can I get to ... ?
  ... yīu dím yéung hūi ā?   ... 要點樣去呀?

Which (bus) do I take to get to ...?
  hūi ... yīu chóh bìn yàt
  gā (bà sí) ā?   去 ... 要坐邊一
                                                   架(巴士)呀?

Is there another way to get there?
  yáuh móh daih yī tìu lóh hūi ā?   有冇第二條路去呀?

GETTING AROUND

What time does	(hǎ yàt bàan) ... géi	(下一班) ... 幾
the (next) ...	dím jùng	點鐘
leave/arrive?	hòi/dò ā?	開/到呀?
bus	bà sí	巴士
ferry	suen	船
shuttle bus	chùen sòh bà sí	穿梭巴士
subway	dèi tìt	地鐵
train	fóh chè	火車
tram	dìn chè	電車
plane	fèi gèi	飛機

FINDING YOUR WAY   問路

There is a Chinese saying lò jói háu bìn, literally translated as 'the road is close to your mouth', which means that all you have to do is ask. Don't hesitate to ask for help.

Where's the ...	chéng mǎn ...	請問 ...
please?	hái bìn dō ā?	喺邊度呀?
airport	gèi cheung	機場
bus stop	bà sí jăam	巴士站
bus terminal	bà sí júng jăam	巴士總站
car park	ting chè cheung	停車場
ferry pier	síu lun mǎ tau	小輪碼頭
helipad	jìk sìng gèi cheung	直升機場
information counter	sùn mǎn chūe	詢問處
light train stop	hìng tìt jăam	輕鐵站
minibus stop	síu bà jăam	小巴站
peak tramway station	lǎam chè jăam	纜車站
pier	mǎ tau	碼頭
subway station	dèi tìt jăam	地鐵站
taxi stand	dìk sí jăam	的士站
ticket office	sǎu pīu chūe	售票處
train station	fóh chè jăam	火車站
tram stop	dìn chè jăam	電車站

Is it far?	yűen m yűen ā?	遠唔遠呀?
Yes, it's far.	hó yűen	好遠
Not that far.	m hāi hó yűen	唔係好遠
It's quite close.	hó kán	好近

Can I walk there?
haang lō hūi m hūi dó ā?   行路去唔去到呀?

How far is it to walk?
haang lō yīu géi női ā?   行路要幾耐呀?

What's the address?
chéng mān déi jí hái bīn
yàt dő ā?   請問地址喺邊
一度呀?

Please write down the address for me.
m gòi sé gōh déi jí béi ngőh   唔該寫個地址俾我

Could you tell the taxi driver the address please?
m gòi wā gōh déi jí béi
dìk sí sì gèi tèng?   唔該話個地址俾
的士司機聽?

Please draw a map for me.
m gòi wǎak gōh déi to
béi ngőh   唔該畫個地圖俾我

Which direction?
bìn yàt gōh fòng hēung ā?   邊一個方向呀?

Directions 方向

after ...	... jì hāu	... 之後
(at) the corner	(hái) gōk lòk táu	(喺)角落頭
behind ...	... hāu bīn	... 後便
direction	fòng hēung	方向
down	hā bīn	下便
downstairs	lau hā	樓下
far away	hó yűen	好遠
go straight ahead	yàt jĭk hūi	一直去
in front of ...	... jì chin	... 之前
inside ...	... lűi bīn	... 便
left	jóh bīn	左便

middle	jùng gàan	中間
near	hó kán	好近
next to ...	... gāak lei	... 隔離
opposite to ...	... dūi mǐn	... 對面
outside	ngòi bǐn	外便
right	yǎu bǐn	右便
that direction	góh gōh fòng hēung	嗰個方向
this direction	nì gōh fòng hēung	呢個方向
turn left ...	... jūen jóh bǐn	... 轉左便
turn right ...	... jūen yǎu bǐn	... 轉右便
at the intersection	hái lǒ háu	喺路口
before the traffic lights	hái gāau tùng dàng chin mǐn	喺交通燈前面
up	sěung bǐn	上便
upstairs	lau sěung	樓上
east	dùng	東
south	naam	南
west	sài	西
north	bàk	北

WALKING   漫步

Walking is an enjoyable, flexible way of getting around and is absolutely free of charge. The long, outdoor escalators connecting Hong Kong Central to Mid-level save you walking up the steep inclines. The underground and flying corridors between buildings and shopping arcades, the many foot bridges, tunnels and elevated walkways are designed to rescue you from the busy traffic. Some main streets are even closed to traffic on Sundays.

elevated walkway	hang yan tìn kiu	行人天橋
escalator	dǐn dǔng lau tài	電動樓梯
flying corridor	fèi long	飛廊

DIRECTIONS

In Chinese the order of directions is east, south, west and north. North-east and north-west become east-north and west-north in Chinese.

foot bridge	hang yan tìn kiu	行人天橋
path	síu gīng	小徑
pedestrian	hang yan	行人
pedestrian underpass	hang yan sŭi dŏ	行人隧道
ramp	chē lŏ	斜路
trail	yau lăam gīng	遊覽徑
zebra crossing	bàan mă sīn	斑馬線

BUYING TICKETS   購票

Most of the buses and trams in Hong Kong require exact fares because no change is given. On buses and trams, you can pay when you board by putting the amount in a slot operated by the driver. Everyone pays the fixed amount no matter how far they travel. Check the correct route and have the exact fare ready before boarding.

Aside from the single ticket, there are prepaid tickets, bāat dăat tùng, Octopus cards available for the subway (MTR), airport express(AEL), light rail transit (LRT), trains (KCR), and some local buses, tunnel buses and ferries.

Where's the ticket office?
    chéng măn său pīu chūe   請問售票處
    hái bìn dŏ ā?   喺邊度呀?

I'd like a (first class) train ticket to Guangzhou.
    ngőh séung yīu yàt jèung   我想要一張
    hūi gwóng jàu gē (tau dáng) 去廣州嘅(頭等)
    fóh chè fèi   火車飛

Do you have any tickets for (Hong Kong) for today?
    yău mŏ gàm yāt hūi   有冇今日去
    (hèung góng) gē fèi ā?   (香港)嘅飛呀?

GETTING AROUND

What's the cheapest fare to Hong Kong (by ferry)?
(chóh dāai súen) hūi hèung (坐大船)去香
góng jūi peng gē fèi yīu géi 港最平嘅飛要幾
dòh chín ā? 多錢呀?

I want to book a train ticket (for next Wednesday).
ngǒh yīu yǔe dēng (hǎ sìng 我要預訂(下星
kei sàam gē) fóh chè fèi 期三嘅)火車飛

I want to change to (soft-seat).
ngǒh séung wòon (yúen jǒh) 我想換(軟座)

What's the price difference?
chà géi dòh chín ā? 差幾多錢呀?

I'd like a/an ...
ngǒh yīu yàt jèung ... fèi 我要一張 ... 飛

How much is a/an ... ticket?	... fèi yīu géi dòh chín ā?	... 飛要幾 多錢呀?
adult	dāai yan	大人
business class	sèung mō hāak wái	商務客位
child's	síu tung	小童
economy class	gìng jāi wái	經濟位
first class	tau dáng	頭等
one-way	dàan ching	單程
platform	jǎam toi	站台
return	loi wooi	來回
second class	yī dáng	二等
student	hǒk sàng	學生

I'd like a window seat.
ngǒh séung yīu gōh 我想要個
chèung háu wái 窗口位

ADDRESSES

When we write addresses in English, the name of the organization or building goes first, followed by the floor, number, street name, suburb, city, state and country. In Chinese, this order is reversed.

Useful Words & Phrases 應用詞句

advance ticket office	yŭe săul chŭe	預售處
berth	chong wái	床位
cabin class	dăai chòng wái	大艙位
cancel	chúi sìu	取消
confirm	kōk yĭng	確認
direct train	jīk tùng chè	直通車
dormitory bunk	chong wái	床位
It's full.	mŏon jŏh	滿座
hard-seat (2nd class)	ngăang jŏh	硬座
hard-sleeper (2nd class)	ngăang ngŏh	硬臥
non-smoking seat	gām yìn wái	禁煙位
Octopus card	băat dăat tùng kàat	八達通卡
ordinary seat	pó tùng wái	普通位
refund	tūi pīu	退票
seat	jŏh wái	座位
second class	yĭ dáng	二等
soft-seat (1st class)	yŭen jŏh	軟座
soft-sleeper (1st class)	yŭen ngŏh	軟臥
standby	hău bó	候補
ticket machine	jĭ dŭng săul pīu gèi	自動售票機
ticket office	săul pīu chŭe	售票處

AT CUSTOMS 通關

Regardless of how you arrive you'll have to go through immigration, quarantine and customs.

We have something/nothing to declare.
ngŏh dēi (yáu yé; mŏ yé) 我哋(有嘢; 冇嘢)
yīu sàn bō 要申報

This is all our luggage.
ngŏh dēi dì hang léi hái 我哋啲行李喺
sāai nì dŏ 哂呢度

GETTING AROUND

All these are our personal items.
chuen bō dò hǎi ngǒh dēi
gē gōh yan yǔng bán

全部都係我哋
嘅個人用品

May we go through?
ngǒh dēi hóh yǐ gwōh
hūi mā?

我哋可以過
去嗎?

Do I have to declare this?
ngǒh yīu m yīu sàn bō
nì dì ā?

我要唔要申報
呢啲呀?

We'd like to declare ...
ngǒh dēi yīu sàn bō ...

我哋要申報 ...

I'd like to call my (embassy/consulate.)
ngǒh yīu dá dǐn wá béi ngǒh
gē (dǎai sī gwóon; lǐng sí gwóon)

我要打電話俾我
嘅(大使館; 領事館)

alien	ngǒi jǐk yan sī	外籍人士
contraband goods	wai gām bán	違禁品
customs	hói gwàan	海關
customs check-point	gwàan kà	關卡
customs clearance	tùng gwàan	通關
customs declaration	hói gwàan sàn bō dàan	海關申報單
customs duties	gwàan sūi	關稅
drugs	dǔk bán	毒品
duty-free	mín sūi	免稅
employment visa	gùng jōk chìm jīng	工作簽證
issue	chìm fāat	簽發
nationality	gwōk jǐk	國籍
passport	wǒ jīu	護照
quarantine	gím yǐk	檢疫
smuggling	jáu sì	走私
tax	sūi	稅
tourism visa	gwòon gwòng chìm jíng	觀光簽證

transit	gwōh gíng	過境
transit visa	gwōh gíng chìm jīng	過境簽證
visa	chìm jīng	簽證
visa-free entry	mín chìm jíng	免簽證
	yǎp gíng	入境

AIR   航空

The Hong Kong International Airport at Chek Lap Kok (chēk lāap gōk), officially opened in June 1998, signifies a new era in air travel. The high-speed AEL, Airport Express railway links up the CBD (Central Business District) to the airport making travelling efficient, comfortable and fast. There is also a complimentary downtown luggage check-in service for some airlines. There are a few more international airports in Macau, Guangzhou and Shenzhen. Together with the local airports located on every corners, they make air travel in the region easy, convenient and efficient.

GETTING AROUND

Arrival & Transit 入境過境

Where is the ... please?	chéng mǎn ... hái bìn dō ā ?	請問 ... 喺邊度呀?
airline office	hong hùng gùng sì bǎan sī chūe	航空公司辦事處
baggage locker	hang lěi chuen fōng gwǎi	行李存放櫃
baggage claim	tai chúi hang lěi chūe	提取行李處
baggage storage	gēi chuen hang lěi chūe	寄存行李處
exit	chùt háu	出口
information centre	sùn mǎn chūe	詢問處
money changer	ngǒi bāi jáau wǒon chūe	外幣找換處
smoking area	kàp yìn kùi	吸煙區
transit service counter	gwōh gíng fūk mǒ gwǎi toi	過境服務櫃台
transit lounge	gwōh gíng hāu gèi sàt	過境候機室

Where can I get a trolley please?
chéng mǎn bìn dō hóh
yí lóh dó sáu tùi chè ā ?

請問邊度可
以攞到手推車呀?

My luggage hasn't arrived.
ngóh gē hang lěi jǔng měi dō

我嘅行李重未到

Is there a bus to (the city) please?
chéng mǎn yǎu mǒ bà
sí hūi (sí kùi) ā ?

請問有冇巴
士去(市區)呀?

Check-In & Departure 離境

Where's the downtown check-in counter?
hái sí kùi bìn dō bāan lěi
hang lěi fōo wǎn sáu jǔk ā ?

喺市區邊度辦理
行李付運手續呀?

What time do I have to check-in by?
géi si yīu hūi bāan léi dàng
gèi sáu jǔk ā?

幾時要去辦理登
機手續呀?

Is there a flight to (Nanking) today?
gàm yāt yǎu mǒ hong bàan
fēi hūi (naam gìng) ā?

今日有冇航班
飛去(南京)呀?

When's the next flight to (Xi'an)?
hā yàt bàan fēi (sài ngòn) gē
hong bàan hǎi géi dím jùng ā?

下一班飛(西安)嘅
航班係幾點鐘呀?

What's the flight number?
hong bàan hǒ mǎ hǎi géi
dòh hǒ ā?

航班號碼係幾
多號呀?

How long does this flight take?
nì gōh hong bàan yīu fēi
géi nǒi ā?

呢個航班要飛
幾耐呀?

Is it a direct flight?
nì bàan hǎi m hǎi jīk
hong gèi ā?

呢班係唔係直
航機呀?

I'd like to check-in my luggage.
ngǒh yīu bāan hang léi fòo
wǎn sáu jǔk

我要辦行李付
運手續

I'd like an aisle/window seat.
ngǒh séung yīu yàt gōh (jáu lóng
tùng dō; chèung háu) jǒh wái

我想要一個(走廊
通道; 窗口)座位

I'm a (Qantas) Frequent Flyer member.
ngǒh hǎi (ngò hong) fēi hang
seung hāak wóoi yuen

我係(澳航)飛行
常客會員

What's the charge for each excess kilogram?
chìu chúng hang léi mǒoi gùng
gàn yīu sàu géi dòh chín ā?

超重行李每公
斤要收幾多錢呀?

How much is the airport tax?
gèi cheung sūi yīu sàu géi
dòh chín ā?

機場稅要收幾
多錢呀?

additional flight	gà bàan gèi	加班機
airbus (plane)	hùng jùng bà sí	空中巴士
air bus (bus)	tùng tìn bà sí;	通天巴士;
	gèi cheung bà sí	機場巴士
aeroplane	fèi gèi	飛機
air ticket	gèi pīu	機票
airline company	hong hùng gùng sì	航空公司
airport	gèi cheung	機場
airport tax	gèi cheung sūi	機場稅
arrival	yǎp gíng	入境
boarding	dàng gèi	登機
boarding pass	dàng gèi jīng	登機證
business class	sèung mǒ hāak wái	商務客位
cancel	chúi sìu	取消
charter flight	bàau gèi	包機
confirm	kōk yǐng	確認
customs	hói gwàan	海關
customs declaration	hói gwàan	海關
	sàn bō dàan	申報單
departure	chùt gíng	出境
departure tax	lei gíng sūi	離境稅
economy class	gìng jāi hāak wái	經濟客位
estimated time of arrival (ETA)	dō dǎat si gāan	到達時間
estimated time of departure (ETD)	héi fèi si gāan	起飛時間
first class	tau dáng	頭等
flight number ...	... hǒ hong bàan	... 號航班
gate	dàng gèi jǎap háu	登機閘口
gate no ...	... hǒ dàng gèi	... 號登機
	jǎap háu	閘口
hand luggage	sáu tai hang léi	手提行李
helicopter	jǐk sìng gèi	直升機
jet	pān sě gèi	噴射機

jumbo	jàn bó hāak gèi	珍寶客機
life jacket	gāu sàng yì	救生衣
no smoking	bàt jún kàp yìn	不准吸煙
non-smoking area	gām yìn kùi	禁煙區
passenger terminal	hāak wǎn dǎai lau	客運大樓
passport	wǒo jīu	護照
propeller	loh suen jéung	螺旋槳
restricted area	gām kùi	禁區
seat belt	ngòn chuen dáai	安全帶
smoking area	kàp yìn kùi	吸煙區
transit	gwōh gíng	過境
Transportation Centre	wǎn sùe jùng sàm	運輸中心
visa	chìm jīng	簽證
waiting lounge	hǎu gèi sàt	候機室

Paperwork 文書

address	děi jí	地址
age	nin ling	年齡
date of birth	chùt sàng nin	出生年
	yǔet yàt	月日
height	sàn gò	身高
itinerary	hang ching bíu	行程表
married	yí fàn	已婚
name	sīng ming	姓名
nationality	gwōk jīk	國籍
occupation	jìk yīp	職業
passport	wǒo jīu	護照
passport number	wǒo jīu hǒ má	護照號碼
place of birth	chùt sàng děi	出生地
profession	jùen yīp	專業
religion	jùng gāau	宗教
single	dàan sàn	單身
transit	gwōh gíng	過境

GETTING AROUND

BUS, TRAM & TROLLEY BUS   陸路交通

It's very cheap to travel by local bus in China. You can also travel long distances by bus on major routes, along all the newly built highways. One of the advantages of regional bus travel is being able to look around little towns and villages that you wouldn't normally see. The drawbacks are that they are usually crowded and noisy, and the ride is often bumpy and uncomfortable in remote areas. If unlucky, you may even have to stand for some or all of the trip. Make good use of your toilet breaks because some buses don't have toilet facilities. Trolley buses are also available in the mainland's major cities, normally cooperating with local buses.

There are many buses in Hong Kong and they serve different purposes. There are also the more luxurious buses with air-conditioning but, of course, they cost more. Buses to and from the mainland are also quite convenient. Trams are only available in Hong Kong Island but they are a good and cheap way to tour the island. Sightseeing buses and open-top buses operate frequently all year round. Book through your hotel counter in advance. There are other franchised buses that run express from one destination to another including the airport, with fixed prices and routes.

The franchised Maxicabs are green and cream in colour, and service minor routes. Exact fares are needed as no change is given.

DID YOU KNOW ...

Traditionally all the thrones of Chinese emperors face south. Being seated facing southward symbolises sovereignty.

For the Chinese, the westerly direction represents the heavenly paradise. To say someone's 'returned to the western paradise' means they have passed away.

GETTING AROUND

Another type of minibus, red and cream coloured, is privately owned. Fares may rise at rush hours and become even more expensive during storms! To give you an indication, their fares are usually more expensive than buses, but much cheaper than taxis. Some minibuses run 24 hours a day. While the destinations are fixed, the routes and the stops are flexible depending on traffic and customers' needs.

Does this minibus go to (... ferry pier)?
nì gā síu bà hūi m hūi
(... mǎ tau) ā?
呢架小巴去唔去
(... 碼頭)呀?

Which bus goes to (... subway station) please?
chéng mǎn bìn yàt gā bà sí
hūi (... děi tīt jāam) ā?
請問邊一架巴士
去 (... 地鐵站)呀?

I want to get off (at the corner).
ngǒh séung (hái gàai háu)
lǒk chè
我想(喺街口)
落車

Please tell me when we've reached that stop.
m gòi chéng nèi dō si gīu
ngǒh lǒk chè
唔該請你到時叫
我落車

air-conditioned bus	hùng tiu bà sí	空調巴士
airbus	gèi cheung bà sí	機場巴士
bus (in China)	gùng gǔng hēi chè	公共汽車
bus (in Hong Kong)	bà sí	巴士
bus stop	bà sí jāam	巴士站
bus terminal	bà sí júng jāam	巴士總站
Citybus	sing bà	城巴
double decker bus	sèung chang bà sí	雙層巴士
feeder bus	jìp bōk bà sí	接駁巴士
First Bus	sàn bà	新巴
franchised bus	jùen lěi bà sí	專利巴士
long-distance bus station	cheung to hēi chè jāam; hāak wǎn jāam	長途汽車站; 客運站

Maxicab	jùen sīn síu bà	專線小巴
minibus (in China)	mĭn bàau chè	麵包車
minibus (in Hong Kong)	síu bà	小巴
section	fàn dũen	分段
shuttle bus	chùen sòh bà sí	穿梭巴士
sightseeing bus	lűi yau bà sí	旅遊巴士
trolley bus	mo gwái dĭn chè	無軌電車
tunnel bus	sũi dŏ bà sí	隧道巴士

TRAIN   鐵路
Trains, LTR & Subways in Hong Kong 港內鐵路

Please give me an Octopus card.
m gòi béi ngŏh yàt jèung   唔該俾我一張
bàat dãat tùng kàat   八達通卡

How much is the fare to (Central) by MTR please?
chòh dĕi tīt hūi (jùng waan)   坐地鐵去(中環)
yīu gēi dòh chín ā?   要幾多錢呀?

How many stations before I reach (Shatin)?
nì dŏ hūi (sà tin) yīu dāap   呢度去(沙田)要搭
géi dòh gŏh jăam ā?   幾多個站呀?

At which station should I changeover?
hái bìn gŏh jăam jūen chè ā?   喺邊個站轉車呀?

Is this the right platform for ...?
chéng mǎn nì gŏh yŭet toi   請問呢個月台
hăi m hăi hūi ... gā?   係唔係去 ... 㗎?

AEL	Airport Express
KCR	Kowloon-Canton Railway East Rail
KMB	Kowloon Motor Bus Company Limited
LRT	Light Rail Transit
MTR	Mass Transit Railway
SF	Star Ferry Company Limited

| electrical train | dĭn hēi fã fóh chè | 電氣化火車 |
| KCR East Rail | gáu tīt dùng sīn | 九鐵東線 |

GETTING AROUND

Light Rail Transit LRT	hìng tīt	輕鐵
LRT stops	hìng tīt jāam	輕鐵站
MTR	děi tīt	地鐵
Octopus card	bāat dǎat tùng	八達通
subway station	děi tīt jāam	地鐵站
subway	děi tīt	地鐵
train station	fóh chè jāam	火車站

Hong Kong Stations 主要站線

Kwun Tong Line	gwòon tong sīn	官塘線
Tsuen Wan Line	chuen wàan sīn	荃灣線
Island Line	góng dó sīn	港島線
Admiralty	gàm jùng	金鐘
Causeway Bay	tung loh waan	銅鑼灣
Central	jùng waan	中環
Chai Wan	chaai wàan	柴灣
Ferry Pier Terminus	tuen moon mǎ tau	屯門碼頭
Kowloon	gáu lung	九龍
Kowloon Tong	gáu lung tong	九龍塘
Kwun Tong	gwòon tong	官塘
Lo Wu	loh woo	羅湖
Mong Kok	wǒng gōk	旺角
Quarry Bay	jàk yue chùng	鰂魚涌
Sam Shing Terminus	sàam sīng júng jāam	三聖 總站
Shatin	sà tin	沙田
Sheung Wan	sěung waan	上環
Tin Shui Wai	tìn súi wai júng jāam	天水圍 總站
Tsim Sha Tsui	jìm sà júi	尖沙咀
Tsuen Wan	chuen wàan	荃灣
Yuen Long Terminus	yuen lǒng júng jāam	元朗 總站

Trains in China 國內鐵路

The local train and subway tickets are relatively cheap in China. If you're not travelling first class, the journey could be noisy and the carriages crowded. Some people may even smoke in the non-smoking section of the train. There are hot water services available on most trains so you can bring your own tea bags, or buy them on the train. For long-distance travellers, food and drinks are available in the dining car.

The fastest long-distance trains, gò chùk lĭt chè, like the fastest train in Mainland China, run from Guangzhou to Kowloon in just a couple of hours. Other long-distance services also provide speedy, comfortable, safe and convenient travelling.

Can you help me find my seat/berth please?

chéng bòng ngőh wán ngőh 請幫我搵我

gē (jőh wái; chong wái) 嘅(座位; 床位)

Excuse me, this is my seat.

dūi m jŭi, nì gōh hăi ngőh 對唔住,呢個係我

gē wái 嘅位

Where is the dining car please?

chéng măn chàan chè hái 請問餐車喺

bìn dŏ ā? 邊度呀?

dining car	chàan chè	餐車
direct train	jĭk tùng chè	直通車
express train	dāk fāai	特快
fast train	fāai chè	快車
first class waiting room	yűen jőh hău chè sàt	軟座候車室
Guangzhou Through Train	gwóng jàu jĭk tùng chè	廣州直通車
hard-sleeper (2nd class)	ngăang ngőh	硬臥
hard-seat (2nd class)	ngăang jőh	硬座
local train	pó tùng chè	普通車
platform ticket	jăam toi pīu	站台票

railway station	fóh chè jāam	火車站
soft-seat (1st class)	yŭen jōh	軟座
soft-sleeper (first class)	yŭen ngöh	軟臥
Through Train	jīk tùng chè	直通車
train	fóh chè	火車

TAXI   的士

You can hail a taxi anywhere in Hong Kong except on some busy streets where boarding taxis is prohibited at certain times. Taxis run on meters, and the customers will have to pay the levy required for crossing most of the tunnels and bridges. It's important to know that taxis can only serve their designated areas. For example, the taxis licensed for the New Territory cannot cross over to the city, but the licence given to the 'city taxis' allows them access throughout Hong Kong. When paying, remember that a tip of about 5% to 10% of the fare is expected.

In China, taxis can be picked up from airport terminals, hotels and even on the streets. Instead of using a meter, some taxi drivers may want to negotiate a fixed price with you for your journey. For daily excursions or journeys to more remote areas, where the return trip is needed, it's possible to charter a taxi for half a day or a whole day. In some cases, the driver could even become your guide, but you'll have to ask for an English-speaking or experienced driver when booking.

I'd like to go to ...
  ngőh séung hūi ...   我想去 ...

How long does it take to go to ...?
  hūi ... yīu géi nŏi ā?   去 ... 要幾耐呀?

I want an English-speaking driver.
  ngőh yīu yàt wái sìk góng   我要一位識講
  yìng mán gē sì gèi   英文嘅司機

How much?
  géi dòh chín ā?   幾多錢呀?

Keep the change.
   m sái jáau lā   唔使找喇

Thank you.
   m gòi sāai   唔該晒

call a taxi	dá dìk	打的
charter (a taxi)	bàau chè	包車
one day charter	bàau yàt yăt chè	包一日車
half day charter	bàau bōon yăt chè	包半日車

Instructions 指示

Please stop here.
   chéng hái nì dŏ ting chè   請喺呢度停車

Please stop before the restricted area.
   chéng hái gām kùi jì chin   請喺禁區之前
   ting chè   停車

First go to (the station), then the airport.
   sìn hūi (fóh chè jăam), jōi   先去(火車站),再
   hūi gèi cheung   去機場

Stop at the next corner.
   m gòi hái hă yàt gōh gàai   唔該喺下一個街
   háu ting chè   口停車

Please hurry.
   m gòi fāai dì   唔該快啲

Please slow down.
   m gòi măan dì   唔該慢啲

Please wait here.
   chéng hái nì dŏ dáng ngŏh   請喺呢度等我

I will get off here.
   ngŏh hái nì dŏ lōk chè   我喺呢度落車

CAR   汽車

You can only drive in Hong Kong and Macau if you have an international licence. Parking could be a problem in the city areas. Most bridges and tunnels carry a levy. There are separate lanes for the drivers with the exact fare (express lanes) and those needing change. It's not advisable for visitors to drive in China.

Where can I rent a car?
　　hái bìn dõ hóh yí jò chè ā?　　　喺邊度可以租車呀?

How much	jò ... yīu géi	租 ... 要幾
is it for ...?	dòh chín ā?	多錢呀?
one day	yàt yãt	一日
three days	sàam yãt	三日
one week	yàt gōh sìng kei	一個星期

Does that include insurance?
　　lin m lin maai bó hím ā?　　　　連唔連埋保險呀?

driving licence	chè paai	車牌
to get in the car	sẽung chè	上車
to get out of the car	lõk chè	落車
international driving licence	gwōk jāi chè paai	國際車牌
rent a car	jò chè	租車
traffic accident	gàau tùng yī ngõi	交通意外

Traffic Signs 交通標誌

Most of the traffic signs are similar to those used internationally. But pay attention to different road laws, the most obvious being that in China you drive on the right-hand side of the road, whilst in Hong Kong you drive on the left.

give way	yẽung	讓
keep left	kāau jóh	靠左
keep right	kāau yãu	靠右
no entry	bàt jún sái yãp	不准駛入

no parking	bāt jún pǎak chè	不准泊車
no waiting	bāt jún ting chè dáng hǎu	不准停車 等候
one-way only	dàan ching lō	單程路
quiet	jìk jíng dẻi dāai	寂靜地帶
railway crossing	ping gàau dō	平交道
restricted area	gām kùi	禁區
slow	mǎan	慢
stop	ting	停
zebra crossing	bàan mǎ sīn	斑馬線

Useful words 應用詞匯

air	dá hēi	打氣
air-conditioning	hùng tiu; lǎang hēi	空調; 冷氣
battery	dǐn chi	電池
brake	sāat chè jāi	煞車掣
diesel	yau jà	油渣
engine oil	gái yáu	偈油
expressway	fāai chùk gùng lō	快速公路
flat tyre	bāau tàai	爆胎
fill up	gà yáu	加油
freeway	gò chùk gùng lō	高速公路
hand brake	sáu jāi	手掣
head light	chè tau dàng	車頭燈
highway	gùng lō	公路
map	dẻi to	地圖
oil	yáu	油
parking meter	ting chè sàu fài bìu	停車收費錶
parking ticket	ting chè kàat	停車卡
petrol	hēi yau; dǐn yau	汽油; 電油
radiator	súi sèung	水箱

rent a car	jò chè	租車
service station	gà yau jăam	加油站
stall	séi fóh	死火
superhighway	chìu kàp gùng lõ	超級公路
towing a car	tòh chè	拖車
traffic jam	sàk chè	塞車
tyre	chè tàai	車胎
unleaded petrol	bàt ham yuen hēi yau	不含鉛汽油
wiper	súi bŏot	水撥

BICYCLE   自行車

Is it within cycling distance?
cháai dàan chè hūi m hūi dó gā?   踩單車去唔去到㗎?

Where can I hire a bicycle?
bìn dŏ yău dàan chè chùt jò ā?   邊度有單車出租呀?

Where can I buy a (secondhand) bike?
bìn dŏ hóh yí máai dó
(yĭ sáu) dàan chè ā?   邊度可以買到
(二手)單車呀?

How much is it for ...?	jò ... yìu géi dòh chín ā?	租 ... 要幾 多錢呀?
one day	yàt yăt	一日
half day	bōon yăt	半日
an hour	yàt gŏh jùng tau	一個鐘頭

Do you have (a/an) ...?	yău mŏ ... ā?	有冇 ... 呀?
front lamps	chè tau dàng	車頭燈
gear lever	bòh gwàn	波棍
gears	chí lun	齒輪
handlebars	bá sáu	把手
helmet	tau kwài	頭盔
hub	lun jŭk	輪軸
inner tube	nŏi tàai	內胎
mountain bike	pàan sàan dàan chè	攀山單車

mudguard	dóng nai báan	擋泥板
padlock	dàan chè sóh	單車鎖
pannier	jàk láam	側籃
pedal	dãap báan	踏板
pump	bàm	泵
puncture	bāau tàai	爆胎
racing bike	chōi chè	賽車
rear lamps	hãu chè dàng	後車燈
reflector	fáan gwòng dàng	反光燈
to rent a bicycle	jò dàan chè	租單車
to repair	sàu léi	修理
saddle	chè jõh	車座
saddlebag	chè jõh hãu dói	車座後袋
spare parts	ling gín	零件
sprocket	lín lun	鏈輪
tandem	sèung yan dàan chè	雙人單車
tricycle	sàam lun chè	三輪車

BOAT   客輪

International cruises normally pick up passengers at the Ocean
Terminal, while regional ferries shipping to Macau and the
mainland have pick up points at almost every corner of Hong
Kong. Scheduled ferries also connect outlying islands of Hong
Kong. The cross harbour ferries include Star Ferry which runs
from early morning until late evening with several routes. Regular
sightseeing cruises also operate for visitors round the year.

China Ferry Terminal	jùng góng sing mã tau	中港城 碼頭
ferry(cross harbour)	dõ hói síu lun	渡海小輪
ferry (to China/Macau)	fàai chùk hāak lun	快速客輪
ferry ticket	suen fèi	船飛
hoverferry	hèi jín suen	氣墊船

DID YOU KNOW ...

The English word 'Rickshaw' comes from Japanese *jinrikisha*, literally meaning human powered vehicle. In Hong Kong, rickshaws once were widely used; but nowadays, there are only a few rickshaws left, mainly for tourists.

hydrofoil	súi yĭk suen	水翼船
jetfoil	pān sĕ suen	噴射船
local village ferry	gàai dó	街渡
Macau Ferry Terminal	góng ngō mă tau	港澳碼頭
Macau Ferry	góng ngō hāak lun	港澳客輪
Ocean Terminal	hói wăn dāai hă	海運大廈
Star Ferry	tìn sìng síu lun	天星小輪

Other Transport 其他工具

boat	tĕng jái	艇仔
funicular railway	sàan déng lāam chè	山頂纜車
junk	faan suen	帆船
motorbike	dĭn dàan chè	電單車
peak tramway	sàan déng lāam chè	山頂纜車
pedicab	sàam lún chè	三輪車
rickshaw	chè jái	車仔
speedboat	fāai tĕng	快艇
tramway	dĭn chè	電車
yacht	yau tĕng	遊艇

ACCOMMODATION 住宿

The main cities have a wide range of accommodation, ranging from five star hotels to simple bunk beds. Most of the luxury hotels have some English-speaking staff, but if you want to stay in cheap local accommodation, you may find this chapter useful.

With most accommodation in China, make sure you know the service hours of restaurants and the availability of the hot water supply.

The general classification of accommodation is as follows:

Luxury Hotel 賓館

hotel	jáu dīm	酒店
	dãai jáu dīm	大酒店
	fãan dīm	飯店
	bàn gwóon	賓館
five star hotel	ng̃ sìng jáu dīm	五星酒店
four star hotel	sēi sìng jáu dīm	四星酒店

Inn/Guesthouse 旅社

Rooms in these only have basic facilities.

inn	lũi gwóon	旅館
	lũi sē	旅舍
	hāak jáan	客棧
guesthouse	jìu dõi sóh	招待所

Apartment/Dormitory 宿舍

apartment	gùng yũe	公寓
dormitory	sùk sē	宿舍
International	gwōk jāi chìng nìn	國際青年
Youth Hostel	hõk sàng lũi gwóon	學生旅館
youth hostel	chìng nìn sùk sē	青年宿舍

FINDING ACCOMMODATION 訪尋住宿

If you need assistance in finding accommodation, the information desk at the airport or railway station will help you.

ACCOMMODATION

I'm looking for a ... hotel.	ngǒh séung wán yàt gàan ... gē jáu dīm	我想搵一間 ... 嘅酒店
cheap	peng	平
clean	gón jěng	干淨
good	hó	好
near the airport	gǎn gèi cheung	近機場
near the city	gǎn sí kùi	近市區
near the station	gǎn chè jāam	近車站
nearby	nì dǒ fǒo gǎn	呢度附近

Where's a ...?	chéng mǎn bìn dǒ yǎu ... ā?	請問邊度有 ... 呀?
hotel	jáu dīm	酒店
guesthouse	jìu dǒi sóh	招待所
youth hostel	chìng nin sùk sē	青年宿舍

What's the address?
dēi jí hái bìn dǒ ā?

地址喺邊度呀?

Could you write down the address for me please?
m gòi sé gōh dēi jí béi ngǒh

唔該寫個地址俾我

Could you tell the taxi driver the address please?
m gòi wǎ gōh dēi jí béi
dìk sí sì géi tèng

唔該話個地址俾
的士司機聽

Could you draw a map for me please?
m gòi wǎak fùk dēi to béi ngǒh

唔該畫幅地圖俾我

Is it possible to walk from here?
haang lō hūi m hūi dó ā?

行路去唔去到呀?

Yes, it isn't far.
hūi dó, hó kán jè

去到, 好近啫

No, it's a long way.
haang lō hūi m dó, hó yǔen gā

行路去唔到, 好遠㗎

Booking Ahead 預訂

Do you have any rooms/beds available?
    chéng màn yǎu mǒ hùng   請問有冇空
    (fong gàan; chong wái) ā?   (房間; 床位)呀?

We'll be arriving (at six o'clock).
    ngǒh děi (lùk dím jùng) dō   我哋(六點鐘)到

I'd like a ...	ngǒh séung yīu yàt gōh ...	我想要一個 ...
bed	chong pò	床舖
big room	dǎai gē fong gàan	大嘅房間
single room	dàan yan fóng	單人房
twin room	sèung yan fóng	雙人房
quiet room	chìng jǐng gē fong gàan	清靜嘅房間

ACCOMMODATION

AT THE HOTEL
Checking In 接待

酒店服務

I don't have a booking.
    ngǒh mǒ yūe děng dō fong gàan   我冇預訂到房間

I've made a reservation.
    ngǒh yǐ gìng děng jóh fong gàan   我已經訂咗房間

I'm a member (of ...).
    ngǒh hǎi (... gē) wōoi yuen   我係(... 嘅)會員

My name is ...
    ngǒh gōh méng gīu jǒ ...   我個名叫做 ...

We're (two) adults and (one) child.
    ngǒh děi yǎu (léung gōh) dǎai   我哋有(兩個)大
    yan tung maai (yàt gōh) sāi lǒ gòh   人同埋(一個)細路哥

This is my ...	nì gōh hǎi ngǒh gē ...	呢個係我嘅 ...
ID card	sàn fán jīng	身份證
membership card	wóoi yuen jīng	會員證
passport	wǒo jīu	護照

Requirements 需求

I want a room with ... (and ...)	ngőh yīu yàt gàan yấu ... (tung maai ...) gē fóng	我要一間 有 ... (同埋 ...) 嘅房
air-conditioning	hùng tiu	空調
bathroom	chùng leung fóng	沖涼房
double bed	sèung yan chong	雙人床
harbour view	hói gíng	海景
heater	nűen lo	暖爐
microwave	mei bòh lo	微波爐
refrigerator	sūet gwǎi	雪櫃
shower	fà sá	花洒
telephone	dīn wá	電話
TV	dīn sĭ	電視
toilet	wǎi sàng gàan	衛生間
window	chèung háu	窗口

ACCOMMODATION

THEY MAY SAY ...

ngőh dĕi yắu hó dòh fóng	We have plenty of rooms.
dūi m jŭe, gàm yầt mőon sāai	Sorry, we're full today.
mő sāai fóng	No vacancies.
néi dĕi yīu jŭe géi dóh mǎan ā?	How many nights will you be staying?
yắu géi dóh yan ā?	How many people?
néi dĕi yīu géi dóh gōh (fóng/chong wái) ā?	How many rooms/beds do you want?
yắu mő jīng gín ā?	Do you have any identification?
chéng tin hó jŭe hāak dàng gēi bíu.	Please fill out the registration forms.
mőoi gōh (yan/fóng) yīu ...	It's ... per person/room.
chéng béi jóh (bó jīng gàm/fóng jò) sìn	Please pay deposit/room charge first.

Negotiation 協商

How much is it per night?
    chéng mǎn yīu géi dòh chín
    yàt mǎan ā?
請問要幾多錢一晚呀?

How much is it per person?
    géi dòh chín yàt gōh yan ā?
幾多錢一個人呀?

Is there a discount for children/students?
    (sāi lō gòh/hōk sàng)
    yǎu mō jìt kāu ā?
(細路哥/學生)
有冇折扣呀?

Would I get a discount if I stayed longer?
    jǔe nōi dì yǎu mō jìt kāu ā?
住耐啲有冇折扣呀?

Does it include (dinner and) breakfast?
    lin m lin (mǎan chàan tung
    maai) jó chàan ā?
連唔連(晚餐同
埋)早餐呀?

Are there any cheaper rooms?
    jǔng yǎu mō peng dì gē fóng ā?
重有冇平啲嘅房呀?

Can I see the room first?
    hóh m hóh yí tái yàt tái
    gàan fóng sìn ā?
可唔可以睇一睇
間房先呀?

Are there any others?
    jǔng yǎu mō kei tà gē?
重有冇其他嘅?

I like this/that room.
    ngōh jùng yī (nì/góh) gàan fóng
我中意(呢/嗰)間房

It's fine, I'll take this room.
    hó, ngōh yīu nì gàan fóng
好, 我要呢間房

I'm going to stay for ... ngōh dá sūen jǔe ... 我打算住 ...
    a night   yàt mǎan   一晚
    two nights   léung mǎan   兩晚
    a few days   géi yǎt   幾日
    a week   yàt gōh sìng kei   一個星期

ACCOMMODATION

ACCOMMODATION

Service 服務

Where's the ...?	chéng màn ... hái bìn dõ ā?	請問 ... 喺邊度呀?
bar	jáu bà	酒吧
business centre	sèung mõ jùng sàm	商務中心
conference room	wŏoi yí sàt	會議室
dining room	chàan tèng	餐廳
gym	gìn sàn sàt	健身室
laundry	sái sàam fong	洗衫房
lounge	yàu sìk sàt	休息室
swimming pool	yau wǐng chi	游泳池
visitor's lounge	wŏoi hãak sàt	會客室

Please take all my luggage to room (123).

m gòi bòng ngŏh bòon dì hang　唔該幫我搬啲行
léi hūi (yàt yí sàam hŏ) fóng　李去(一二三號)房

Please wake me up at (6:30 am) tomorrow morning.

m gòi tìng jìu (lŭk dím bōon)　唔該聽朝(六點半)
gìu séng ngŏh　叫醒我

I need (a/an) ...	ngŏh séung yīu ...	我想要 ...
adapter	dĭn jāi bīn wŏon hēi	電掣變換器
dryer	chùi fùng túng	吹風筒
fan	dĭn fùng sīn	電風扇
some hangers	géi gŏh yì gá	幾個衣架
table lamp	tói dàng	檯燈

Do you have a/an ...?	chéng màn néi dẽi yãu mŏ ... ā?	請問你 哋有冇 ... 呀?
computer	dĭn nŏ	電腦
copy machine	yíng yān gèi	影印機
internet (provider)	yàn dãk mŏng	因特網
internet café	mŏng lŏk gā fè	網絡咖啡
fax machine	chuen jàn gèi	傳真機
stationery	man gŭi	文具
type writer/	dá jĭ gèi	打字機

| No visitors. | jē jūet tāam fóng | 謝絕探訪 |
| Please do not disturb. | chèng măt sò yĭu | 請勿騷擾 |

Requests & Queries 問訊

The key for room ... please.
  m gòi béi ... hŏ fóng gē
  sóh si ngŏh

唐該俾 ... 號房嘅
鎖匙我

Is hot water available all day?
  hāi m hāi seng yăt yáu
  yĭt súi ā?

係唔係成日有
熱水呀?

Please fill up the flask with boiling water.
  m gòi gà mŏon gōh
  nŭen súi wóo

唔該加滿個
暖水壺

Please call a taxi for me.
  m gòi bòng ngŏh gīu gā dĭk sí

唔該幫我叫架的士

Any (bikes) for rent here?
  nì dŏ yáu mŏ (dàan chè)
  chùt jò ā?

呢度有冇(單車)
出租呀?

Any ... for me please?	chéng măn yáu mŏ ngŏh gē ... ā?	請問有冇我嘅 ... 呀?
fax messages	chuen jàn	傳真
letters	sūn	信
telegrams	dĭn bō	電報
telephone messages	dĭn wá lau yĭn	電話留言

I'll be back in (a half/one) hour.
  ngŏh (bōon/yàt) gōh jùng
  tau jì hāu fàan lei

我(半/一)個鐘
頭之後番嚟

Please keep it in the safe.
  chéng sàu maai hái bó hím
  sèung bó gwóon

請收埋喺保險
箱保管

ACCOMMODATION

Laundry 洗熨

Could I have these clothes ... please?	m gòi bòng ngőh ... nì dì yì fŭk	唔該幫我 ... 呢啲衣服
drycleaned	gòn sái	干洗
ironed	tōng hó	熨好
washed	sái gòn jěng	洗干淨

Is my laundry ready?
ngőh dì yì fŭk dàk mēi ā?   我啲衣服得未呀?

There's something missing.
síu jóh yàt gìn   少咗一件

I need it ...	ngőh ... yīu	我 ... 要
this afternoon	gàm yàt ngāan jāu	今日晏晝
tonight	gàm màan	今晚
tomorrow	tìng yàt	聽日

Complaints 不滿

The room needs to be cleaned.
chéng dá sō fong gàan   請打掃房間

Please change the sheets/pillow case.
chéng wŏon (chong dàan; jám tau tō)   請換(床單; 枕頭套)

The room is too ...	nì gàan fóng tāai gwōh ...	呢間房 太過 ...
big	dáai	大
cold	dūng	凍
dark	ngām	暗
dirty	wòo jò	污糟
hot	yĭt	熱
noisy	cho cháau	嘈吵
small	sāi	細
windy	dáai fùng	大風

There's no hot/boiling water.
  mő (yĭt/gwán) súi — 冇(熱/滾)水

I don't like this room.
  ngőh m jùng yĭ nì gàan fóng — 我唔中意呢間房

Can I change rooms?
  chéng wőon dǎi yĭ gàan
  fóng béi ngőh — 請換第二間
房俾我

The ... doesn't work.	... wāai jóh	... 壞咗
TV	dĭn sĭ	電視
shower	fà sá	花洒
telephone	dĭn wá	電話
light	dàng	燈
tap	súi hau	水喉
electrical outlet	chāap sò	插蘇

The ... is blocked.	... sàk jŭe jóh	... 塞住咗
bath-tub	yŭk gòng	浴缸
sink	sái sáu poon	洗手盆
toilet	chi sóh	廁所

I can't open/ close the ...	ngőh (hòi/sàan) m dó ...	我(開/門) 唔到 ...
curtain	chèung lím	窗簾
door	fóng moon	房門
wardrobe	yì gwǎi	衣櫃
window	chèung	窗

I can't turn on the ...	ngőh hòi m dò ...	我開唔到 ...
cooler	lǎang hēi gèi	冷氣機
fan	dĭn fùng sīn	電風扇
heater	nűen hēi	暖氣
light	dàng	燈
shower	fà sá	花洒
tap	súi hau	水喉
TV	dĭn sĭ	電視

This room smells.
> nì gàan fóng yáu gwāai mēi   呢間房有怪味

The door's locked.
> fóng moon sóh jūe jóh   房門鎖住咗

Please have it fixed as soon as possible.
> m gòi jūn fāai sàu léi   唔該儘快修理

CHECKING OUT   退房

I'd like to check out ...	ngőh ... tūi fóng	我 ... 退房
now	yi gà	而家
tomorrow	tìng yàt	聽日
in a while	dáng yàt jān gàan	等一陣間

Do you accept ...?	néi dēi sàu m sàu ... à?	你哋收唔收 ...呀?
US dollars	méi gàm	美金
travellers' cheques	lūi hang jì pīu	旅行支票
credit card	sūn yúng kàat	信用卡

I'm returning ...	ngőh ... fàan lei	我...番嚟
tomorrow	tìng yàt	聽日
in two/three days	léung sàam yàt	兩三日
next week	hā gőh sìng kei	下個星期

I'd like to settle the account.
> ngőh yi gà béi chín jáau sō   我而家俾錢找數

Can I leave my luggage here for a few days?
> hóh m hóh yí bòng ngőh bó   可唔可以幫我保
> gwóon géi yàt ngőh dì hang léi   管幾日我啲行李

Thank you for your hospitality.
> dòh jē néi dēi gē fūk mō   多謝你哋嘅服務

Some Useful Words 應用詞匯

| air-conditioning | hùng tiu | 空調 |
| babysitter | lam si bó mő | 臨時褓姆 |

baggage	hang léi	行李
balcony	lõ toi	露台
basin	sái mǐn poon	洗面盆
bathroom	chùng leung fóng	沖涼房
bed	chong	床
blanket	mo jìn	毛氈
bucket	túng	桶
candle	lãap jùk	蠟燭
chair	dāng	凳
checking in	hòi fóng	開房
checking out	tūi fóng	退房
cooler	lǎang hēi gèi	冷氣機
cot	yǔk yìng chong	育嬰床
curtain	chèung lím	窗簾
dining room	fãan tèng	飯廳
double bed	sèung yan chong	雙人床
dryer	chùi fùng túng	吹風筒
duty manager	jīk bàan gìng léi	值班經理
English newspaper	yìng mán bō jí	英文報紙
hangers	yì gá	衣架
heating	nŭen hēi	暖氣
hot water	yĭt súi	熱水
iron	tōng dáu	熨斗
key	sóh si	鎖匙
lift (elevator)	sìng gōng gèi; lìp	升降機; 軐
light bulb	dàng dáam	燈膽
lobby	dăai tong	大堂
lock	sóh	鎖
luggage	hang léi	行李
massage	ngōn mòh	按摩
mattress	chong jín	床墊
mirror	gēng	鏡
mosquito net	màn jēung	蚊帳

operator	jīp sīn sàng;	接線生;
	júng gèi	總機
pillow	jám tau	枕頭
pillowcase	jám tau tō	枕頭套
porter	moon fóng;	門房;
	fūk mŏ yuen	服務員
reception desk	fūk mŏ toi	服務台
registration card	jŭe hāak dàng gēi kàat	住客登記卡
room	fong gàan	房間
room service	hāak fóng sūng	客房送
	chàan fūk mŏ	餐服務
sauna	sòng na yŭk	桑拿浴
service charge	fūk mŏ fài	服務費
shower	fa sá	花洒
sleeping bag	sūi dói	睡袋
soap	fàan gáan	番枧
suitcase	hang léi sèung	行李箱
suite room	tō fóng	套房
swimming pool	yau súi chi	游水池
telephone	dīn wá	電話
TV	dīn sī	電視
toilet paper	chī jí	廁紙
towel	mo gàn	毛巾
twin room	sèung yan fóng	雙人房
valuables	gwāi jŭng màt bán	貴重物品
wardrobe	yì gwāi	衣櫃
water	súi	水

AROUND TOWN　　市內

The cities in the Cantonese-speaking regions offer endless activities, they are cities that never sleep. These cities harmoniously blend modern life with culture and tradition. Things can happen on any street corner at any time. No matter what time of the day it is, you are sure to have something to do and see.

STREET LIFE　　街景

What's this?
　nì dì hāi màt yé lei gā?　　呢啲係乜嘢嚟㗎?

What's happening?
　fāat sàng màt yé sĭ ā?　　發生乜嘢事呀?

What's happened?
　fāat sàng jóh màt yé sĭ ā?　　發生咗乜嘢事呀?

What's she/he doing?
　kŭi jŏ gán dì màt yé ā?　　佢做緊啲乜嘢呀?

What are they selling?
　kŭi dĕi măai gán dì màt yé ā?　　佢哋賣緊啲乜嘢呀?

Do I need to call the police/ambulance?
　yīu m yīu bòng néi gīu
　(gíng chāat; sǎp jĭ chè) ā?　　要唔要幫你叫
　　(警察; 十字車)呀?

Can I help you?
　ngőh hóh yí bòng
　néi dì màt yé ā?　　我可以幫
　　你啲乜嘢呀?

Can I have one please?
　hóh m hóh yí béi yàt
　gőh ngőh ā?　　可唔可以俾一
　　個我呀?

cooked food stall	sŭk sĭk dōng	熟食檔
kiosk	síu sĭk dìm	小食店
market	sí cheung	市場
newspaper kiosk	bō tàan	報攤

parade	yau hang	遊行
public toilet	gùng chī	公廁
rubbish bin	lāap sāap túng	垃圾桶
stall	tàan dōng	攤檔
tobacco kiosk	yìn dōng	煙檔

AROUND TOWN

AT THE BANK   银行

The banks in Hong Kong are well known for their efficiency
and the variety of tasks which they can perform. Besides the
import and export banking businesses, foreign currency exchange
is another major function. If you are planning to stay longer,
you may even open an account. You can use your bank card to
withdraw money from ATMs throughout the area. After business
hours, money exchange shops and the service desks of hotels can
exchange money, but they may charge higher rates than the banks'
official rates.

Credit cards are quite popular and convenient, and travellers
cheques may get an even better rate of exchange than cash.

In Macau, currency rates are worth marginally less than the Hong
Kong dollar. However, Hong Kong dollars are often more welcome
than the Macau dollar. So if you're coming from or going on to
Hong Kong, skip the Macau money. Likewise in some areas of
southern China, Hong Kong dollars and other foreign currencies
are often more welcome than the local Renminbi.

Where can I exchange money?
    bìn dõ hóh yí dūi wõon   邊度可以兌換
    ngõi bāi ā?   外幣呀?

Can I change money here?
    nì dõ hóh m hóh yí dūi   呢度可唔可以兌
    wõon ngõi bāi ā?   換外幣呀?

Can I cash the (travellers cheque; bankdraft)?
    nì dõ hóh m hóh yí dūi wõon   呢度可唔可以兌換
    (lúi hang jì pīu; ngan hong   (旅行支票; 銀行
    bóon pīu) ā?   本票)呀?

I want to exchange (US$) (cash; travellers cheque).
    ngõh séung dūi wõon (méi   我想兌換(美
    gàm) (yĭn chàau; lúi hang jì pīu) 金)(現鈔; 旅行支票)

How much can I get for (US$100)?
    (méi gàm yàt bàak màn) hóh   (美金一百文)可
    yí wõon dó géi dòh chín ā?   以換到幾多錢呀?

What's the exchange rate?
wǒoi lút hǎi géi dòh ā?　　　　匯率係幾多呀?

What's your commission?
néi dēi yīu sàu géi dòh　　　　你哋要收幾多
chín yúng gàm ā?　　　　　　錢佣金?

Please write it down.
m gòi chéng sé dài　　　　　唔該請寫低

I'd like some smaller notes.
ngǒh séung yīu dì sāi chàau　　我想要啲細鈔

Can I transfer money overseas?
ngǒh hóh m hóh yí wǒoi　　　我可唔可以匯
chín hūi ngǒi gwòk ā?　　　　錢去外國呀?

Can I have money transferred here from (Canada)?
ngǒh hóh m hóh yí hái (gà na　　我可唔可以喺(加拿
dǎai) wǒoi chín lei nì dō ā?　　大)匯錢嚟呢度呀?

Has my money arrived yet?
ngǒh dì chín dō jóh měi ā?　　我啲錢到咗未呀?

account	wǒo háu	戶口
airwaybill	hùng wǎn tai dàan	空運提單
ATM	jǐ dǔng tai fóon gèi	自動提款機
amount	ngan mǎ	銀碼
bank	ngan hong	銀行
bankdraft	ngan hong bóon pīu	銀行本票
bank manager	ngan hong gìng léi	銀行經理
banknote	jí bǎi	紙幣
black market	hàk sí	黑市
buying rate	mǎai yǎp gā	買入價
cash	yīn gàm	現金
cashier	chùt nǎap	出納
cheque	jì pīu	支票
coins	sūi ngán	碎銀
commission	yúng gàm	佣金
counter	gwǎi tói	櫃檯

credit card	sūn yŭng kàat	信用卡
deposit	chuen fóon	存款
draft	wŏoi pīu	匯票
exchange	jáau wŏon;	找換;
	dūi wŏon	兌換
exchange rate	ngŏi wŏoi paai gā;	外匯牌價;
	wŏoi lút	匯率
foreign currency	ngŏi bǎi	外幣
identification card	sàn fán jīng	身份證
interest	lĕi sìk	利息
invoice	fāat pīu	發票
letter of credit	sūn yŭng jīng	信用證
remittance	wŏoi fóon	匯款
selling rate	mǎai chùt gā	賣出價
signature	chìm méng	簽名
telegraphic transfer	dĭn wŏoi	電匯
travellers' cheque	lŭi hang jì pīu	旅行支票
waybill	tai dàan	提單
withdrawal	tai fóon	提款

Currency 外幣

Australian A$	ngō yuen	澳元
Canadian $	gà na dǎai yuen	加拿大元
Deutschmarks	mǎ hàk	馬克
Euro	ngàu loh	歐羅
French franc F	fāat long	法朗
HK$	góng yuen	港元
Japanese yen ¥	yăt yuen	日元
Macau pataca M$	po bǎi	葡幣
New Taiwan NT$	sàn toi bǎi	新台幣
Renminbi ¥	yan man bǎi	人民幣
UK £	yìng bóng	英鎊
US$	mĕi gàm	美金

Black Market 黑市

There is a high risk when exchanging Renminbi on the black market. If you have exchanged money at a bank or an authorised outlet, you should always keep the official receipts.

black market	hàk sí	黑市
black market rate	hàk sí gā	黑市價
exchange rate	ngői wōoi paai gā	外匯牌價
official rate	gùng gā	公價

AT THE POST OFFICE   郵政

Besides sending mail at post offices in China, you can send cables and make long-distance and international phone calls (although making calls from your hotel may save precious time as queues often form at the post office). Commemorative stamps and first-day covers can become good souvenirs. The main post offices in large cities are more experienced in sending international mail, especially the express, parcel and registered mails. When filling out any forms or writing addresses, write all the English words in block letters to avoid unnecessary misunderstandings.

There should be no communication problems in post offices in Hong Kong and Macau.

I'd like to send a/an	ngőh séung	我想
... (to Australia).	... (hūi ngõ jàu)	... (去澳洲)
aerogram	gēi gōh hong hùng yau gáan	寄個航空郵束
cable	dá dīn bō	打電報
card	gēi jèung kàat	寄張卡
Christmas card	gēi jèung sīng dāan kàat	寄張聖誕卡
express mail	gēi gōh fāai yau	寄個快郵
fax	fāat yàt fān chuen jàn	發一份傳真
letter	gēi fùng sūn	寄封信
parcel	gēi gōh bàau gwóh	寄個包裹

postcard	gēi jèung ming sūn pín	寄張明信片
telegram	dá dīn bō	打電報

How much is the postage?
géi dòh chín yau fài ā? 幾多錢郵費呀?

What's the weight of this?
nì gōh yáu gēi chńg ā? 呢個有幾重呀?

I'd like some stamps.
ngőh séung yīu dì yau pīu 我想要啲郵票

Are there any	yáu mő	有冇
... restrictions?	... hãan jāi ā?	... 限制呀?
size	dãai sāi chēk chūen	大細尺寸
thickness	háu dő	厚度
weight	chńg lēung	重量

address	dēi jí	地址
aerogram	hong hùng yau gáan	航空郵柬
airmail	hùng yau	空郵
consignee	sàu gín yan	收件人
envelope	sūn fùng	信封
express mail	fàai yau	快郵
fax	chuen jàn	傳真
general post office	yau jīng júng gúk	郵政總局
insurance	bó hím	保險
letter	sūn	信
letter box	yau túng	郵筒
PO box	yau jīng sūn sèung	郵政信箱
parcel	bàau gwóh	包裹
postcard	ming sūn pín	明信片
postcode	yau jīng pìn hő	郵政編號
poste restante	yau gín dői líng	郵件待領
post office	yau jīng gúk	郵政局
printed matter	yān chāat bán	印刷品
registered mail	gwā hő	掛號

AROUND TOWN

stamps	yau pīu	郵票
surface mail	ping yau	平郵
telegram	dǐn bō	電報
urgent telegram	gán gàp dǐn bō	緊急電報

TELECOMMUNICATIONS   電訊
Telephone 電話

Using the telephone is extremely convenient in Hong Kong. Phone calls are reasonably priced, readily available and technologically advanced. Dialling your home country is as easy as dialing locally. Some families even set up other lines for the children's private use. Public phones are not as widely used as in other countries because most of the restaurants and stores allow the customers to use their phones free of charge. The popularity of mobile phones is almost unequalled anywhere else in the world. If you are doing business, hiring a pager or a mobile phone would be a good idea.

Out of the major cities, private phones are still uncommon in China. Some families have to share a line and in some remote areas there may only be a few phones per village. Making a long-distance call through the operator may take a very long time. Most cities now have their own area codes, enabling people to dial direct to anywhere in the world.

What's the area code for (France) please?
chéng mǎn (fàat gwōk) gē děi   請問(法國)嘅地
kùi jǐ tau hǎi géi dòh hǒ ā?   區字頭係幾多號呀?

I want to ring (Spain).
ngǒh yīu dá gōh dǐn wá   我要打個電話
hūi (sài bàan nga)   去(西班牙)

The number is ...
dǐn wá hǒ mǎ hǎi ...   電話號碼係 ...

I'd like to make a long-distance call to (Xi'an).
ngǒh yīu dà gōh cheung to   我要打個長途
dǐn wá hūi (sài ngòn)   電話去(西安)

Have you got a telephone interpreting service here?
　　nì dŏ yáu mŏ dĭn wá chuen　　呢度有冇電話傳
　　yĭk fŭk mŏ ā?　　譯服務呀?

Where can I rent a mobile phone?
　　chéng mān bìn dŏ hóh yĭ　　請問邊度可以
　　jò dó sáu tai dĭn wá ā?　　租到手提電話呀?

Where can I send a fax?
　　chéng mān bìn dŏ hóh yĭ　　請問邊度可以
　　fàat chuen jàn ā?　　發傳真呀?

area code	dēi kùi jĭ tau	地區字頭
beeper	chuen fŏo gèi	傳呼機
collect call	dūi fòng fŏo fóon	對方付款
country code	gwōk jāi pìn hŏ	國際編號
direct dial	jĭk bŏot dĭn wá	直撥電話
directory	dĭn wá bó	電話簿
engaged	dĭn wá m tùng	電話唔通
(China)	jìm sīn	佔線
extension	fàn gèi	分機
extension number	nŏi sín hŏ má	內線號碼
international call	gwōk jāi dĭn wá	國際電話
local call	sí nŏi dĭn wá	市內電話
long-distance call	cheung to dĭn wá	長途電話
make a phone call	dá dĭn wá	打電話
mobile phone	dăai gòh dăai;	大哥大;
	sáu tai dĭn wá	手提電話
operator	jĭp sīn sàng	接線生
(in China)	júng gèi	機總
pager	chuen fŏo gèi	傳呼機
person to person	gĭu yan dĭn wá	叫人電話
public telephone	gùng jūng dĭn wá	公眾電話
return a call	fŭk dĭn wá	覆電話
station (of beeper)	chuen fŏo toi	傳呼台

AROUND TOWN

telephone	dīn wá	電話
telephone booth	dīn wá ting	電話亭
telephone card	dīn wá kàat	電話卡
telephone charge	dīn wá fāi	電話費
telephone number	dīn wá hō mǎ	電話號碼
wrong number	dá chōh dīn wá	打錯電話
yellow page directory	wong yǐp dīn wá bó	黃頁電話簿

Making a Call 搭線

Hello!
  wái/wéi   喂

Is (Mrs Hung) at home please?
  chéng mǎn (hung tāai táai)   請問(洪太太)
  hái ngùk kéi mā?   喺屋企嗎?

I'm looking for (Mr Lee).
  ngőh séung wán (léi sìn sàang)   我想搵(李先生)

I'm calling from (New Zealand).
  ngőh hái (náu sài laan) dà lei gē   我喺(紐西蘭)打嚟嘅

What time will she/he be back?
  kűi wōoi géi sí fàan lei ā?   佢會幾時番嚟呀?

Thank you!
  m gòi sāai   唔該晒

I'll call again ...   我 ... 會再
  ngőh ... wōoi jōi   打電話嚟
  dá dīn wá lei

  at two o'clock   hái léung dím jùng   喺兩點鐘
  half an hour later bōon gōh jùng   半個鐘
                    tau hǎu   頭後
  soon   yàt jǎn   一陣
  tomorrow   tìng yàt   聽日
  tonight   gàm màan   今晚

AROUND TOWN

THEY MAY SAY ...

néi hãi bìn yàt wái ā?	Who's calling please?
bìn gōh ā?	Who is it?
wán bìn gōh ā?	Who are you calling for?
kéui m hái dõ	He/She's not here.
chéng néi dáng yàt jãn	Just a minute please.
chéng néi dàng yàt jãn jōi dá lei	Please call again later.
chéng lau dài sīng ming tung maai dīn wá hõ mã	Please leave your name and telephone number.
yãu màt yẽ sĩ chéng néi góng dài là	Please leave a message.
jīm sīn	The line's busy.
dāap chōh sīn; dá chōh dĩn wá	Wrong number.
kéui dẽi bòon jáu jóh lā	They've moved.

AROUND TOWN

SIGHTSEEING 觀光

Excuse me, what is this/that?
chéng mãn (nì/góh) dì hãi màt yẽ ā?
請問(呢/嗰)啲係
乜嘢呀?

What are the special attractions?
yãu màt yẽ dãk bĩt gē dẽi fōng ā? 有乜嘢特別嘅地方呀?

Am I allowed to take photos here?
chéng mãn nì dõ béi m béi yíng séung ā?
請問呢度俾唔俾
影相呀?

Do you have a/an ... ?	chéng mãn néi dẽi yãu mõ ... ā?	請問你 哋有冇 ... 呀?
English guidebook	yìng mán sũet ming sùe	英文説 明書
guidebook	sũet ming sùe	説明書
local map	dòng dẽi dẽi to	當地地圖

What time does it (open/close)?

géi dím jùng (hòi/sàan) moon ā? 幾點鐘(開/閂)門呀?

How much is ... ?	... géi dòh chín ā?	... 幾多錢呀?
the admission fee	yàp cheung fài	入場費
the guidebook	sūet ming sùe	説明書
the postcard	ming sūn pín	明信片
this	nì gōh	呢個

ancient	góo dói	古代
archaeology	háau góo	考古
art gallery	méi sùt gwóon	美術館
building	gīn jùk	建築
lookout	gwòon gíng toi	觀景台
market	sí cheung	市場
monument	góo jìk	古跡
museum	bōk màt gwóon	博物館
old city	gàu sing sí	舊城市
pagoda	tāap	塔
ruins	wai jìk	遺跡
sculpture	sōk jēung	塑像
sightseeing	gwòon gwòng	觀光
souvenirs	gēi ním bán	紀念品
statues	sōk jēung	塑像
theatre	kēk yúen	劇院

Guided Tours 導遊

You can book most local tours through travel agents and hotel service desks.

Where can I book the tour?

hái bìn dò hóh yí yūe dēng
lúi hang tuen ā?

喺邊度可以預訂
旅行團呀?

Do you organise (English speaking) group tours?

néi dēi yáu mó bāan (góng
yìng mán gē) lúi hang tuen ā?

你哋有冇辦(講
英文嘅)旅行團呀?

I want to join this (half-day) tour.
　ngőh séung chàam gà nì
　gōh (bōon yǎt) tuen

我想參加呢
個(半日)團

What is the departure time?
　géi dím jùng chùt fāat ā?

幾點鐘出發呀?

Where is the pick-up point?
　hái bìn dō jāap hǎp ā?

喺邊度集合呀?

I'm with this group.
　ngőh tung maai nì gōh tuen gē

我同埋呢個團嘅

I've lost my group.
　ngőh jáu sàt jóh ngőh gōh tuen

我走失咗我個團

Have you seen a group of (Australians)?
　chéng mǎn yǎu mő gīn dó
　yàt gōh (ngő jàu) tuen ā?

請問有冇見到
一個(澳洲)團呀?

How long will we stop for?
　ngőh dēi wōoi ting géi női ā?

我哋會停幾耐呀?

What time do we have to be back?
　ngőh dēi yīu géi dím
　jùng fàan lei ā?

我哋要幾點
鐘番嚟呀?

I don't want too many shopping stops.
　ngőh m séung ngòn paai gām
　dòh mǎai yế gé si gāan

我唔想安排咁
多買嘢嘅時間

I want to buy some (Chinese herb medicine; handicrafts).
　ngőh séung mǎai dì (jùng
　yếuk; sáu gùng ngǎi bán)

我想買啲(中
藥; 手工藝品)

AROUND TOWN

day tour	chuen yǎt yau	全日遊
half-day tour	bōon yǎt yau	半日遊
night tour	mǎan sěung gwòon gwòng	晚上觀光
city tour	sí női gwòon gwòng	市內觀光
cruise	yau suen hóh	遊船河
guide (person)	dő yau	導遊

ENTERTAINMENT & NIGHTLIFE   娛樂

The Cantonese attitude towards nightlife is 'eat, drink, play and enjoy' or hēk, hōt, wŏon, lŏk, with 'eat' being the most important aspect.

There are hundreds of nightspots some of which are expensive. Movies however, remain the most popular entertainment night or day.

Sometimes traditional Peking opera, Cantonese opera, comedy or 'witty dialogue' in different dialects is performed. However, local favourites would be the concerts given by popular singers, the horse races and soccer games.

Besides these, most of the local people also enjoy playing mahjong, ma jēuk, or watching the local and international TV programs.

The well-known night view from Victoria Peak in Hong Kong, said to be worth a million dollars, is free of charge.

What's there to do in the evenings?
  yé mǎan yǎu màt jīt mǔk ā?   夜晚有乜節目呀?

Is there a (karaoke bar) here?
  nì dǒ yǎu mǒ (kà làai OK) ā?   呢度有冇(卡拉OK)呀?

I'd like to see (a/an) ...	ngőh séung tái ...	我想睇 ...
acrobatic show	jăap gĕi bíu yín	雜技表演
dog racing	páau gáu	跑狗
horse racing	páau mǎ	跑馬
movie	dǐn yíng	電影

I'd like to (go to) ...	ngőh séung hūi ...	我想去 ...
a (singing) concert	tèng yín chēung	聽演唱
a casino	dó cheung	賭場
go on a night tour	chàam gà mǎan	參加晚
	sĕung gwòon gwòng	上觀光
play mahjong	dá ma jēuk	打麻雀

Some Useful Words 應用詞匯

acrobat	jăap gēi	雜技
Cantonese opera	yŭet kēk	粵劇
cinema	hēi yúen	戲院
circus	mă hēi	馬戲
dance	tĭu mŏ	跳舞
disco	dìk sĭ gò	的士高
dog racing	páau gáu	跑狗

SIGNS 標誌	
BEWARE OF DOGS	提防惡犬
BEWARE OF PICK POCKETS	提防小手
COLD/HOT	冷/熱
CLOSED	關閉
DANGER	危險
EMERGENCY	緊急
ENTRANCE	入口
EXIT	出口
INFORMATION	詢問處
KEEP QUIET	蕭靜
MEN/WOMEN	男/女
NO ADMITTANCE	不准進入
NO ENTRY	不准駛入
NO FLASHLIGHTS	不准用閃光燈
NO PARKING	不准停車
NO PHOTOGRAPHY	禁止攝影
NO SMOKING	不准吸煙
OPEN	開
PROHIBITED	禁止
RESTRICTED AREA	禁區
TOILETS	洗手間
MALE	男
FEMALE	女

AROUND TOWN

floor show	fòh sò	科騷
folk dance	tó fùng mő	土風舞
local opera	dĕi fòng hēi	地方戲
magic show	mòh sŭt bíu yín	魔術表演
movie	dīn yíng	電影
night club	yĕ júng wóoi	夜總會
nightlife	yĕ sàng wõot	夜生活
night tour	mấan sĕung	晚上
	gwòon gwòng	觀光
Peking opera	gìng kĕk	京劇
song & dance troupe	gòh mő tuen	歌舞團
theatre	kĕk yúen	劇院
witty dialogue	sēung sìng	相聲

INTERESTS

興趣

COMMON INTERESTS

同樂

It is common to see tens to hundreds of people in the morning doing group Tai Chi. They may be up as early as dawn. These people are mostly elderly Chinese. Some other people prefer walking tracks, whilst others do slow (wooden) sword exercises. Other common interests are similar to those in other cities in the world.

OPINIONS & INTERESTS

喜好

While some Cantonese people are blunt and will tell you how or what they feel, others prefer not to express their opinion. One way of telling these people apart is by observing their facial expressions. A polite smile and a nod probably means that you have crossed the line and that you should stop. By the same token, you may find it hard to stop some enthusiastic Cantonese people from talking!

What do you like?
néi jùng yī dì màt yế ā?　　　　你中意啲乜嘢呀？

What's your hobby?
néi yǎu màt yế sī hō ā?　　　　你有乜嘢嗜好呀？

Would you like to ...?
néi jùng m jùng yī ... ā?　　　　你中唔中意 ... 呀？

I (don't) like ...	ngỗh (m) jùng yī ...	我(唔)中意 ...
chess	jùk kéi	捉棋
dancing	tīu mố	跳舞
football (playing)	tèk jùk kau	踢足球
football (watching)	tái jùk kau	睇足球
going shopping	haang gùng sì	行公司
Hong Kong	hèung góng	香港
music	tèng yàm ngōk	聽音樂
photography	sīp yíng	攝影
reading	tái sùe	睇書

sport	wǎn dǔng	運動
swimming	yau súi	游水
travelling	lǚi hang	旅行

MAHJONG   麻雀

Although Mahjong, ma jēuk, literally means 'sparrow', it actually has nothing to do with the bird. Mahjong is quite a common game within the Cantonese community and its popularity is spreading to most Chinese and Japanese communities internationally. The Mahjong tiles have pictures and numbers on one side. People play Mahjong to kill time, some do it for fun, some as a social or business activities, or for gambling. Some even think it is good for the health since you can exercise both hands. In Hong Kong, some gambling dens are even called Mahjong School, ma jēuk hōk hǎau. An experienced player can recognise the different tiles simply by touching them. Playing Mahjong is a common way for guests to get to know each other before weddings or birthday banquets.

There are four players (number of players and tiles may vary among different regions) in this game. Every one initally gets 13 páai, or tiles. They pick up a new tile and surrender one thus maintaining 13 throughout the game. The first person who can use all their 13 tiles, plus the new one, to arrange a specified series wins. A Marathon Mahjong game can sometimes last for days and nights with only toilet and meal breaks.

to be a banker	jō jòng	做莊
banker	jòng gà	莊家
Mahjong	ma jēuk	麻雀
Mahjong tile	páai	牌
Mahjong den	ma jēuk gwóon	麻雀館
Mahjong party	jēuk gǔk	雀局
Mahjong player (col)	ma jēuk gēuk	麻雀腳
to play Mahjong	dá ma jēuk	打麻雀
a playing cycle	hùen	圈

There are 144 Mahjong tiles including:

萬子
măn jí — craks (from 1 to 9, each x 4 = 36)

索子
sōk jí — bams (from 1 to 9, each x 4 = 36)

筒
tung — dots (from 1 to 9, each x 4 = 36)

花(梅蘭菊竹)
fà — flowers: plum, orchid, chrysanthemum, bamboo (= 4)

四季(春夏秋冬)
sēi gwāi — seasons: spring, summer, autumn, winter (= 4)

風(東南西北)
fùng — wind: east, south, west, north (each x 4 = 16)

中/發/白
jùng/fāat/bǎak — dragons: centre, produce, white (each 4 x 3 = 12)

GEOMANCY – FUNG-SHUI   勘輿

The Cantonese phrase fung-shui literally 'wind and water' first derived from a form of divination to select the good sites for burial or for construction. Later it became an art of creating harmony between humans and their environment (specially mountains and water). It involves a certain arrangement of furniture or mirrors in the home. Fung-shui experts were even consulted when a subway was built! Some of the practices are quite logical, creating a comfortable working environment so that you may concentrate better, thus creating wealth. But most of the practices seem superstitious. A specified direction or spot is supposed to make more money. The professional practitioner of this geomancy is referred to as the geomancy master fūng súi sìn sàang. He knows how to examine the site and find the real dragon's den, the good fung-shui, for you. They are also commonly called fũng súi ló, 'the fung-shui guy'.

In Hong Kong, there are morning fung-shui tours with commentary on the local geomancy which include some well known buildings in town.

dragon's den	lung yǔet	龍穴
to examine (fung-shui)	tái (fũng súi)	睇(風水)
fung-shui	fũng súi	風水
fung-shui compass	loh gàng	羅更
geomancer	fũng súi ló	風水佬
geomancer master	fũng súi sìn sàng	風水先生

MUSICAL INSTRUMENTS   國樂

The Chinese classical instruments are classified by the materials they are made from. It is called bāat yàm, (literally eight sounds); they are:

金 gàm, metalware	鐘 jùng, bronze bells
石 sěk, stoneware	磬 hīng, tuned stone slabs
絲 sì, string	二胡 yī wóo, *er-hu* a two-string lute
竹 jùk, bamboo	簫笛 sìu and dēk, flutes
匏 paau, bottle gourd	笙 sàng, reed pipe mouth-organ
土 tó, ceramics	
革 gāak, leatherware	鼓 góo, drums
木 mǔk, wooden	木魚 mǔk yue, fishmouth-like knocker

Among these, the stoneware, ceramics and wooden instruments are not common nowadays. Wooden knockers can be found in temples where monks knock them rhythmically while reading the scriptures.

China developed many musical instruments over thousands of years, the majority of which have been adopted by the Cantonese people. Traditionally, bronze bells (similar to chimes) were the most popular instruments used in the Emperor's court.

There were also woodwind instruments called sìu and dĕk, which are very similar to flutes and the sàng, a gourd-shaped hand-held instrument with a row of 13 (or more) reed pipes.

Common stringed instruments include the butterfly harp yeung kám, the *er-hu*, yĭ wóo and the *pi-pa*, pei pá. The jàng is a flat stringed zither with 13 strings similar to the Japanese *koto*. Woodwinds and strings form the main portion of traditional Cantonese music instruments, making sì jùk, strings and woodwinds, the alternative name of Cantonese music. This sound is often enriched by combining with violins and other Western musical instruments. Drums, góo, gongs, loh, and cymbals, bāt, are played during the New Year celebrations and on other festive events.

One characteristic of traditional Chinese music is its omission of the fourth note of the scale, fa, and the seventh note, ti. This leaves only the pentatonic scale of do, re, mi, so and la – likened to only playing the black notes of the piano.

Where can I see the Cantonese opera?
  bìn dŏ yáu dāai hēi tái ā?   邊度有大戲睇呀?

Which musical instrument do you play?
  néi wáan màt yé ngŏk hēi ā?   你玩乜嘢樂器呀?

I (don't) like ...	ngŏh (m) jùng yī ...	我(唔)中意 ...
Cantonese music	gwóng dùng yàm ngŏk	廣東音樂
string/woodwind music	gòng naam sì jùk	江南絲竹
classical music	góo dín yàm ngŏk	古典音樂
Chinese music	jùng gwŏk yàm ngŏk	中國音樂
music	yàm ngŏk	音樂
popular music	lau hang yàm ngŏk	流行音樂
Western music	sài yeung yàm ngŏk	西洋音樂

INTERESTS

Cantonese Opera 粵劇

粵劇	yũet kēk	Cantonese opera
大戲	dãai hēi	Cantonese opera (Col)
京劇	gìng kēk	Peking opera
地方戲	dẽi fòng hēi	local opera
潮劇	chiu kēk	Chaozhou opera
梨園	lei yuen	theatre (traditional name)
梨園子弟	lei yuen jí dãi	actors of the troupe
小生	síu sàng	actor or actress who takes male parts in Cantonese opera
花旦	fà dāan	actor or actress who takes female parts in Cantonese opera
丑角	cháu gōk	clown
大花面	dãai fà mín	1st clown
二花面	yĩ fà mín	2nd clown

POLITICS   政治

Like anywhere else in the world, politics can be a touchy subject.
It's probably best not to discuss politics when meeting people for
the first time, however once you've made friends you can try
some of the phrases below.

What do you think of the current government?
  néi yĩng wai yĩn jĩng fóo　　你認為現政府
  hó m hó ā?　　　　　　　好唔好呀?

Politicians are all the same.
  jĩng jí gà dò hãi gám　　　政治家都係咁

In my country, we have a left-wing/conservative government.
  ngõh dẽi gwōk gà hãi (gùng　我哋國家係(工
  dóng; bó sáu dóng) jàp jĩng　黨; 保守黨)執政

Did you hear about ...?
  yáu mõ tèng dó gwàan　　　有冇聽到關
  yùe ... gē sìu sìk ā?　　　　於 ... 嘅消息呀?

What do you think?
  néi yĩng wai dím ā?　　　　你認為點呀?

I (don't) agree with this policy on ...

ngőh (m) jāan sing nì gõh ... jīng chāak	我(唔)贊成呢個 ... 政策

I am against/in favour of the ... policy.

	ngőh (fáan dūi; jāan sing) ... jīng chāak	我 (反對; 贊成) ... 政策
drugs	dŭk bán	毒品
environment	waan bó	環保
free education	yǐ mő gāau yŭk	義務教育
immigration	yi man	移民
military service	bīng yĭk	兵役
social welfare	sế wóoi fūk lẽi	社會福利
tax	sūi mő	稅務

Useful Words 應用詞匯

candidate	hãu súen yan	候選人
commonwealth	luen bòng	聯邦
Commonwealth (British)	yìng luen bòng	英聯邦
Communist Party	gũng cháan dóng	共產黨
Conservative Party	bó sáu dóng	保守黨
constitution	hīn fãat	憲法
constitutional monarchy	gwàn júe lãap hīn	君主立憲
democracy	man júe	民主
Democratic Party	man júe dóng	民主黨
direct election	jĩk jĩp súen gúi	直接選舉
election	súen gúi	選舉
Government	jīng fóo	政府
Labour Party	gùng dóng	工黨
left-wing	jóh yĭk	左翼
local government	dễi fòng jīng fóo	地方政府
Liberal Party	jĩ yau dóng	自由黨
Monarchy	gwàn júe jīng jāi	君主政制

National People's Congress (NPC)	chuen gwōk yan man dŏi bíu dăai wóoi	全國人民代表大會 (人大)
Opposition Party	fáan dūi dóng	反對黨
	jīng dóng	政黨
political apathy	jīng jī láang gám	政治冷感
politically neutral	jīng jī jùng lăap	政治中立
political propaganda	jīng jī sùen chuen	政治宣傳
political system	jīng jāi	政制
politician	chung jīng yan sĭ	從政人士
politics	jīng jī	政治

SHOPPING   購物

Hong Kong is great for shopping. There's a huge variety of goods available and, best of all, there are no import duties for most goods. The period between December and the Chinese New Year is the best time for shopping. To avoid counterfeits, rejects and defective goods in Hong Kong, shop in HKTA-recommended shops, or those offering international guarantees.

Shopping in Macau is similar to Hong Kong although the range offered is smaller. Liquor and tobacco don't have import duties.

In Mainland China, there is a limited range of imported goods, but the shops are full of traditional Chinese artefacts. China is the mother country of tea, silk products and chinaware, and still the world leader in these fields.

There are markets on every street corner and they have reasonable quality goods at low prices. The street markets in Hong Kong sell practically anything and are worth visiting just for the experience. The famous Ladies' Street, nűi yán gàai is an excellent example of such markets.

LOOKING FOR ...   寻询

Where's the nearest ...?

	chéng mǎn jūi kán gē	请问最近嘅
	... hái bìn dõ ā?	... 喺边度呀?
I'm looking for a/an ...	ngóh yīu wán ...	我要搵 ...
7-Eleven store	chàt sǎp yàt bīn léi dīm	7-Eleven 便利店
antique shop	góo wóon dīm	古玩店
bakery	mǐn bàau gùng sì	面包公司
bank	ngan hong	银行
barber	léi fãat dīm	理发店
bookshop	sùe dīm	书店
butcher	yǔk sǐk gùng sì	肉食公司
camera shop	sīp yíng hēi choi gùng sì	摄影器材公司

SHOPPING

Chinese product emporium	jùng gwōk gwōk fōh gùng sì	中國國貨公司
department store	bāak fōh gùng sì	百貨公司
dress shop	si jòng dīm	時裝店
duty free shop	mín sūi dīm	免稅店
electrical appliance shop	dīn hēi pó	電器舖
florist	fà dīm	花店
free market	jí yau sí cheung	自由市場
fruit shop	sàang gwóh dīm	生果店
goldsmith	gàm hóng	金行
grocer's shop	jāap fōh pó	雜貨舖
hairdresser	fāat long	髮廊
handicraft shop	gùng ngái bán dīm	工藝品店
jade free market	yúk hēi sí cheung	玉器市場
Japanese department store	yàt bóon bāak fōh gùng sì	日本百貨公司
jeweller's shop	jùe bó hóng	珠寶行
laundry	sái yì dīm	洗衣店
lunar New Year's Eve free market	nin sìu sí cheung	年宵市場
market	sí cheung	市場
money exchange	jáau wóon dīm	找換店
musical instrument shop	ngŏk hēi hóng	樂器行
pharmacy	yĕuk fong	藥房
public square	dāai dāat déi	大笪地
salon	méi yung yúen	美容院
shoe shop	haai pó	鞋舖
shop	gùng sì	公司
shopping arcade	sèung cheung	商場
shopping centre	kāu māt jùng sàm	購物中心
souvenir shop	lái bán dīm	禮品店

SHOPPING

stall	tàan dōng	攤檔
stationers	man gǔi dīm	文具店
store	sǐ dòh	士多
supermarket	chìu kàp sí cheung	超級市場
tailor	choi fúng dīm	裁縫店
trading firm	sèung hóng	商行
travel agency	lǔi hang sé	旅行社
vegetable shop	sòh chōi sèung dīm	蔬菜商店

MAKING A PURCHASE
採購

Where can I find ...?
hái bīn dǒ hóh yí wán dó ... ā?
喺邊度可以搵到 ... 呀?

I'd like to buy ...
ngǒh séung mǎai ...
我想買 ...

I'm just looking around.
ngǒh jàu wai tái yàt tái sìn
我周圍睇一睇先

How much does this/that cost?
(nì/góh) gōh géi dòh chín ā?
(呢/嗰)個幾多錢呀?

This is very expensive.
nì gōh gā chin hó gwāi
呢個價錢好貴

That's cheap.
nì gōh gā chin hó peng
呢個價錢好平

Do you have others?
jǔng yáu mǒ dǎi yǐ dì ā?
重有冇第二啲呀?

Do you have a better/cheaper one?
jǔng yáu mǒ (hó dì; peng dì) gē?
重有冇(好啲; 平啲)嘅?

Do you accept credit cards?
néi dēi sàu m sàu sùn
yǔng kàat ā?
你哋收唔收信
用卡呀?

I'd like a receipt in English.
ngǒh séung yīu jèung yǔng
yìng mán sé gē sàu gǔi
我想要張用
英文寫嘅收據

Does it have an international guarantee?
yáu mǒ gwōk jāi bó yǔng gā?
有冇國際保用㗎?

SHOPPING

Returning Goods 退換

I'd like to return this, please.
m gòi, ngőh yīu tūi fōh   唔該, 我要退貨

I'd like to change this, please.
m gòi, ngőh yīu wőon nì yàt gīn   唔該, 我要換呢一件

I don't like this ...	ngőh m jùng yī	我唔中意
	nì yàt gōh ...	呢一個 ...
colour	ngaan sìk	顏色
pattern	fà yéung	花樣
style	fóon sìk	款式

I've found a better/cheaper one.
ngőh wán dò lĩng yàt gōh   我搵到另一個
(hó/peng) dì gē   (好/平)啲嘅

It's faulty.
wăai jóh   壞咗

It's broken/damaged.
lăan jóh   爛咗

I'd like my money back.
ngőh yīu lóh fàan ngőh dì chín   我要攞返我啲錢

BARGAINING & PRICES   議價

Bargaining is an art. Some people bargain while others don't, but you could ask if you could negotiate prices by saying yáu mő gā gòng ā? Normally, at privately owned shops or stalls, you stand a better chance of bargaining. Also, buying more will increase your negotiating power. Before doing so, however, make sure you have the things you want, and don't bother buying poor quality goods, even if they are cheap.

You may also express the amount you wish to pay for the goods by keying the figure in the calculator and showing it to the vendor. It's also advisable to check other prices before buying.

Department stores are not ideal places for bargaining. However, they have occasional sales which offer many bargain goods.

SHOPPING

It's too expensive!		
gā chin tāai gwāi lā	價錢太貴喇	

Can you reduce the price a bit?
peng síu síu dàk m dàk ā? 平少少得唔得呀?

Do you have something cheaper?
yǎu mó peng dì gē? 有冇平啲嘅?

I don't have much money.
ngǒh mó gām dòh chín 我冇咁多錢

Do you give discounts?
yǎu mó jīt tau dá ā? 有冇折頭打呀?

(100) dollars per ...	mǒoi ... (yàt bàak) màn	每 ... (一百)文
dozen	dà	打
piece	gǐn/gōh	件/個
set	tō/fǎn	套/份

Can you give me a ... discount?	dá gōh ... dàk m dàk ā?	打個 ... 得唔得呀?
5%	gáu ńg jīt	九五折
10%	gáu jīt	九折
15%	bāat ńg jīt	八五折
20%	bāat jīt	八折
30%	chàt jīt	七折

THEY MAY SAY ...

séung yīu dì màt yě ā?	What would you like?
yīu géi dòh ā?	How many/much do you want?
chéng chui bín tái la	Please take your time.
sūe bàt tūi wòon dòh jě	Sorry, no refund and no exchange. Thank you.
măai sāai!	Sold out!
mó fōh!	Not in stock!
mó dǎai/jùng/sāi mǎ.	No L/M/S size.
jūi hǎu yàt gǐn!	Last one!

I'll buy this if you make it cheaper.
   peng dì ngőh jāu mǎai   平啲我就買

No bargain.
   mő gā góng   冇價講

No second price.
   bàt yǐ gā   不二價

bargaining	góng gā	講價
buy (two) get one free	mǎai (yǐ) sūng yàt	買(二)送一
clearance sale	chìng fōh dāai	清貨大
	gáam gā	減價
discount	dá jīt kāu	打折扣
half price	bōon gā	半價
on sale	dāai gáam gā	大減價
sale	dāai peng mǎai	大平賣

DISCOUNTS

When talking about a discount, the number applies to the amount paid rather than the amount being taken off. For example, instead of saying 15% off, the Cantonese say 85%.

10% discount – 90%	gáu jīt	九折
15% discount – 85%	bāat nǵ jīt	八五折

SOUVENIRS   禮品

calligraphy	sùe fāat	書法
carpets	děi jìn	地氈
chinaware	chi hēi	瓷器
chopsticks	fāai jí	筷子
curios	góo wóon	古玩
dolls	gùng jái	公仔
earrings	yí wáan	耳環

SHOPPING

embroidery	chī sāu	刺繡
fabrics	bō lĭu	布料
fans	sīn	扇
foods	sĭk bán	食品
furniture	gà sì	傢俬
gold products	gàm hēi	金器
handbag	sáu dói	手袋
handicrafts	sáu gùng ngăi bán	手工藝品
jade products	yŭk hēi	玉器
jewellery	jùe bó	珠寶
lacquerware	chàt hēi	漆器
leatherwork	pei gŭi	皮具
musical instruments	ngōk hēi	樂器
necklace	géng lín	頸鏈
paintings	wá	畫
paper cuts	jín jí	剪紙
pearl	jàn jùe	珍珠
personal seal	to jèung	圖章
porcelain	chi hēi	瓷器
postcard	ming sūn pín	明信片
pottery	to hēi	陶器
scrolls	gúen jŭk	卷軸
sculpture	dìu hàk	雕刻
shuttle-cock	yín	毽
silk products	sì jìk	絲織
silver products	ngan hēi	銀器
souvenirs	gēi nĭm bán	紀念品
toys	wŏon gŭi	玩具

ELECTRICAL APPLIANCES   影音

Hong Kong is one of the best Audio/Video markets in the world.
Here, you can find the latest and the most advanced model of
almost any product at a reasonable price.

amplifier	kwōng yàm gèi	擴音機
audio/video shop	yíng yàm hēi choi gùng sì	影音器材公司
blank tapes	hùng bāak chi dáai	空白磁帶
cable TV	yáu sīn dǐn sǐ	有線電視
cassette tapes	kà sìk lǔk yàm dáai	卡式錄音帶
copy machine	yìng yān gèi	影印機
DVD	sō mǎ yíng díp	數碼影碟
DVD player	sō mǎ yíng díp gèi	數碼影碟機
eight mm video tape	bāat mǎi lei lǔk yíng dáai	八米厘錄影帶
fax machine	chuen jàn gèi	傳真機
hair dryer	fùng túng	風筒
headphone	yǐ túng	耳筒
microphone	mài gò fùng	咪高峰
microwave oven	mei bòh lo	微波爐
minidisc player	síu yíng díp gèi	小影碟機
monitor	hín sǐ hēi	顯示器
multi system	gwōk jāi sīn lō	國際線路
NTSC system	NTSC sīn lō	NTSC線路
plug	chāap táu	插頭
power cord	dǐn sīn	電線
recorder	lǔk yàm gèi	錄音機
remote control	yiu hūng	遙控
speakers	lā bà	喇叭
tape recorder	kà sìk lǔk yàm gèi	卡式錄音機
VCD	yíng díp	影碟
VCD player	yíng díp gèi	影碟機
video camera	sīp lǔk gèi	攝錄機
video tape	lǔk yíng dáai	錄影帶
VCR	lǔk yíng gèi	錄影機

SHOPPING

MUSIC 音樂

I'm looking for a CD by ...
ngốh wán gán ... gē CD díp 我搵緊 ... 嘅CD碟

Do you have the latest recording by ...
yấu mố ... gē jūi sàn lǔk yàm ā? 有冇 ... 嘅最新錄音呀?

Where can I find the ... section?
chéng mǎn ... bō hái bìn dõ ā? 請問 ... 部喺邊度呀?

Can I listen to this here?
ngốh hóh m hóh yí hái 我可唔可以喺
nì dõ sī tèng ā? 呢度試聽呀?

Do you have this on ...?	nếi dēi yấu mố nì jēk gē ... ā?	你哋有冇呢 隻嘅 ... 呀?
CD	CD díp	CD碟
cassette	kà sìk dáai	卡式帶
record	chēung pín	唱片

Cantonese music	gwóng dùng yàm ngốk	廣東音樂
Chinese music	jùng gwōk yàm ngốk	中國音樂
choral	hắp chēung	合唱
classical music	góo dín yàm ngốk	古典音樂
guitar	gīt tà	結他
hit song	lau hang kùk	流行曲
jazz	jēuk sī yàm ngốk	爵士音樂
keyboard (piano)	dīn jí kam	電子琴
music	yàm ngốk	音樂
musical instrument	ngốk hēi	樂器
opera	gòh kếk	歌劇
piano	gōng kam	鋼琴
popular music	lau hang yàm ngốk	流行音樂
rock & roll	yiu báai ngốk	搖擺樂
singing	gòh chēung	歌唱
soft music	hìng yàm ngốk	輕音樂
soprano	nűi gò yàm	女高音

| tenor | naam gò yàm | 男高音 |
| vocal | sìng ngõk | 聲樂 |

SHOPPING

RENTING VIDEOS 租賃

Make sure you have adequate equipment and the correct PAL or NTSC systems before you rent video tapes, VCD and DVD.

I'd like to rent a (videotape/VCD).
ngõh séung jò (lŭk yíng 我想租(錄影
dáai; yíng díp). 帶; 影碟)

Do you have a/an ... (video/VCD)?	yáu mő ... (lŭk yíng dáai; yíng díp) ā?	有冇 ... (錄影帶; 影碟)呀?
cartoon	kà tùng	卡通
Chinese	jùng mán	中文
English	yìng mán	英文
French	fãat mán	法文
karaoke	kà làai OK	卡拉 OK
Kung-Fu	gùng fòo	功夫
musical	yàm ngõk	音樂

When is this due back?
géi si yīu waan ā? 幾時要還呀?

How much for renting it for (one/two) nights?
jò (yàt/léung) mán yīu 租(一/兩)晚要
géi dòh chín ā? 幾多錢呀?

How much is the deposit?
yīu géi dòh chín bó jìng gàm ā? 要幾多錢保證金呀?

DVD	sō mã yíng díp	數碼影碟
DVD player	sō mã yíng dĩp gèi	數碼影碟機
minidisc	síu yíng díp	小影碟
VCR	lŭk yíng gèi	錄影機
VCD	yíng díp	影碟
VCD player	yíng dĩp gèi	影碟機
videotape	lŭk yíng dáai	錄影帶

PHOTOGRAPHY 攝影

SHOPPING

How much is it to process this film?
chùng sāai nì tung fèi lám
yīu gèi dòh chín ā?
沖晒呢筒菲林
要幾多錢呀?

Do you have one-hour processing?
néi dèi yáu mő yàt síu si
chùng sāai fúk mő ā?
你哋有有一小
時沖晒服務呀?

When will it be ready?
géi si dàk ā?
幾時得呀?

I'd like to have some passport photos taken.
ngőh yīu yíng wőo jīu séung
我要影護照相

I'd like a film/battery for this camera.
ngőh yīu wán jēk ngàam nì gőh
séung gèi gē (fèi lám; dǐn chi)
我要搵隻啱呢個
相機嘅(菲林; 電池)

Would you insert the film/battery for me please.
m gòi néi tung ngőh yǎp
nì gőh (fèi lám; dǐn chi)
唔該你同我入
呢個(菲林; 電池)

I'd like to buy (two rolls of) film.
ngőh yīu mǎai (léung tung)
fèi lám
我要買(兩筒)
菲林

automatic camera	chuen jí dũng	全自動
	yíng séung gèi	影相機
battery	dǐn chi	電池
B/W film	hàk bǎak fèi lám	黑白菲林
camera	yíng séung gèi	影相機
colour	chói sìk	彩色
colour film	chói sìk fèi lám	彩色菲林
colour slide	chói sìk wǎan dàng pín	彩色幻燈片
digital camera	sō mǎ yíng séung gèi	數碼影相機
enlarge	fōng dāai	放大
film	fèi lám	菲林
film speed	fèi lám chùk dõ	菲林速度
flash	sím gwòng dàng	閃光燈

SHOPPING

Fuji film	fōo sĭ fèi lám	富士菲林
instant camera	jìk yíng jìk yáu séung gèi	即影即有相機
Kodak film	òh dāat fèi lám	柯達菲林
lens	gēng tau	鏡頭
lens cap	séung gèi gōi	相機蓋
lens paper	māat gēng tau jí	抹鏡頭紙
light metre	chàk gwòng bìu	測光錶
negative film	fèi lám dái pín	菲林底片
photo	jìu pín	照片
photography	sīp yíng	攝影
slide	wăan dàng pín	幻燈片
slide projector	wăan dàng gèi	幻燈機
telephoto lens	cheung gēng	長鏡
timer	si gāan jāi	時間掣
tripod	sàam gēuk gá	三腳架
video camera	sīp lŭk gèi	攝錄機
waterproof	fong súi	防水
wide angle lens	gwóng gōk gēng	廣角鏡
zoom lens	san gēng	神鏡

COMPUTERS   電腦

applications	yīng yŭng yúen gín	應用軟件
bit	wăi yuen	位元
byte	jĭ jĭt	字節
CD	gwòng díp	光碟
CPU	mei chúe léi hēi	微處理器
computer	dĭn nó	電腦
computer shop	dĭn nó gùng sì	電腦公司
floppy disc	chi díp	磁碟
hard disc	ngăang chi díp	硬磁碟
hard drive	ngăang chi póon	硬磁盤
hardware	ngăang gín	硬件
keyboard	gīn poon	鍵盤

SHOPPING

modem	tiu jāi gáai tiu hēi	調制解調器
monitor	hín sī hēi	顯示器
motherboard	hǎi túng júe báan	系統主板
mouse	wǎat súe	滑鼠
PC	gōh yan dǐn nő	個人電腦
ports	lin jīp fǎu	連接埠
printer	yān bíu gèi	印表機
program	ching sìk	程式
screen	ying mŏk	螢幕
software	yűen gín	軟件
switching power supply	dǐn yuen bīn ngäat hēi	電源變壓器
terminal	jùng dùen gèi	終端機
virus	běng dǔk	病毒
Windows	sī chèung	視窗

DUTY FREE SHOP　　　　　　免稅商店

Hong Kong established the first modern duty free shop right after the Korean War. Nowadays, they supply not only duty exempted liquor and tobacco but also all the usual imported products like perfumes, and so on.

a bottle (of ...)	yàt jùn (...)	一樽(...)
a box	yàt hǎp	一盒
a carton of cigarettes	yàt tiu yìn	一條煙
cologne	góo lung hèung súi	古龍香水
cosmetics	fā jòng bán	化妝品
duty free	mín sūi	免稅
duty free concession	mín sūi yàu dōi	免稅優待
duty free shop	mín sūi dīm	免稅店
duty paid	fōh sūi	課稅
imported liquor	yeung jáu	洋酒
lipstick	sun gò	唇膏
liqour	līt jáu	烈酒
one ounce	yàt ngòn sí	一盎士

SHOPPING

| perfume | hèung súi | 香水 |
| watch | sáu bìu | 手錶 |

SMOKING   菸草

A packet of cigarettes, please.
m gòi béi ngő̕h yàt bàau yìn jái

唔該俾我一包煙仔

Do you have any Chinese cigarettes?
yẫu mố̕ bóon dẽi gwōk cháan
yìn jái ā?

有冇本地國產
煙仔呀?

Are these cigarettes strong/mild?
nì dì yìn hã̕i m hã̕i hó
(nung/sun) gā?

呢啲煙係唔係好
(濃/醇)㗎?

Do you have a/an ashtray/light?
chèng mãn yẫu mố̕ (yìn fòoi
gòng; dá fóh gèi) ā?

請問有冇(煙灰
缸; 打火機)呀?

Can I smoke here?
nì dõ hóh m hóh yỉ sỉk yìn ā?

呢度可唔可以食煙呀?

Do you mind if I smoke?
nẽi gãai m gãai yī ngố̕h
sỉk yìn ā?

你介唔介意我
食煙呀?

Please don't smoke here.
m gòi nẽi m hó hái nì
dõ sỉk yìn

唔該你唔好喺呢
度食煙

Would you like one?
nẽi yīu m yīu yàt jì ā?

你要唔要一支呀?

No, thank you. I don't smoke.
dòh jē sāai la, ngố̕h m sỉk yìn gē

多謝晒喇,我唔食煙嘅

Can I have one?
ngő̕h hóh m hóh yỉ yīu yàt jì ā?

我可唔可以要一支呀?

I'm trying to give up.
ngố̕h sī gán gãai yìn

我試緊戒煙

No smoking!
bàt jún kàp yìn

不准吸煙

SHOPPING

a carton of cigarettes	yàt tiu yìn jái	一條煙仔
cigar	sūet gà	雪茄
cigarette end	yìn táu	煙頭
cigarette holder	yìn júi	煙咀
cigarette machine	jì dūng sāu yìn gèi	自動售煙機
cigarette papers	gúen yìn jí	捲煙紙
cigarettes	hèung yìn	香煙
extra mild	dāk sun	特醇
filtered	lūi júi	濾咀
give up smoking	gāai yìn	戒煙
lighter	dá fóh gèi	打火機
matches	fóh chaai	火柴
menthol	bŏk hoh	薄荷
mild (cigarettes)	sun (yìn)	醇(煙)
pipe	yìn dáu	煙斗
smoking area	kàp yìn kùi	吸煙區
strong (cigarettes)	nung yùk	濃郁
tobacco	yìn sì	煙絲

FOOTWEAR 鞋襪

Where is the ...	chéng mǎn ... bŏ	請問 ... 部
section please?	moon hái bìn dŏ ā?	門喺邊度呀?
children's shoes	tung jòng haai	童裝鞋
ladies' shoes	nűi jòng haai	女裝鞋
men's shoes	naam jòng haai	男裝鞋
sport shoes	wǎan dŭng haai	運動鞋

My size is (seven).
ngőh hǎi (chàt hŏ) mǎ   我係(七號)碼

I want a larger/smaller size.
ngőh yīu (dǎai dì/sǎi dì) gē mǎ   我要(大啲/細啲)嘅碼

I'd like to have my shoes resoled/reheeled.
ngőh yīu wŏon gōh haai   我要換個鞋
(jéung/jàang)   (掌/踭)

SHOPPING

boot	cheung hèuh	長靴
high heel shoes	gò jàang haai	高踭鞋
pantyhose	fōo màt	褲襪
sandals	leung haai	涼鞋
shoes	haai	鞋
shoelaces	haai dáai	鞋帶
shoe polish	haai yáu	鞋油
shoe repair	bó haai	補鞋
shoe shop	haai pó	鞋舖
slippers	tòh háai	拖鞋
socks	màt	襪
sport shoes	wǎn dǔng haai	運動鞋
stockings	sì màt	絲襪

CLOTHING   服裝

Imported and locally made clothes for men, women, children and aged people are abundant and can be bought at realistic prices, especially at the markets. Tailors exist in profusion as made-to-measure is popular and relatively cheap.

My collar size is (36 cm/14¹/2").
  ngǒh gē sàam lěng hǎi (sàam sǎp lǔk gùng fàn; sǎp sēi chūen bōon)   我嘅衫領係(36公分; 14吋半)

I'd like a larger/smaller size.
  ngǒh yīu (dàai dì/sāi dì) gē mǎ   我要(大啲/細啲)嘅碼

I'd like a S/M/L/XL size.
  ngǒh yīu (sāi/jùng/dàai/dǎk dàai) mǎ   我要(細/中/大/特大)碼

Can I try it on?
  hóh m hóh yí sī jēuk ā?   可唔可以試着呀?

belt	yìu dáai	腰帶
blazer	sài jòng sēung yì	西裝上衣
blouse	nűi jòng sēung yì	女裝上衣
casual dress	bǐn jòng	便裝

clothing	fūk jòng	服裝
coat	ngŏi tō	外套
dress	sàam kwan	衫裙
dressing gown	san làu	晨褸
evening wear	mǎan jòng	晚裝
fitting room	sī sàn sàt	試身室
formal dress	lǎi fūk	禮服
gloves	sáu tō	手套
garment	sing yì	成衣
handkerchief	sáu gàn	手巾
hat	mó	帽
jacket	sĕung yì	上衣
jeans	ngau jái fōo	牛仔褲
jumper/sweater	làp táu tō sàam	笠頭套衫
long gown (Manchu lady style)	kei pó	旗袍
long sleeves	cheung jǎu	長袖
man's long gown (traditional)	cheung sàm	長衫
to mend clothing	fung bó yì fūk	縫補衣服
nightdress	sǔi po	睡袍
nightwear	sǔi yì	睡衣
pants	dúen fōo	短褲
pyjamas	sǔi yì	睡衣
raincoat	yǔe yì	雨衣
scarf	wai gàn	圍巾
shirt	sùt sàam	裇衫
shorts	dúen fōo	短褲
skirt	kwan	裙
sport wear	wǎn dǔng yì	運動衣
suit	sài jòng	西裝
sweater	mo sàam	毛衫
sweatshirt	wǎn dǔng yì	運動衣

SHOPPING

swimming suit	yau wǐng yì	游泳衣
tracksuit	wǎn dǔng tō jòng	運動套裝
T-shirt	T-sùt	T-裇
tie	lěng tàai	領呔
trousers	fōo	褲
umbrella	yǔe jè	雨遮
underwear	nǒi yì	內衣
uniform	jāi fǔk	制服
Western style suit	sài jòng	西裝
zipper	làai lín	拉鍊

Materials 衣料

angora	tō mo	兔毛
corduroy	dàng sàm yúng	燈芯絨
cashmere	kè sǐ mè	茄士咩
cotton	min	棉
cotton milling	fóng min	紡棉
dacron	dìk kōk leung	的確涼
fabric	bō lǐu	布料
handmade	sáu gùng jǒ	手工做
leather	péi	皮
linen	ā ma	亞麻
nylon	nei lung	尼龍
polyester	jǔi jì chìm wai	聚脂纖維
ramie	chǔe ma	苧麻
satin	dǔen	緞
silk	sì	絲
silk blend fabrics	gāap sì wǎn fóng	夾絲混紡
velvet	tìn ngoh yúng	天鵝絨
wool	mo	毛

SHOPPING

JEWELLERY 珠寶

Traditionally, Chinese prefer pure gold (24K) than 11K or 18K gold. Jade and diamonds also are quite popular among Chinese.

amber	fóo pāk	琥珀
bracelet	sáu ngáak	手鈪
brooch	hùng jàm	胸針
coral	sàan woo	珊瑚
crystal	súi jìng	水晶
diamonds	jūen sēk	鑽石
earrings	yí wáan	耳環
emerald	lūk bó sēk	綠寶石
gemstone	bó sēk	寶石
gold	gàm	金
gold bar	gàm tíu	金條
gold coins	gàm bǎi	金幣
gold plated	dō gàm	鍍金

jade	féi chūi; yúk	翡翠; 玉
jewellery	jùe bó	珠寶
necklace	géng lín	頸鏈
opal	ngō bó; dáan bǎak sēk	澳寶; 蛋白石
pearl	jàn jùe	珍珠
pendant	lín jūi	鏈錘
platinum	bǎak gàm	白金
rings	gāai jí	戒指
ruby	hung bó sēk	紅寶石
silver	ngán	銀
silverware	ngan hēi	銀器
stone	sēk	石

COLOURS 色澤

bright ...	sìn ...	鮮 ...
dark ...	sàm ...	深 ...
light ...	chín ...	淺 ...
beige	mấi sìk	米色
black	hàk sìk	黑色
blue	laam sìk	藍色
brown	fè sìk	啡色
golden	gàm sìk	金色
green	lũk sìk	綠色
grey	fòoi sìk	灰色
indigo	dīn laam sìk	靛藍色
orange	cháang sìk	橙色
pink	fán hung sìk	粉紅色
red	hung sìk	紅色
silver	ngan sìk	銀色
violet	jí sìk	紫色
white	bãak sìk	白色
yellow	wong sìk	黃色

Descriptions 物色

It fits.
　　nì gōh ngàam ngốh gē mấ　　呢個啱我嘅碼

It doesn't fit.
　　nì gōh m ngàam ngốh gē mấ　　呢個唔啱我嘅碼

It's too ...
　　nì gōh tāai ...　　呢個太 ...

It's (not) very ...	nì gōh (m) hãi hó ...	呢個(唔)係好 ...
big	dãai	大
cheap	peng	平
expensive	gwāi	貴
good	hó	好
hard	ngãang	硬

SHOPPING

heavy	chúng	重
light	hèng	輕
long	cheung	長
loose	fōot	闊
narrow/tight	jāak	窄
pretty	lēng	靚
short	dúen	短
soft	yűen	軟
small	sāi	細
tight	gán	緊

STATIONERY & PUBLICATIONS 文房

Is there an English-language bookshop nearby?
nì dŏ fŏo găn yắu mŏ
yìng mán sùe dīm ā?
呢度附近有冇
英文書店呀?

Where is the (English/French) book section please?
chéng mǎn (yìng mán/fāat
mán) sùe hái bìn dŏ ā?
請問(英文/法
文)書喺邊度呀?

Do you have the latest novel/book by ...?
néi dĕi yắu mŏ ... jūi sàn
gē (síu sūet/sùe) ā?
你哋有冇 ... 最新
嘅(小說/書)呀?

Do you sell ...?
néi dĕi yắu mŏ mǎai ... ā?
你哋有冇賣 ... 呀?

I'd like a/an ... ngőh séung yīu ... 我想要 ...
ballpoint pen	yuen jí bàt	原子筆
book	sùe jīk	書籍
calculator	gāi sŏ gèi	計數機
calendar	yàt līk	日曆
calligraphic model	jī típ	字帖
correction fluid	gói chōh súi	改錯水
crayons	lăap bàt	蠟筆
dictionary	jī dín	字典

SHOPPING

envelope	sūn fùng	信封
file holder	man gín gáap	文件夾
ink	mǎk súi	墨水
ink stone	mǎk yín	墨硯
ink tablet	mǎk	墨
letter pad	sūn jí	信紙
magazine	jǎap jì	雜誌
map	děi to	地圖
newspaper	bō jí	報紙
newspaper in English	yìng mán bō jí	英文報紙
novel	síu sūet	小說
paper	jí	紙
pencil	yuen bàt	鉛筆
scissors	gāau jín	較剪
stapler	dèng sùe gèi	釘書機
sticky tape	gàau jí	膠紙
weekly magazine	jàu hón	週刊
weekly TV magazine	dīn sī jàu hón	電視週刊
writing brush	mo bàt	毛筆

DID YOU KNOW ...

The paper, writing brush, ink tablet and ink stone, or jí, bàt, mǎk and mǎk yín are the four treasures of Chinese stationery. They have been used by Chinese for thousands of years. Together with the calligraphy and calligraphic model, or jì típ they make good souvenirs.

SHOPPING

TOILETRIES

盥洗

brush	chāat	刷
comb	sòh	梳
condoms	bēi yǎn tō	避孕套
conditioner	woo fāat sō	護髮素
dental floss	nga sīn	牙線
deodorant	chui chāu jài	除臭劑
distilled water	jìng lāu súi	蒸餾水
hair cream	fāat yǔe	髮乳
hairbrush	fāat chāat	髮刷
insect repellent	sāat chung súi	殺蟲水
iodine	dìn jáu	碘酒
laxative	sē yěuk	瀉藥
lipstick	háu sun gò	口唇膏
mirror	gēng	鏡
moisturising cream	yǔn fòo sèung	潤膚霜
razor	tāi dò	剃刀
sanitary napkins	wāi sàng gàn	衛生巾
shampoo	sái tau súi	洗頭水
shaving cream	tāi sò gò	剃鬚膏
soap	fàan gáan	番梘
sunblock cream	tāai yeung yau	太陽油

tissues	jí gàn	紙巾
toilet paper	chī jí	廁紙
tooth-brush	nga chāat	牙刷
tooth-paste	nga gò	牙膏
nail clippers	jí gāap kím	指甲鉗
perfume	hèung súi	香水
vaseline	fà sī líng	花士令

SHOPPING

FOR THE BABY

育嬰

baby soap	yìng yi fàan gáan	嬰兒番梘
baby powder	yìng yi sóng sàn fán	嬰兒爽身粉
baby food	yìng yi sīk bán	嬰兒食品
baby's bottle	nǎai jùn	奶樽
bib	háu súi gìn	口水墊
disposable nappies	jí nǐu pín	紙尿片
dummy	nǎai júi	奶咀
milk	ngau nǎai	牛奶
nappy	nǐu pín	尿片
nappy rash cream	yìng yi sàp chán gò	嬰兒濕疹膏
playpen	yau hēi chong	遊戲床
powdered milk	nǎai fán	奶粉
soy milk	dǎu nǎai	豆奶
talcum powder	sóng sàn fán	爽身粉
teat	nǎai júi	奶咀
toy	wǒon gūi	玩具

SIZES & COMPARISONS

比較

a little bit	yàt dì	一啲
big	dǎai	大
bigger	dǎai dì	大啲
biggest	jūi dǎai	最大
discount	jīt kāu	折扣
enough	gāu	夠
heavy	chúng	重
less	síu dì	少啲
light (weight)	hèng	輕
long	cheung	長
many	dòh	多
more	dòh dì	多啲
none	mǒ	冇
short	dúen	短

SHOPPING

small	sāi	細
smaller	sāi dì	細啲
smallest	jūi sāi	最細
tall	gò	高
the most ...	jūi ...	最 ...
too many/much	tāai dòh	太多

FOOD

餐飲

There is an old saying in Chinese, man yí sīk wai sìn, literally meaning 'eating is people's first priority'. To Cantonese people, eating is not only a need, it's an art. On special occasions, they may spend hours, days or even weeks preparing extravagant dishes. Over many centuries the Chinese have perfected their own unique style of cooking. Cantonese cuisine has largely inherited China's extensive range of cooking styles and methods, and the Cantonese are known for their ability to cook and eat virtually anything. The dishes are many and varied. Unlike many other national cuisines, there isn't any one dish that can capture the total essence of the cuisine in itself. However, there is one distinctive characteristic of the Cantonese style – all the ingredients in the dishes keep their original flavours.

Hong Kong's convenient location, being the centre point of east and west, north and south, in Asia, is a significant reason for its inhabitants' multicultural eating habits. Transporting of ingredients is convenient and this, in turn, attracts chefs from China and all over the world. Many visitors consider Hong Kong to be a food paradise, and Cantonese people agree. Eating is a very significant part of their lives. For many of the island's inhabitants, Cantonese meals are social events.

afternoon tea	hā ng̊ cha	下午茶
banquet	yīn wǒoi	宴會
breakfast	jó chàan	早餐
dinner	mǎan chàan	晚餐
lunch	ng̊ chàan	午餐
midnight snack	sìu yé	宵夜
snack	síu sīk	小食
supper	mǎan chàan	晚餐
tea	cha dím	茶點

VEGETARIAN & SPECIAL MEALS   素食

Traditionally, the reasons for Chinese vegetarian habits were religious, and not due to health or preference. Monasteries were the first true vegetarian restaurants, providing visitors with vegetarian dishes, most of which resembled meat in colour, shape and even taste, although they were still strictly vegetarian. This tradition dates back thousands of years!

Nowadays, as more and more people become vegetarian, more vegetarian restaurants are being established. Due to the influence of the Western culture, you can now find health food shops scattered all around the region. Also, most restaurants do serve some vegetarian dishes.

FOOD

I'm a vegetarian.
ngőh hǎi sō sǐk gē   我係素食嘅

I like healthy food.
ngőh jùng yī gǐn hòng sǐk mǎt   我中意健康食物

I'd like a ... meal.	ngőh yīu sǐk ...	我要食...
diabetic	mő tong sǐk mǎt	無醣食物
halal	chìng jàn sǐk mǎt	清真食物
health food	gǐn hòng sǐk mǎt	健康食物
kosher	yau tāai sǐk mǎt	猶太食物
low-sodium	dài yim sǐk mǎt	低鹽食物
vegan	mő dáan mő	無蛋無
	nǎai bán sō sǐk	奶品素食
vegetarian	sō sǐk	素食

Is there a ... near by?	nì dō fōo gǎn yǎu mő ... ā?	呢度附近 有冇 ... 呀?
health food restaurant	gǐn hòng sǐk bán chàan tèng	健康食品 餐廳
health food shop	gǐn hòng sǐk bán dīm	健康食品店
vegetarian restaurant	jàai chōi gwóon; sō sǐk gwóon	齋菜館; 素食館

I don't eat (fish/meat).
   ngőh m sĭk (yúe/yŭk lũi)   我唔食(魚/肉類)

I'm allergic to (egg).
   ngőh dūi (dáan) mấn gám   我對(蛋)敏感

Don't include	chéng m hó	請唔好
any ...	gà yăm hoh ...	加任何 ...
egg	dáan	蛋
meat	yŭk lũi	肉類
MSG	mẽi jìng	味精
oil	yau	油
salt	yim	鹽
soybean sauce	sĭ yau	豉油
sugar	tong	糖

FOOD

FAST FOOD   快餐

chips	sue tíu	薯條
cup noodles	bòoi mĭn	杯麵
donut	dùng làt	冬甩
fried fish and chips	jā yúe sue tíu	炸魚薯條
fried chicken	jā gài	炸雞
fried potato	jā sue tíu	炸薯條
hamburger	hōn bó bàau	漢堡包
hot dog	yĭt gáu	熱狗
instant noodles	jìk sĭk mĭn	即食麵
macaroni	tùng sàm fán	通心粉
pizza	yī dăai lẽi bŏk béng	意大利薄餅
potato chips	sue pín	薯片
sandwich	sàam man jĭ	三文治
spaghetti	yī dăai lẽi fán	意大利粉
fast food shop	fāai chàan dīm	快餐店

EATING OUT   堂吃

It's said that 'wherever there are people, there is going to be a Chinese person, wherever there is a Chinese person, there is going to be a Chinese restaurant'. Hong Kong not only has many restaurants that specialise in the cuisines of the regions of China, it also has restaurants that specialise in other nations' cuisines, from the Mediterranean to Japanese dishes. The Portuguese and African food in Macau is among the best in the region.

The Cantonese people go to restaurants on all occasions, from weddings to funerals, birthday parties to farewell parties. Or for no particular reason at all.

Unlike some Western restaurants, Cantonese eateries are usually crowded and extremely noisy. Expect to wait for a table on arrival, even if you have booked one. Sometimes you may even be asked to share a table, but this is an exception rather than the rule. One Cantonese custom that you could easily get used to; they fight to pay for the meal! It's an amusing scene. The Cantonese will go to almost any length to be the host. Sometimes they even sneak to the reception desk to pay the bill.

FOOD (side tab)

EATERIES   食肆

I want to go to a ...	ngőh yīu hūi ...	我要去 ...
bar	jáu bà	酒吧
canteen	fãan tong	飯堂
Chinese restaurant	jáu lau; jáu gà	酒樓; 酒家
Chinese teahouse	cha lau	茶樓
coffee house	gā fè tèng	咖啡廳
cooked food stall	sŭk sĩk dōng	熟食檔
floating restaurant	hói sìn fóng	海鮮舫
food centre	yám sĩk jùng sàm	飲食中心
food court/street	sĩk gàai	食街
health food restaurant	gĩn hòng sĩk	健康食
	bán chàan tèng	品餐廳
herb teahouse	leung cha pó	涼茶舖

kiosk	síu sīk dím	小食店
lounge	jáu long	酒廊
pub	jáu bà	酒吧
restaurant	chàan tèng	餐廳
seafood restaurant	hói sìn jáu gà	海鮮酒家
vegetarian restaurant	jàai chōi gwóon;	齋菜館;
	sō sīk gwóon	素食館
VIP room	gwāi bàn tèng	貴賓廳
Western-style restaurant	sài chàan tèng	西餐廳

Chinese Regional Cuisines 地方菜式

I want to go to a restaurant serving ...	ngőh séung hūi sīk ...	我想 去食 ...
Beijing food	gìng chōi	京菜
Cantonese food	gwóng dùng chōi; yŭet chōi	廣東菜; 粵菜
Chaozhou food	chiu jàu chōi	潮州菜
Chinese food	jùng gwōk chōi	中國菜
Eastern Chinese food	waai yeung chōi	淮揚菜
Hu-nan food	séung chōi	湘菜
Kejia food	dùng gòng chōi; hāak gà chōi	東江菜; 客家菜
Northern Chinese food	bàk fòng chōi	北方菜
Shandong food	sàan dùng chōi	山東菜
Shanghai food	sēung hói chōi	上海菜
Sichuan food	chùen chōi	川菜
Taiwanese food	toi wàan chōi	台灣菜

Other National Cuisines 東西食譜

| French food | fàat gwōk chōi | 法國菜 |
| Indian food | yàn dō chōi | 印度菜 |

FOOD

Japanese teppanyaki	yǎt bóon tīt báan sìu	日本鐵板燒
Japanese food	yǎt bóon lǐu léi	日本料理
Korean food	hon gwōk chōi	韓國菜
Portuguese food	po gwōk chōi	葡國菜
South-East Asian food	naam yéung chōi	南洋菜
Thai food	tāai gwōk chōi	泰國菜
Vietnamese food	yǔet naam chōi	越南菜
Western food	sài chàan	西餐

FOOD

At the Restaurant 餐館

A table for ... please.
   m gòi ... wái   唔該 ... 位

Can I see the menu please?
   m gòi béi gōh chàan   唔該俾個餐
   páai ngǒh tái   牌我睇

Do you have an English menu?
   yǎu mǒ yìng mán chàan páai ā?   有冇英文餐牌呀?

We'd like this set menu please.
   ngǒh děi yīu nì gōh tō chàan   我哋要呢個套餐

Can you recommend any dishes?
   yǎu màt yě hó gāai sǐu ā?   有乜嘢好介紹呀?

What's the speciality here?
   néi děi yǎu màt yě na sáu   你哋有乜嘢拿手
   hó chōi sìk ā?   好菜式呀?

What are they eating?
   kǔi děi sǐk gán màt yě ā?   佢哋食緊乜嘢呀?

What's in this dish?
   nì gōh chōi lǔi bǐn yǎu   呢個菜裡便有
   dì màt yě ā?   啲乜嘢呀?

Are the (fish/prawns/crabs) fresh today?
   gàm yǎt dì (yúe/hà/hǎai)   今日啲(魚/蝦/蟹)
   sàn m sàn sìn ā?   新唔新鮮呀?

The bill please.
   m gòi maai dàan   唔該埋單

Can you please bring me a/some ...?	m gòi lóh ... béi ngóh	唔該攞 ... 俾我?
bread	mĭn bàau	麵包
chilli sauce	lăat jìu jēung	辣椒醬
highchair	yàt jèung gò dāng	一張高凳
knife and fork	yàt fō dò chà	一副刀叉
rice	fāan	飯
salt	yim	鹽
tea	cha	茶
(cold) water	(dūng) súi	(凍)水
pepper	woo jìu fán	胡椒粉

FOOD

WAITER!

Captain! (head waiter)	bŏ jéung	部長
Chef!	dăai chúe	大廚
Waiter!	fóh gēi	伙記
Waitress!	síu jé	小姐
waiter (in China)	fŭk mŏ yuen	服務員

Staples 主食

bread	mĭn bàau	麵包
noodles	mĭn	麵
fried rice	cháau fāan	炒飯
rice	fāan	飯
rice noodles	lāai fán	瀬粉
rice vermicelli	mǎi fán	米粉
shredded rice noodles	hóh fán	河粉
steamed bun	bàau	飽

MEALS 餐點

Dinner is traditionally the main meal. It's a time for families to get together. Some people prefer a rich breakfast to get their energy for the day, some enjoy a yám cha lunch. Most foods are only available at a certain time of the day. For example, it wouldn't be easy for you to find breakfast dishes or dim sims in the evening. Chinese banquets are mostly held late in the evening.

Breakfast 早點
A huge variety of breakfasts exist. You can have the convenient takeaway of the many fast food chains, buy traditional congee rice porridge from the cooked food stalls (sūk sīk dōng) or, try a morning yám cha.

Cantonese people don't normally eat rice for breakfast, unless it's in the form of congee.

Cantonese Breakfast

dim sim	dím sàm	點心
fried bread stick	yau jā gwái; yau tíu	油炸鬼; 油條
fried noodle	cháau mīn	炒麵
rice noodles	chéung fán	腸粉

FOOD

rice noodles with shrimp	hà chéung	蝦腸
rice noodles with beef	ngau chéung	牛腸
rice porridge	jùk	粥
rice porridge with beef	ngau yŭk jùk	牛肉粥
sesame seed pancake	sìu béng	燒餅
steamed bun	bàau	飽
soybean milk	dǎu jèung	豆漿

Lunch 午膳

Cantonese people's favourite lunch is, you guessed it, yám cha! Another section of this chapter has been devoted to this important aspect of eating.

Other people may opt for a simple, hot lunch. This may be a plate of rice with something on top or maybe fried noodles, available from the fast food shops. The lunches are relatively light and quick.

fried noodle	cháau mìn	炒麵
fried rice	cháau fāan	炒飯
noodle in soup	tòng mìn	湯麵
set menu	tō chàan	套餐
set menu (full course)	chuen chàan	全餐
set menu (ordinary)	seung chàan	常餐

Yum Cha   飲茶

Yám cha literally means 'drink tea', but it implies eating dim sims and other food while the tea is served. This the origin of what is now a feast on dim sims. Yum cha is a hot meal (breakfast, brunch or lunch, but not dinner) that is comprised mostly of dim sims. It's so popular among Cantonese people it has become the symbol of socialising. People yum cha for breakfast, lunch, business deals and whatever reasons they can think of, not solely for the meal.

I want to go to/for yum cha.
  ngőh séung hūi yám cha   我想去飲茶

FOOD

I'd like (a plate of beef rice noodles) and (two baskets of Shrimp dumplings).

m gòi, ngőh yīu (yàt dĭp ngau
chéung) tung maai (léung lung
hà gáau)

唔該, 我要(一碟牛
腸)同埋(兩籠
蝦餃)

The first is the favourite saying of the ever hungry Cantonese people.

Tea 名茶

Ordering tea at yám cha is a must. There are many types of teas that exist, all taste distinctly different. Don't be afraid to try new flavours. (see page 173)

I would like a pot of (Jasmin) tea please.

m gòi, ngőh yīu yàt woo
(hèung pín) cha

唔該, 我要一壺
(香片)茶

Savoury Steamed 蒸點

[Steamed buns filled with ...]

assorted meat	dāai bàau	大飽
barbecue pork	chà sìu bàau	叉燒飽
chicken	gài bàau	雞飽
Chinese sausage	lāap cheung gúen	臘腸卷

[Dumplings filled with ...]

bamboo shoots, pork and prawns	sìn hà fán gwóh	鮮蝦粉粿
coriander and pork	hèung sài gáau	香茜餃
crab, pork and prawn	hăai wong sìu máai	蟹黃燒賣
seafood	hói sìn gáau	海鮮餃
shark fin	yue chī gáau	魚翅餃
shrimp	hà gáau	蝦餃
soup	gwōon tòng gáau	灌湯餃

[Rice noodle roll filled with ...]

barbecue pork	chà sìu chéung fán	叉燒腸粉
beef	ngau yŭk chéung fán	牛肉腸粉

FOOD

fried bread stick	jā léung	炸兩
prawns	hà chéung fán	蝦腸粉
scallop	dāai jí chéung fán	帶子腸粉

Here are some more savoury steamed dishes and others:

beef ball	gòn jìng ngau yŭk	干蒸牛肉
chicken claws with black bean sauce	sī jàp fūng jáau	豉汁鳳爪
chicken wrap	gài jaat	雞紮
pork chop with black bean sauce	sī jàp paai gwàt	豉汁排骨
rice porridge	jùk	粥
shark's fin soup	wóon jái chī	碗仔翅
sticky rice dumpling	nŏh măi gài	糯米雞
squid with curry sauce	gā lèi sìn yáu	咖喱鮮魷
webbed feet wrap	ngāap gēuk jaat	鴨腳紮

FOOD

Savoury Fried & Deep Fried 煎炸

dumpling with taro fillings	wŏo gōk	芋角
egg-shaped dumpling with fillings	haam súi gōk	鹹水角
pan stick fried dumpling	wòh tīp	窩貼
rice noodle roll	jìn chéung fán	煎腸粉
sesame prawn on toast	jì ma hà	芝麻蝦
spring roll	jā chùn gúen	炸春卷
taro cake	wŏo táu gò	芋頭糕
turnip cake	loh bāak gò	蘿蔔糕

Sweets – Steamed 糕點

| buns with egg yoke and cream | năai wong bàau | 奶黃飽 |
| buns with lotus seed filling | lin yung bàau | 蓮蓉飽 |

buns with sesame seed filling	ma yung bàau	麻蓉鮑
Malayan style sponge cake	mǎ làai gò	馬拉糕
sponge cake	sùng gò	鬆糕

Sweets Fried & Deep Fried 甜點

cakes with waterchestnut	mǎ tái gò	馬蹄糕
sesame ball	jìn dùi	煎堆
toffee apple	bǎt sì ping gwóh	拔絲萍果

Sweets – Soup 甜羹

almond fruit jelly	hāng yan dàu fõo	杏仁豆腐
almond milk	hāng yan cha	杏仁茶
beancurd jelly	dàu fõo fà	豆腐花
Chinese agaragar jelly	leung fán	涼粉
red bean soup	hung dáu sà	紅豆沙
sago milk with coconut	ye jàp sài mǎi lõ	椰汁西米露
sago milk with honeydew melon	mǎt gwà sài mǎi lõ	蜜瓜西米露
sesame seed dumpling	jì ma tòng yúen	芝麻湯丸

Sweets – Others 雜類

coconut custard jelly	ye jàp gò	椰汁糕
coconut tart	ye tàat	椰撻
custard tart	dàan tàat	蛋撻
fruit jelly	jǎap gwóh jè léi	雜果這喱
fruit pudding	jǎap gwóh bō dìn	雜果布甸
mango pudding	mòng gwóh bō dìn	芒果布甸
sago pudding	sài mǎi bō dìn	西米布甸
sesame roll	jì ma gúen	芝麻卷

FOOD

Snacks & Afternoon Tea 茶點

The British tradition of an afternoon tea at about 3.15pm is a must for most people in Hong Kong. It could range from a cup of tea and some biscuits, to a bowl of noodles at the restaurant or a mini-lunch.

I'd like a ...	ngốh séung yìu ...	我想要 ...
barbecue pork bun	chà sìu bàau	叉燒飽
biscuit	béng gòn	餅乾
cake	sài béng	西餅
club sandwich	gùng sì sàam man jí	公司三文治
coconut tart	ye tàat	椰撻
congee	jùk	粥
cream cake	gēi lìm dāan gò	忌廉蛋糕
croissant	ngau gōk bàau	牛角包
dessert	tìm bán	甜品
dim sim	dím sàm	點心
dinner roll	chàan bàau	餐包
dumpling	gáau jí	餃子
egg cake	dāan gò	蛋糕
egg tart	dāan tàat	蛋撻
French toast	sài dòh sí	西多士
garlic bread	sūen yung bàau	蒜蓉包
ice cream	sūet gò	雪糕
noodle with shrimp dumplings	wan tàn mín	雲吞麵
noodle with dumplings	súi gáau mín	水餃麵
omelette	ngàm līt	菴列
pancake	bŏk béng	薄餅
sweet bread	tìm mīn bàau	甜麵包
toast	dòh sí	多士

FOOD

Dinner 晚餐

Dinner is considered to be the most important meal of the day. Many Cantonese people believe that you should always go to bed on a full stomach. Here are some common dishes:

I'd like to order ... and ...

ngőh séung gīu ... tung maai ...　　我想叫 ... 同埋 ...

bāak fà yeung dāai jí　　百花釀帶子
grilled, stuffed scallops in white sauce

bàk gìng tin ngāap　　北京填鴨
also known as Peking Duck. The crispy skin of the freshly roasted duck is sliced and served in pancakes with leek or cucumber and sauce.

chà sìu　　叉燒
barbecued pork

chèng jìu ngau yŭk　　青椒牛肉
shredded beef stir-fried with capsicum

chìng jìng yúe　　清蒸魚
steamed whole fish

chìng jìng dāai jí　　清蒸帶子
steamed scallop

chōi yűen pa ngāap　　菜薳扒鴨
braised duck and green vegetables

chōi yűen sĕk bàan kau　　菜薳石斑球
garoupa(fish) fillets and green vegetables

dāai leung wòh sìu ngāap　　大良窩燒鴨
deep fried, stuffed duck in crabmeat sauce

gèung chùng hăi　　薑蔥蟹
baked crab in ginger and spring onion sauce

gèung chùng ngau yŭk　　薑蔥牛肉
beef stir-fried with ginger and spring opion

gìng dò gwàt　　京都骨
spare rib, Beijing style

FOOD

gòn sìu ming hà 干燒明蝦
  dry-fried spicy king prawns

gòo lò yǔk 咕老肉
  sweet and sour pork

gǔk hǎai gōi 焗蟹蓋
  crabmeat crumbs, deep-fried in the shell

gùng bó gài dìng 宮保雞丁
  diced chicken stir-fried with peanuts, pepper and chilli flakes

hàt yì gài 乞兒雞
  also known as 'beggar's chicken'. The whole chicken is rubbed
  with spices and stuffed. It's wrapped in lotus leaves and clay-
  dough, then baked.

ho yau bàau pó 蠔油鮑脯
  abalone in oyster sauce

ho yau ngau yǔk 蠔油牛肉
  sliced beef in oyster sauce

FOOD

THEY MAY SAY ...

géi dòh wái ā?	How many people?
dūi m jūe, mǒon jōh	Sorry, full house!
chéng dáng yàt jǎn	Please wait for a while.
jùng m jùng yī sǐk (hói sìn) ā?	Do you like (sea food)?
gàm yàt dì (yúe/hà/hǎai) hó sàn sìn.	The (fish/prawns/crabs) are fresh today.
ngǒh tùi jǐn něi děi sǐk nì gōh ...	I recommend this ...
lei gán	Coming!
hó fāai dàk la	It'll be ready soon.
sǐng wǎi; dòh jē sāai	Thank you.

FOOD

hói sìn jēuk chaau   海鮮雀巢
a combination of prawns, scallops and fish in a fried potato
or taro tray that resembles a bird's nest

jā jí gài   炸子雞
deep fried chicken

jā sàang ho   炸生蠔
deep fried oysters

jā sìn náai   炸鮮奶
deep fried milk mixture with egg white

jí bàau gwàt/gài   紙包骨/雞
spare rib/chicken wrapped with rice paper

jìn yéung dàu fõ   煎釀豆腐
grilled fish, prawns or meat stuffed in beancurds

jìu yim sìn yáu   椒鹽鮮魷
fried calamari in spicy peppery salt

ké jàp hà lùk   茄汁蝦碌
broiled king prawns in tomato sauce

loh hōn jàai   羅漢齋
assorted vegetables

ma po dàu fõ   麻婆豆腐
braised beancurd with minced beef and chillies

ngan woo bāak fà pó   銀湖百花脯
prawn patties in crabmeat sauce

sàang chōi bàau   生菜包
minced pork or seafood wrapped in lettuce

sēung tòng gài   上湯雞
chicken boiled in stock soup

sī jàp gùk háai   豉汁焗蟹
crab baked in black bean sauce

wooi wòh yúk   回窩肉
broiled pork slice cooked with garlic, peppers and soya bean sauce

yue hèung ké jí   魚香茄子
chunks of eggplants and pork batons sauteed in a spicy
vinegary sauce

Soups 湯羹

There are endless varieties of Cantonese tonic soups, too many to name in the following list. They are good for your health, although to first-timers and especially foreigners, some may taste odd.

asparagus	lõ sún tòng	露筍湯
beancurd claypot	dãu fõo bò	豆腐煲
broth	shēung tòng	上湯
chicken	gài tòng	雞湯
chicken & shark fin	gài bàau chī tòng	雞鮑翅湯
Chinese dried mushroom	dùng gòo tòng	冬菇湯
Ching-bo-leung tonic	chìng bó léung	清補涼
combination beancurd	bāak jàn dãufõo gàng	八珍豆腐羹
consomme	chìng tòng	清湯
corn	sùk mãi gàng	粟米羹
corn with chicken	gài yung sùk mãi gàng	雞蓉粟米羹
corn with crab meat	hãai yũk sùk mãi gàng	蟹肉粟米羹
cream	gẽi lìm tòng	忌廉湯
dried scallop	yiu chũe gàng	瑤柱羹
duckling	ngāap sì gàng	鴨絲羹
egg-drop	dāan fà tòng	蛋花湯
fish	yúe tòng	魚湯
ginseng	yan sàm tòng	人參湯
green pea	chèng dáu tòng	青豆湯
hot-and-sour	sùen lãat tòng	酸辣湯
Japanese miso	yãt bóon mĭn sí tòng	日本麵豉湯
Japanese osuimono	yãt bóon chìng tòng	日本清湯
lobster	lung hà tòng	龍蝦湯
lotus root	lin ngãu tòng	蓮藕湯
mushroom	moh gòo tòng	蘑菇湯
onion	yeung chùng tòng	洋蔥湯
oxtail	ngau mẽi tòng	牛尾湯
Russian broth	loh sũng tòng	羅宋湯
seafood	hói sìn tòng	海鮮湯

FOOD

FOOD

seafood beancurd	hói sìn dāu fōo gàng	海鮮豆腐羹
shark fin	yue chī gàng	魚翅羹
snake gravy	se gàng	蛇羹
soup	tòng	湯
soup of the day	lāi tòng	例湯
steam boat	dá bìn lo	打邊爐
tomato	fàan ké tòng	番茄湯
vegetable	jāap chōi tòng	雜菜湯
whole wax gourd	dūng gwà jùng	冬瓜盅

Banquets 飲宴

Drinks, prawn crackers, nuts or pickles are usually served as appetisers. Cantonese banquets usually start with a combination platter of salad – or at wedding banquets, a platter of suckling pig – followed by two hot dishes. A thick soup is then served, during which the host will propose a toast.

This is followed by five main dishes: seafoods, meats, poultries, vegetables and fish which is served last. Fried rice and noodles will be served again to fill up the last little space of your stomach. Fruits, sweets and more snacks come at the end.

The following is a list of the more common entrees or appetisers served at Chinese and Western banquets (For main dishes, see page 154).

appetiser	chàan chìn síu sīk	餐前小食
Chinese combination platter	jùng sìk pīng póon	中式拼盤
cold dishes	lāang chōi	冷菜
cold hors d'oeuvre	lāang póon	冷盤
combination platter	pīng póon	拼盤
fruit salad	jāap gwòh sà lūt	雜果沙律
hot dishes	yīt fàn	熱葷
hot entrees	tau pòon	頭盤
Japanese combination platter	yàt sìk pīng póon	日式拼盤

jellyfish and sliced hocks	hói jīt fàn tai	海蜇醮蹄
roast meat combination platter	sìu méi pīng póon	燒味拼盤
salad	sà lūt	沙律
salad with lobster	lung hà sà lūt	龍蝦沙律
salad with prawns	dāai hà sà lūt	大蝦沙律
salmon	sàam man yúe	三文魚
seafood combination platter	hói sìn pīng póon	海鮮拼盤
suckling pig combination platter	yúe jùe pīng póon	乳豬拼盤
vegetable salad	jāap chōi sà lūt	雜菜沙律

FOOD

SELF-CATERING 自炊

The following lists can be used when ordering at a restaurant or shop at the markets.

Measurements 斤兩

There are different measurements used. The Chinese catty/tael system is widely used, as are the pound/ounce and the gram/kilogram systems.

1 catty	= 16 taels	
3 catties	= 4 pounds	= 1.82Kg
1 tael	= 1.34 oz	= 38.5g
1 lb	= 12 taels	
1 oz	= 28.4g	= 0.75 tael
1Kg	= 26 taels	
100g	= 4.8 taels	

How much does this weigh?
nì gōh yáu géi chúng ā? 呢個有幾重呀?

How much is it (per catty)?
géi dòh chín (yàt gán) ā? 幾多錢(一斤)呀?

At the Market 市集

Where is the nearby ... please?	chéng mān fõo gān gē ... hái bīn dō ā?	請問附近嘅 ... 喺邊度呀?
fish market	yue sí cheung	魚市場
market	gàai sí	街市
meat stalls	yŭk dōng	肉檔
roadside stalls	gàai bìn dōng	街邊檔
supermarket	chìu kàp sí cheung	超級市場
vegetable market	chōi sí cheung	菜市場

How much is it (per catty)?
géi dòh chín (yàt gán) ā?　　幾多錢(一斤)呀?

Do you have anything cheaper?
yáu mő dăi yī yĕung peng dì gē?　有冇第二樣平啲嘅?

Give me a catty/pound please.
m gòi béi ngőh yàt (gàn/bõng)　唔該俾我一(斤/磅)

I'd like ...	ngőh yīu ...	我要...
(half catty of) tomatoes	(bōon gàn) fàan ké	(半斤)番茄
(a dozen) eggs	(yàt dà) gài dáan	(一打)雞蛋
(six slices of) ham	(lŭk pīn) fóh túi	(六片)火腿

Meat 肉類

bacon	yìn yŭk	煙肉
barbecue pork	chà sìu	叉燒
beef	ngau yŭk	牛肉
beef ball	ngau yŭk yúen	牛肉丸
beef fillet	ngau láu	牛柳
Chinese sausage	lãap chéung	臘腸
crispy pork	sìu yŭk	燒肉
crocodile meat	ngŏk yue yŭk	鱷魚肉
dried shredded meat	yŭk sùng	肉鬆
ham	fóh túi	火腿
lean meat	sāu yŭk	瘦肉

marinated meat	lŏ méi	滷味
meat	yŭk	肉
meat ball	yŭk yúen	肉丸
minced beef	mín jī ngau yŭk	免治牛肉
mutton	yeung yŭk	羊肉
pork	jùe yŭk	豬肉
roasted meat	sìu méi	燒味
roasted suckling pig	sìu yŭe jùe	燒乳豬
sausage	hèung chéung	香腸
spare rib	paai gwàt	排骨

Poultry 三鳥

baby pigeon	yŭe gáp	乳鴿
chicken	gài yŭk	雞肉
chicken wings	gài yĭk	雞翼
drum sticks	gài béi	雞髀
duck	ngāap yŭk	鴨肉
goose	ngóh	鵝
Peking duck	bàk gìng tin ngāap	北京填鴨
quail	ngàm chùn	鵪鶉
roast duck	sìu ngāap	燒鴨
roast goose	sìu ngóh	燒鵝
turkey	fóh gài	火雞

FOOD

Seafood 海鮮

The most important part of the Cantonese cuisine is fresh seafood. Unlike other cuisines, all ingredients in Cantonese dishes keep their original flavour. It's believed that merely from tasting, it's possible to know which fish was used, how fresh the catch was, or even whether they have been frozen. One of the good places to taste fresh seafood is in a floating restaurant.

Some seafood restaurants and markets keep tanks on their premises so that the seafood is as fresh as possible.

abalone	bàau yue	鮑魚
baby eel	sín	鱔
barramundi cod	ló súe bàan	老鼠斑
bream	lǎap yúe	鱲魚
butter fish	chèung yúe	鯧魚
carp	léi yúe	鯉魚
clam	pőng	蚌

crab	hǎai	蟹
crabmeat (minced)	hǎai fán	蟹粉
crab roe	hǎai wong	蟹黃
crayfish	lung hà	龍蝦
cuttlefish	mǎk yue	墨魚
dace	leng yúe	鯪魚
dried oyster	ho sí	蠔豉

FOOD

dried scallop	gòng yiu chűe	干瑤柱
eel	mǎan	饅
fish	yúe	魚
fishball	yue dáan	魚旦
fish maw (bladder)	yue tő	魚肚
fish meat	yue yūk	魚肉
fish roe	yue jí	魚子
flag fish	sàam dò	三刀
flounder	jóh háu yúe	左口魚
garoupa	sēk bàan	石斑
geoduck	jěung bāt pőng	象拔蚌
giant grouper	lung dán	龍躉
goby (freshwater)	sún hōk yúe	筍殼魚
green wrasse	chèng yì	青衣
humphead wrasse	sò mei	蘇眉
jellyfish	hói jīt	海蜇
lobster	lung hà	龍蝦
mackerel	gàau yúe	鮫魚
mullet	wòo táu	烏頭
mussel	chèng háu	青口
octopus	bāat jáau yue	八爪魚
oyster	ho	蠔
parrot fish	ngàng gòh léi	鸚歌鯉
perch	lo yúe	鱸魚
prawn	dāai hà	大蝦
raw fish	yue sàang	魚生
salmon	sàam man yúe	三文魚
salted fish	haam yúe	鹹魚
scallop	dāai jí	帶子
sea bass	maang cho	盲鰽
sea bream	lāap yúe	鱲魚
sea cucumber	hói sàm	海參
sea snails	héung lóh	響螺

FOOD

sea urchin	hói dáam	海膽
shad	si yúe	鰣魚
Shanghai crab	dāai jăap hăai	大閘蟹
shark fin	yue chī	魚翅
shellfish	lóh	螺
shrimp	hà	蝦
shrimp ball	hà yúen	蝦丸
snakehead	sàang yúe	生魚
snapper	hung lăap	紅鱲
soft-shelled turtle	súi yúe	水魚
sole	tāat sà	撻沙
squid	yau yúe	魷魚
top shell	héung lóh	響螺
trout	jùn yúe	鱒魚
tuna	gàm chèung yúe	金鎗魚
white herring	cho băak	鯧白

Vegetables 蔬菜

asparagus	lō sún	露筍
bamboo shoots	jùk sún	竹筍
beancurd (tofu)	dău fŏo	豆腐
beans	dău gōk	豆角
bean sprouts	nga chōi	芽菜
beetroot	hung chōi tau	紅菜頭
bitter melon	fóo gwà	苦瓜
broccoli	sài laan fà	西蘭花
cabbage	ye chōi	椰菜
capsicum	chèng jìu	青椒
carrot	hung loh băak	紅蘿蔔
cauliflower	ye chōi fà	椰菜花
celery	sài kán	西芹
Ceylon spinach	saan chōi	潺菜
Chinese cabbage	băak chōi	白菜

FOOD

Chinese kale	gāai láan	芥蘭
Chinese leek	gáu chōi	韮菜
Chinese spinach	yĭn chōi	莧菜
chayote/choko	fāt sáu gwà	佛手瓜
corn	yŭk máí	玉米
cucumber	chèng gwà	青瓜
dried seaweed	jí chōi	紫菜
dried vegetables	chōi gòn	菜干
eggplant	ngái gwà	矮瓜
flowering cabbage	chōi sàm	菜心
gourd	sì gwà	絲瓜
green radish	chèng loh bāak	青蘿蔔
kudzu	fán gōt	粉葛
leek	dāai sūen	大蒜
leek (yellow)	gáu wong	韮黄
lettuce	sàang chōi	生菜
lotus root	lin ngáu	蓮藕
lotus seed	lin jí	蓮子
melon	gwà	瓜
mung bean	lŭk dáu	綠豆
mushroom	moh gòo	蘑菇
olive	gāam láam	橄欖
onion	yeung chùng	洋蔥
peanuts	fà sàng	花生
peas	dáu	豆

FOOD

| **DID YOU KNOW ...** | The Cantonese are known for their ability to eat anything. It's said that the only four-legged thing they won't eat is a table, and the only thing that flies that they won't eat is an airplane! |

FOOD

pea sprouts	dău miu	豆苗
potato	sue jái	薯仔
pumpkin	naam gwà	南瓜
salted vegetables	haam chōi	鹹菜
seaweed	jí chōi	紫菜
shallot	sūen	蒜
snap bean	sēi gwāi dáu	四季豆
snow peas	hoh làan dáu	荷蘭豆
spinach	bòh chōi	菠菜
spring onion	chùng	蔥
sweet potato	fàan súe	番薯
sugar pea	chèng dáu	青豆
taro	wŏo táu	芋頭
tomato	fàan ké	番茄
turnip	loh băak	蘿蔔
vegetable	sòh chōi	蔬菜
water-cress	sài yeung chōi	西洋菜
water spinach	ngūng chōi	甕菜
wax gourd	dùng gwà	冬瓜
yam bean	sà gōt	沙葛

Fruit & Nuts 水果

apple	ping gwóh	萍果
apricot	hāng	杏
avocado	ngau yau gwóh	牛油果
banana	hèung jìu	香蕉
cashew nut	yìu gwóh	腰果
cherries	chè lei jí	車厘子
chestnuts	lŭt jí	栗子
Chinese peach	súi mặt to	水蜜桃
Chinese plum	móoi	梅
coconut	ye jí	椰子
corn	sùk mặi	粟米

dates	jó	棗
dried fruit	gòn gwóh	干果
durian	lau lin	榴蓮
fig	mo fà gwóh	無花果
fresh fruit	sàn sìn súi gwóh	新鮮水果
fruit	sàang gwóh	生果
grapefruit	sài yáu	西柚
grapes	tai jí	提子
guava	fàan sēk láu	番石榴
Hami melon	hà māt gwà	哈密瓜
honeydew melon	māt gwà	蜜瓜
jackfruit	dāai sūe bòh loh	大樹菠蘿
Japanese nashi pear	súi jìng léi	水晶梨
juice	gwóh jàp	果汁
kiwifruit	kei yī gwóh;	奇異果;
	nei hau to	彌猴桃
lemon	ning mùng	檸檬
lime	chèng ning mùng	青檸檬
longan	lung ngán	龍眼
(similar to lychee)		
loquat	pei pá	枇杷
lychee	lāi jì	荔枝
mandarin	gàm	柑
mango	mòng gwóh	芒果
melon	gwà	瓜
mixed fruit platter	sàang gwóh pìng póon	生果拼盤
nectarine	yau tó	油桃
nuts	gwóh yan	果仁
olive	gāam láam	橄欖
orange	cháang	橙
papaya (pawpaw)	mūk gwà	木瓜
peach	tó	桃
peanut	fà sàng	花生

FOOD

FOOD

pear	bè léi	啤梨
persimmon	chí	柿
pineapple	bòh loh	菠蘿
pinenut	chung jí	松子
plum	léi	李
pomegranate	sěk láu	石榴
pomelo	sà tin yáu	沙田柚
raisins	po to gòng	葡萄干
star apple	yeung tó	楊桃
strawberries	sī dòh bè léi	士多啤厘
sugar cane	gàm jē	甘蔗
tangerine	gàm	柑
walnut	hăp to	合桃
water chestnut	mă tái	馬蹄
watermelon	sài gwà	西瓜

Dairy Products 乳酪

butter	ngau yau	牛油
cheese	jì sí	芝士
cream	năi yau	奶油
evaporated milk	fà năi	花奶
ice cream	sūet gò	雪糕
margarine	jīk mǎt yau	植物油
milk	ngau năi	牛奶
milk powder	năi fán	奶粉
milkshake	năi sìk	奶昔
skim milk	tūet jì năi	脱脂奶
soy milk	dău năi	豆奶
sweet condensed milk	tim lǐn năi	甜煉奶
yoghurt	sùen năi	酸奶

Spices & Condiments 調味

barbecue sauce	sìu hàau jēung	燒烤醬
bean sauce	mǐn sí jēung	麵豉醬
black bean	dǎu sǐ	豆豉
chicken essence	gài jìng	雞精
chilli	làat jìu	辣椒
chilli sauce	làat jìu jēung	辣椒醬
cinnamon	yǔk gwāi	玉桂
cloves	dìng hèung	丁香
coriander	yuen sài	芫茜
curry	gā lèi	咖喱
dark soy sauce	ló chàu	老抽
fish soy	yue lō	魚露
five-spices powder	nǧ hèung fán	五香粉
garlic	sūen tau	蒜頭
ginger	gèung	薑
Hoisin sauce	hói sìn jēung	海鮮醬
honey	mǎt tong	蜜糖
horseradish, green (wasabi)	yǎt bóon gāai làat	日本芥辣
leek	dǎai chùng	大蔥
lemongrass	hèung maau	香茅
malt sugar	mǎk nga tóng	麥芽糖
mint	bǒk hoh	薄荷
MSG	měi jìng	味精
mustard	gáai làat	芥辣
mustard sauce	gáai jēung	芥醬
nutmeg	dǎu kāu	豆蔻
oil	yau	油
olive oil	gāam lǎam yau	橄欖油
onion	yeung chùng	洋蔥
oyster sauce	ho yau	蠔油
paprika	hung làat jìu	紅辣椒

FOOD

parsley	hèung chōi; yeung yuen sài	香菜; 洋芫茜
pepper	woo jiu	胡椒
peppered-salt	jiu yim	椒鹽
plum sauce	mooi jí jēung	梅子醬
red vinegar	jīt chō	浙醋
rice wine	máí jáu	米酒
salt	yim	鹽
satay	sā dè	沙茶
sesame oil	ma yau	麻油
soy sauce	sī yau	豉油
spring onion	chùng	蔥
star aniseed	bāak gōk	八角
sugar	tong	糖
sunflower oil	kwai fā yau	葵花油
sweet sauce	tim jēung	甜醬
sweet savoury sauce	jā jēung	炸醬
tomato sauce	ké jàp	茄汁
vinegar	chō	醋
wasabi	yāt bóon gāai lãat	日本芥辣
wild pepper	fā jiu	花椒

Other Foods 雜貨

agar-agar jelly	leung fán	涼粉
baby food	yìng yi sīk bán	嬰兒食品
bean vermicelli	fán sì	粉絲
chocolate	jùe gòo lìk	朱古力
corn flour	sàang fán	生粉
congee (rice porridge)	jùk	粥
egg	dáan	蛋
flour	mīn fán	麵粉
instant noodles	jìk sīk mīn	即食麵
Japanese udon	wòo dùng	烏冬

macaroni	tùng sàm fán	通心粉
rice vermicelli	máai fán	米粉
self raising flour	jī fāat fán	自發粉
spaghetti	yī dāai lěi fán	意大利粉
yeast	fāat fán	發粉

Cooking Methods 烹調

baked	gǔk	焗
baked by slow fire	wòoi	煨
barbecue	sìu hàau	燒烤
boil	gwán	滾
braised	pa	扒
brine	yīp	醃
broil	chēuk	灼
cook	júe	煮
deep-fried	jā	炸
decoct	ngaau	熬
dry-fried	gòn sìu	干燒
fried	jìn	煎
grilled	sìu	燒
marinated	lǒ	滷

FOOD

DID YOU KNOW ...

The Chinese believe that eating snake gall bladder dispels wind, promotes blood circulation, dissolves phlegm and soothes one's breathing. Snake meat is said to remedy all sorts of ailments including anaemia, rheumatism, arthritis and asthenia (abnormal loss of strength).

FOOD

pan-fried	jìn	煎
quick-fried	bāau	爆
roasted	hàau	烤
simmer	màn	炆
smoked	fàn	燻
steam boat	dá bìn lo	打邊爐
steam in close vessel	dūn	燉
steamed	jìng	蒸
stew	hung sìu	紅燒
stir-fried	cháau	炒
stir mix	leung bõon	涼拌
teppanyaki	tīt báan sìu	鐵板燒

BEVERAGES 飲品
Cold Drinks 冷飲

apple juice	ping gwóh jàp	萍果汁
beverage	yám bán	飲品
chocolate milk	jùe gòo lìk nãai	朱古力奶
coconut juice	ye jàp	椰汁
cold water	dūng súi	凍水
fizzy drink	hēi súi	汽水
fresh juice	sìn gwóh jàp	鮮果汁
fruit juice	gwóh jàp	果汁
ginger beer	gèung bè	薑啤
grapefruit juice	sài yáu jàp	西柚汁
hot water	yīt súi	熱水
iced coffee	dūng gā fè	凍咖啡
iced lemon tea	dūng ning mùng cha	凍檸檬茶
iced water	bìng súi	冰水
juice	gwóh jàp	果汁
lemonade	ning mùng hēi súi	檸檬汽水
milk	ngau nãai	牛奶
milkshake	nãai sìk	奶昔

mineral water	kwōng chuen súi	礦泉水
orange juice	cháang jàp	橙汁
pineapple juice	bòh loh jàp	菠蘿汁
soda water	sòh dá súi	梳打水
soft drink	hēi súi	汽水
soya bean	dāu jèung	豆漿
soya bean milk	dāu nǎai	豆奶
sugar cane juice	jē jàp	蔗汁
tomato juice	fàan ké jàp	番茄汁
tonic	tòng līk	湯力
water	súi	水

Alcoholic Drinks 酒類

beer	bè jáu	啤酒
brandy	bāt làan déi	拔蘭地
champagne	hèung bàn	香檳
Chinese wine	sìu jáu	燒酒
draught beer	sàang bè	生啤
Japanese rice wine (sake)	yāt bóon jáu	日本酒
Mao Tai (Chinese)	maau toi	茅台
red wine	hung jáu	紅酒
spirits	jáu	酒
whisky	wài sǐ géi	威士忌
white wine	bǎak jáu	白酒
wine	po to jáu	葡萄酒

Hot Drinks 熱飲

almond milk	hǎng yan cha	杏仁茶
black coffee	jàai fē	齋啡
boiling water	gwán súi	滾水
camomile tea	gùk fà cha	菊花茶
Chinese herbal tea	leung cha	涼茶
Chinese tea	jùng gwōk cha	中國茶

FOOD

FOOD

coffee	gā fe	咖啡
green tea	lūk cha	綠茶
Horlicks	hó lāap hàk	好立克
hot chocolate	yìt jùe gòo lìk	熱朱古力
hot fresh milk	yìt sìn nǎai	熱鮮奶
hot Shaoxing wine	yìt sīu hīng jáu	熱紹興酒
jasmine tea	fà cha	花茶
lemon tea	ning mùng cha	檸檬茶
milk	ngau nǎai	牛奶
Ovaltine	òh wa tin	柯華田
Pu-er tea	pó léi cha	普洱茶
Pu-er and camomile	gùk pó	菊普
soya bean milk	dǎu nǎai	豆奶
sweet herb tea	ng fà cha	五花茶
tea	cha	茶
tea with milk	nǎai cha	奶茶
Tieguanyin tea	tīt gwóon yàm cha	鐵觀音茶
Wulong tea	wòo lúng cha	烏龍茶

TYPES OF TEA

Green Tea: New or fresh tea is better.

Bi-luo-chun and most Japanese tea.	bík loh chun	碧螺春

Black Tea: The older the better.

Pu-er	pó léi	普洱

Red Tea (semi-fermented):

Wulong	wòo lúng cha	烏龍茶
Tieguanyin	tīt gwóon yàm cha	鐵觀音茶

Other Tea:

Jasmin	huèng pín;	香片
	mōot lei;	茉莉
	fà cha	花茶

SOME USEFUL WORDS
Cutlery & Accessories 餐具

應用詞匯

ashtray	yìn fòoi jùng	煙灰盅
basket	lung	籠
bottle	jùn	樽
bowl	wóon	碗
box	hãp	盒
can	gwõon	罐
chair	dãng	凳
chopsticks	fãai jí	筷子
cup	bòoi	杯
fork	chà	叉
knife	dò	刀
napkin	jí gàn	紙巾
packet	bàau	包
plate	dĩp	碟
pot	woo	壺

FOOD

rice bowl	fãan wóon	飯碗
scoop (for rice)	fãan hõk	飯殼
scoop (for soup)	tòng gàng	湯羹
spoon	chi gàng	匙羹
table	tói	檯
tablecloth	tói bō	檯布
teapot	cha wóo	茶壺
teaspoon	cha gàng	茶羹
toothpick	nga chìm	牙簽
tray	poon	盤
wet towel	sàp mo gàn	濕毛巾
wine glass	jáu bòoi	酒杯

FOOD

Others 雜項

The bill please.

maai dàan　　　　　埋單

10% service charge	gà yàt síu jēung	加一小賬
bill	dàan	單
chef	dăai chúe	大廚
delicious	hó sīk	好食
fresh	sàn sìn	新鮮
full house	mőon jŏh	滿座
guest	yan hāak	人客
manager	gìng léi	經理
parking service	dŏi hāak pāak chè	代客泊車
service charge	fūk mŏ fài	服務費
to share a table	dāap tói	搭檯
to smell nice	hó hèung	好香
tips	tìp sí	貼士
toilet	sái sáu gàan	洗手間
VIP	gwāi bàn	貴賓
waiter (f)	nűi sĭ yīng	女侍應
waiter (m)	sĭ yīng	侍應
waiter (in China)	fūk mŏ yuen	服務員

The main attractions are the many historical monuments, temples of different religions, street markets and of course, the food. There are also ample opportunities to relax on the beach, cruise on the Pearl River or go walking in the White Cloud Hills, Lotus Mountain and Yuexiu Park.

The magnificent scenery in Guangxi has long been a source of traditional ink paintings, particularly around Guilin and Yanshuo. This is where you'll get the most out of trekking and river excursions.

In Hong Kong, a few traditional walled villages called wai still remain. They're completely surrounded by high and strong brick walls, with narrow entrances, which were originally built for protection against invaders. With an afternoon or day to spare away from the city you can visit a fishing village, go hiking in the country parks or visit the outlying islands.

Macau is like a model of what happens when a European city is combined with Chinese culture. Here, the temples of Chinese gods and European cathedrals often coexist.

WEATHER 天氣

It's important to know the weather forecast before you travel into the country, as the weather may change dramatically from one moment to another. Make sure you are fully equipped and have enough clothes and rain gear. Sunglasses, sunscreen and hats are a necessity when travelling in the tropical areas.

What's the weather like today/tomorrow?

(gàm/tìng) yǎt tìn hēi dím ā? (今/聽)日天氣點呀?

The weather's nice today/tomorrow.

(gàm/tìng) yǎt tìn hēi
wōoi hó hó

(今/聽)日天氣
會好好

Will it rain today/tomorrow?

(gàm/tìng) yǎt wōoi m
wōoi lǒk yúe ā?

(今/聽)日會唔
會落雨呀?

It's (not) going to rain today/tomorrow.

(gàm/tìng) yằt (m)		(今/聽)日(唔)
wŏoi lŏk yűe		會落雨

Today's very ...	gàm yằt hó ...	今日好 ...
cold	dūng	凍
cool	leung	涼
fine	ching lőng	晴朗
gloomy	yàm ngām	陰暗
hot	yĭt	熱
warm	nuễn	暖
windy	dāai fùng	大風

Useful Words

bright	gwòng mẳang	光猛
clear	ching lőng	晴朗
cloud	wan	雲
cloud free	mo wan	無雲
cloudy	yàm tìn	陰天
cyclone	suen fùng	旋風
dew	lŏ súi	露水
drizzle	mo mo yűe	毛毛雨
evening glow	mẳan ha	晚霞
fine weather	ching tìn	晴天
flood	hung súi	洪水
fog	mŏ	霧
frost	sèung	霜
halo	wẳn	暈
hail	bìng bŏk	冰雹
heavy rain	dāai yűe	大雨
humid	chiu sàp	潮濕
lightning	sím dīn	閃電
mist	ha	霞
mud	nai	泥

observatory	tìn man toi	天文台
rain	yűe	雨
rainbow	chói hung	彩虹
raining	lők yűe	落雨
rainy season	yűe gwāi	雨季
shower	jăau yűe	驟雨
sky	tìn hùng	天空
snow	süet	雪
snowing	lők süet	落雪
storm	bō fùng yűe	暴風雨
sunny	hó yeung gwòng	好陽光
sunrise	yăt chùt	日出
sunset	yăt lők	日落
thunder	lui	雷
tornado	lung gúen fùng	龍卷風
tropics	yīt dāai	熱帶
typhoon	toi fùng	颱風
weather	tìn hēi	天氣
weather forecast	tìn hēi yűe bō	天氣預報
wet	chiu sàp	潮濕
wind	fùng	風

IN THE COUNTRY

Seasons 季節

It's usually humid, gloomy and drizzling endlessly during the 'plum ripes season' in early spring.

spring	chùn gwāi	春季
summer	hă gwāi	夏季
autumn	chàu gwāi	秋季
winter	dùng gwāi	冬季
dry season	hőn gwāi	旱季
rainy season	yűe gwāi	雨季
monsoon	gwāi hău fùng	季候風

plum season	wong mooi tìn	黃梅天
swimming season	wǐng gwāi	泳季
horse racing season	mǎ gwāi	馬季

HIKING   遠足

There are numerous hikes to be undertaken within a short distance of central Hong Kong.

Where are we going?
    ngőh dēi wōoi hūi bìn dő ā?   我哋會去邊度呀?

When do we go?
    ngőh dēi géi si chùt fāat ā?   我哋幾時出發呀?

Where do we meet?
    ngőh dēi hái bìn dő jāap hāp ā?   我哋喺邊度集合呀?

Is the trail steep?
    tiu lő hǎi m hǎi hó chē ā?   條路係唔係好斜呀?

Is it a difficult climb?
    hǎi m hǎi hó naan pa ā?   係唔係好難爬呀?

Have you brought the ...?
    dāi jóh ... mĕi ā?   帶咗 ... 未呀?

Do you need to bring the ...?
    yīu m yīu dāi ... ā?   要唔要帶 ... 呀?

We'll come back ...	ngőh dēi ... fàan	我哋 ... 番
at (9) o'clock tonight	gàm mǎan	今晚
	(gáu) dím jùng	(九)點鐘
tomorrow	tìng yǎt	聽日
tomorrow evening	tìng mǎan	聽晚
the day after tomorrow	hǎu yǎt	後日

Useful Words

binoculars	mőng yűen gēng	望遠鏡
boots	cheung hèuh	長靴
camera	yíng séung gèi	影相機
climb	pa	爬

climbing boots	pa sàan haai	爬山鞋
compass	jí naam jàm	指南針
distance marker (pole)	lõ ching jí sĩ bìu	路程指示標
experienced	gìng yĩm	經驗
hat	mó	帽
hiking	yũen jùk	遠足
inexperienced	gìng yĩm m gāu	經驗唔夠
insect repellent	màn pā súi	蚊怕水
map	dẽi to	地圖
mountaineering	pàan sàan wăn dũng	攀山運動
orienteering	yẽ ngõi dĩng hēung	野外定向
raincoat	yũe yì	雨衣
sunscreen	tāai yeung yau	太陽油
sunglasses	tāai yeung ngắan gēng	太陽眼鏡
umbrella	jè	遮
walkie talkie	dūi góng gèi	對講機
walking stick	gwáai jéung	柺杖
water bottle	súi wóo	水壺

On The Path 沿路

Where are we now?
ngõh dẽi yi gà hái bìn dõ ā?   我哋而家喺邊度呀?

Are there any famous monuments here?
nì dõ yắu màt yế ming   呢度有乜嘢名
sīng góo jĩk ā?   勝古跡呀?

Can you please tell me how to get to ...?
chéng mắn ... dím yéung hūi ā?   請問 ... 點樣去呀?

What will we pass on the way?
wōoi gìng gwõh dì màt   會經過啲乜
yế dẽi fòng ā?   嘢地方呀?

How far is it from here to ...?
chéng mắn hūi ... jũng   請問去 ... 重
yắu géi yũen ā?   有幾遠呀?

Are there any things to see here/there?
    (nì/góh) dõ yáu màt dãk bĩt   (呢/嗰)度有乜特別
    gē yế tái ã?   嘅嘢睇呀?

Which is the (shortest/easiest) trial?
    bìn yàt tiu lõ jũi   邊一條路最
    (dúen; yung yĩ) ã?   (短; 容易)呀?

Let's take a rest here.
    ngőh dēi sìn hái nì dõ   我哋先喺呢度
    yàu sìk yàt jãn   休息一陣

Is this water OK to drink?
    nì dì súi yám m yám dãk ã?   呢啲水飲唔飲得呀?

Can I have a cup of water/tea?
    hóh m hóh yí béi bòoi   可唔可以俾杯
    (súi/cha) ngőh ã?   (水/茶)我呀?

What's this/that?
    (nì/góh) dì hãi màt yế lei gã?   (呢/嗰)嘅係乜嘢嚟㗎?

We've lost our way.
    ngőh dēi dõng sàt jóh lõ   我哋蕩失咗路

fitness trail	gĩn sàn gĩng	健身徑
hiking trail	yűen jùk gĩng	遠足徑
jogging track	woon páau gĩng	緩跑徑
lookout	gwòon gíng toi	觀景台
private property	sì yan dēi fòng	私人地方
pavilion	leung tíng	涼亭
shelter	bẽi yűe ting	避雨亭
steep	chē	斜
trail	lõ gĩng	路徑
scene	fùng gĩng	風景
scenic spot	gĩng dím	景點

Directions 方向

Which direction is the ... please?
chéng màn ... hái bìn yàt
gōh fòng hēung ā?

請問 ... 喺邊一
個方向呀?

direction	fòng hēung	方向
east	dùng	東
south	naam	南
west	sài	西
north	bàk	北
south-east	dùng naam	東南
north-west	sài bàk	西北
uphill	séung chē	上斜
downhill	lòk chē	落斜
left	jóh bìn	左便
right	yàu bìn	右便

Country Parks in Hong Kong 郊野公園

There are four main types of country parks in Hong Kong. Some are specifically for light recreational purposes, with playgrounds, lookouts, pavillions, trails for bushwalking, barbecue facilities, picnic areas and even campsites. Rangers patrol the areas and are there to assist you if any problems may occur.

Other parks accommodate serious walkers, rock climbers and hikers. The popular cliff of Lion Rock is one of the steepest cliffs in South-East Asia.

There are also wildlife observatories. Mai Po Marsh nature reserve is a world-famous wetland of international importance, and permission is needed before you are allowed entry.

Other reserves are used mainly for scientific research. Plants and animals are kept in their natural habitat and access is restricted.

Generally, the facilities in Hong Kong's parks are outstanding. Detailed maps are available, and signposts are common.

There are several trails in the country parks which you may like to try. The Maclehole Trail, which is 100 km long, the Lantau

Trail, stretching 70 km and Hong Kong Trail, a modest 50 km. All the trails are separated into sections, depending on how far you wish to walk. The views are magnificent – in some places you could be enjoying ocean views on one side of the trail while overlooking the modern city on the other.

country park	gàau yế gùng yúen	郊野公園
Ocean Park	hói yeung gùng yúen	海洋公園
sanctuary	bó wǒo kùi	保護區
Mai Po Bird Sanctuary	mắi bō níu lũi bó wǒo kùi	米埔鳥類 保護區
Mai Po Nature Reserve	mắi bō jī yin wǒo lếi kùi	米埔自然 護理區
MacLehole Trail	mắk lếi hǒ gīng	麥理浩徑
Lantau Trail	fũng wong gīng	鳳凰徑
Hong Kong Trail	góng dó gīng	港島徑
section	dũen	段

IN THE COUNTRY

CAMPING   露營

There are many opportunities to camp in the country areas surrounding Hong Kong.

Is there a campsite nearby?
nì dõ fõo gần yắu mố ying dẽi ā?   呢度附近有冇營地呀?

Am I allowed to camp here?
ngốh hóh m hóh yí hái nì dõ jaat ying ā?   我可唔可以喺呢 度紮營呀?

How much do you charge?
nếi yīu sàu géi dòh chín ā?   你要收幾多錢呀?

Where can I hire a tent?
bìn dõ hóh yí jò dó jẽung mók ā?   邊度可以租到 帳幕呀?

Do you have (a/any) ... here?	nì dõ yấu mố ... ā?	呢度有冇 ... 呀?
cooking facilities	júe sĩk hēi gũi	煮食器具
electricity	dĩn	電
first aid kit	gàp gāu sèung	急救箱
hot water	yĩt súi	熱水
showers	fā sá	花洒
toilets	chī sóh	廁所
washing machines	sái yì gèi	洗衣機

Useful Words

backpack	bōoi nong	背囊
camping	lõ ying	露營
camp fire	ying fóh	營火
campsite	ying dẽi	營地
can opener	gwōon tau dò	罐頭刀
firewood	mũk chaai	木柴
hammock	dīu chong	吊床
huricane lamp	fong fùng dàng	防風燈
kettle	súi wóo	水壺
knife	dò	刀
matches	fóh chaai	火柴
rope	sing sōk	繩索
rucksack	bōoi bàau	背包
sleeping bag	sũi dói	睡袋
stove	fóh lo	火爐
tent	jēung mõk	帳幕
tent pegs	ying dèng	營釘
torch	sáu dĩn túng	手電筒

GEOGRAPHICAL TERMS 地理

altitude	hói bằt gò dõ	海拔高度
bay	wàan	灣
beach	sà tàan	沙灘
bridge	kiu	橋
cave	sàan lùng	山窿
cliff	yuen ngaai	懸崖
coast	hói ngõn	海岸
countryside	gàau ngõi	郊外
country park	gàau yế gùng yúen	郊野公園
creek	kài gãan	溪澗
desert	sà mõk	沙漠
earth	tó dẽi	土地
earthquake	dẽi jãn	地震
farm	nung cheung	農場
fishery	yue yĩp	漁業
forest	sàm lam	森林
forestry	lam yĩp	林業
gap	sàan hãap	山峽
grassy plains	chó yuen	草原
harbour	góng háu	港口
high plateau	gò yuen	高原
hill	sàan gòng	山崗
hot spring	wàn chuen	溫泉
island	dó	島
jungle	chung lam	叢林
lake	woo	湖
landslide	sàan bàng	山崩
lookout	gwòon gíng toi	觀景台
mountain (range)	sàan (mãk)	山(脈)
mountain trail	sàan lõ	山路
mudslide	sàan nai kìng sē	山泥傾瀉
ocean	hói yeung	海洋

park	gùng yúen	公園
peak	sàan déng	山頂
peninsula	bōon dó	半島
pond	chi tong	池塘
puddle	súi tấm	水氹
ricefield	dō tin	稻田
river	hoh	河
road	dō lō	道路
rock	ngaam sĕk	岩石
sand	sà	沙
sea	hói	海
soil	nai tó	泥土
stone	sĕk	石
swamp	jíu jăak	沼澤
tide	chiu jĭk	潮汐
valley	sàan gùk	山谷
village	hèung chùen	鄉村
waterfall	bŭk bō	瀑布
well	jéng	井

THE STARS 天文

The Chinese legend has it that the Cowboy (Altair) and the Spinster's Maid (Vega) are allowed to meet once a year. On the seventh evening of the seventh lunar month, all the Joyful Birds fly across the Milky Way to form a bridge so that the lovers can meet.

Altair	ngau long	牛郎
Big Dipper	bàk dáu chàt sìng	北斗七星
comet	sō bá sìng	掃把星
constellation	sìng jōh	星座
Earth	dĕi kau	地球
full moon	mŏon yŭet	滿月
Jupiter	mŭk sìng	木星
lunar eclipse	yŭet sĭk	月蝕

Mars	fóh sìng	火星
Mercury	súi sìng	水星
meteor	lau sìng	流星
Milky Way	ngan hoh	銀河
Moon	yüet	月
nebula	sìng wan	星雲
new moon	sàn yüet	新月
Orion	lĭp wŏo sìng jŏh	獵戶座星
planet	hang sìng	行星
Polaris	bàk gĭk sìng	北極星
Saturn	tó sìng	土星
solar eclipse	yàt sĭk	日蝕
Southern Cross	naam sǎp jī sìng	南十字星
star	sìng	星
Sun	tāai yeung	太陽
universe	yǔe jǎu	宇宙
Venus	gàm sìng	金星
Vega	jìk nǚi	織女

THE ENVIRONMENT   應用詞句

What's it called?
nì gōh gīu jŏ màt yé ā?   呢個叫做乜嘢呀?

Is this a/an/the ...?
nì gōh hǎi m hǎi ... ā?   呢個係唔係 ... 呀?

acid rain	sùen yǔe	酸雨
animal welfare	dǔng mǎt fùk lēi	動物福利
cage	lung	籠
caged birds	lung jùng nǚu	籠中鳥
chemical waste	fà hŏk fài mǎt	化學廢物
cruel	chaan yán	殘忍
dangerous	ngai hím	危險
ecology	sàng tāai	生態
ecosystem	sàng tāai hǎi túng	生態系統

endangered species	pan ngai sūk júng	瀕危屬種
environmental protection	waan gíng bó wōo	環境保護
Friends of the Earth	dēi kau jì yáu	地球之友
greenhouse effect	wàn sàt hāau yīng	溫室效應
Greenpeace	lūk sìk woh ping	綠色和平
natural habitat	jī yin chài sìk dēi	自然棲息地
ozone layer	chāu yéung chang	臭氧層
pet	chúng māt	寵物
poisonous	yáu dūk	有毒
tame	sun leung	馴良
tropical rainforest	yīt dāai yúe lam	熱帶雨林

FAUNA 動物

amphibian	léung chài dūng māt	兩棲動物
birds	níu lūi	鳥類
domestic animals	gà chùk	家畜
domestic poultry	gà kam	家禽
fish	yue lūi	魚類
insects	kwàn chung	昆蟲
marsupial	yáu dói dūng māt	有袋動物
nocturnal	yē hang dūng māt	夜行動物
reptiles	pa chung	爬蟲
wild animal	yé sàng dūng māt	野生動物

Animals 走獸

bat	bìn fùk	蝙蝠
boar	yé jùe	野豬
camel	lōk toh	駱駝
cat	màau	貓
cow	ngau	牛
deer	lúk	鹿
dog	gáu	狗
domestic animals	gà chùk	家畜

IN THE COUNTRY

elephant	jēung	象
fox	woo léi	狐狸
gibbon	cheung bēi yuen	長臂猿
goat	sàan yeung	山羊
hare	yế tō	野兔
horse	mấ	馬
kangaroo	dōi súe	袋鼠
koala	sũe hung	樹熊
leopard	pāau	豹
lion	sì jí	獅子
monkey	mấ làu	馬騮
mouse	lố súe	老鼠
ox	gùng ngau	公牛
panda	hung màau	熊貓
pangolin	chùen sàan gāap	穿山甲
pig	jùe	豬
rabbit	tō	兔
sheep	yeung	羊
squirrel	chung súe	松鼠
tiger	lố fóo	老虎
wild animal	yế sàng dũng mất	野生動物
wolf	long	狼

Birds 禽鳥

birds	jēuk nĩu	雀鳥
chicken	gài	雞
crane	hōk	鶴
crow	wòo ngà	烏鴉
duck	ngāap	鴨
eagle	yìng	鷹
goose	ngóh	鵝
ibis	lố chī	鷺鷥
lark	wan jéuk	雲雀

Mandarin duck	yìn yèung	鴛鴦
parrot	yìng mő	鸚鵡
peafowl(peacock)	húng jēuk	孔雀
pelican	tong ngóh	塘鵝
penguin	kếi ngóh	企鵝
pigeon	bāak gāp	白鴿
rooster	gài gùng	雞公
sea gull	hói ngàu	海鷗
shearwater	sūn tìn yùng	信天翁
sparrow	ma jēuk	麻雀
swallow	yīn jí	燕子
swan	tìn ngoh	天鵝
turkey	fóh gài	火雞
woodpecker	dēuk mŭk nĭu	啄木鳥

Aquatic Creatures 水產

abalone	bàau yue	鮑魚
bream	lăap yúe	鱲魚
carp	lếi yúe	鯉魚
coral	sàan woo	珊瑚
crab	hăai	蟹
dace	leng yúe	鯪魚
dolphin	hói tuen	海豚
eel	măan	鰻
fish	yúe	魚
fresh water fish	tăam súi yúe	淡水魚
globe fish	gài pő yúe	雞泡魚
jelly fish	bāak jā	白鮓
oyster	ho	蠔
prawn	dāai hà	大蝦
salt water fish	hăam súi yúe	鹹水魚
sea cucumber	hói sàm	海參
sea horse	hói mã	海馬

sea urchin	hói dáam	海膽
seal	hói pāau	海豹
shark	sà yúe	鯊魚
shrimp	hà	蝦
skate fish	mòh gwái yúe	魔鬼魚
starfish	hói sìng	海星
tropical fish	yĭt dāai yúe	熱帶魚
whale	king yue	鯨魚

Insects & Reptiles 爬虫

ant	má ngái	螞蟻
bee	mĕt fùng	蜜蜂
beetle	gāap chung	甲蟲
butterfly	woo díp	蝴蝶
centipede	ng gùng	蜈蚣
cicada	sim	蟬
cobra	ngáan gēng se	眼鏡蛇
cockroach	găat jăat	甲由
crocodile	ngŏk yue	鱷魚
dragonfly	chìng ting	蜻蜓
earth worm	yàu yán	蚯蚓

GREEN TURTLES

Sham Wan (Deep Bay), in the south of Lama island – one of the outlying islands of the Hong Kong region – is the only remaining beach in the whole region where endangered Green Turtles are still known to struggle onto the sand to lay their eggs. In other areas, the turtles have been repulsed in their attempts to deposit eggs by a nefarious alliance of real estate developers, construction noise, and pollution.

firefly	ying fóh chung	螢火蟲
fly	wòo yìng	烏蠅
frog	tin gài	田雞
lice	sàt	虱
lizard	sìk yĭk	蜥蜴
mosquito	màn	蚊
moth	ngoh	蛾
poisonous snake	dŭk se	毒蛇
python	mŏng se	蟒蛇
rattle snake	héung méi se	響尾蛇
scorpion	dŭk kĭt	毒蠍
silk worm	chaam chúng	蠶蟲
snake	se	蛇
spider	jì jùe	蜘蛛
spider web	jì jùe mŏng	蜘蛛網
termite	băak ngăi	白蟻
turtle	gwài	龜
wasp	wong fùng	黃蜂

FLORA   植物
Trees 樹木

In rural China, you will often see village people gathering and socialising under the huge banyan trees after dinner. These gatherings are so common and popular that the banyan tree area, yung sŭe tau, has become a symbol for social gatherings.

Hong Kong people like to buy and decorate peach trees bought from the New Year's Eve free market. They believe that the more blossoms the tree produces, the more prosperity the new year will bring them.

bamboo	jùk	竹
banyan	yung sŭe	榕樹
camphor tree	jèung tree	樟樹
Christmas tree	sīng dāan sŭe	聖誕樹
cotton tree	mŭk min sŭe	木棉樹

cypress	pāak sūe	柏樹
elm	yue sūe	榆樹
eucalyptus	ngòn sūe	桉樹
fig tree	mo fà gwóh sūe	無花果樹
forest	sàm lam	森林
Hong Kong orchid tree	yeung jí gìng sūe	洋紫荊樹
locust tree	waai sūe	槐樹
maple	fùng sūe	楓樹
oak	jĕung sūe	橡樹
oleander	gāap jùk to	夾竹桃
palm	jùng lui	棕櫚
pine	chung sūe	松樹
shrub	gwōon mŭk	灌木
stem	gīng	莖
sugar cane	gàm jē	甘蔗
tree	sūe	樹
white champak	bāak láan	白蘭
willow	yeung láu	楊柳

Flowers 花卉

The plum flower is a Chinese favourite because it survives all the hardships of the cold winter, and its blossoms survive for a long time.

The beautiful purple flower, *bauhinia blakeana*, from the Hong Kong orchid tree, is Hong Kong's floral emblem.

bauhinia	yeung jí gìng	洋紫荊
bonsai	poon jòi	盆栽
cactus	sìn yan jéung	仙人掌
camellia	cha fà	茶花
carnation	hòng nǎai hìng;	康乃馨;
	dìng hèung	丁香
cherry blossom	yìng fà	櫻花
chrysanthemum	gùk fà	菊花

cymbidium orchid	wăi laan	蕙蘭
daffodil	yeung súi sìn	洋水仙
dandelion	po gùng yìng	蒲公英
flower	fà	花
forget-me-not	mo mong ngőh	毋忘我
gladiolus	gĩm laan	劍蘭
grass	chó	草
iris	chèung po	菖蒲
jasmin	mŏot léi fà	茉莉花
jonquil	súi sìn fà	水仙花
leaf	yĭp	葉
lily	bāak hăp	百合
lotus	lin fà; hoh fà	蓮花; 荷花
orchid	laan fà	蘭花
peach flower	to fà	桃花
peony	mắau dàan	牡丹
petal	fà fáan	花瓣
petunia	hìn ngau fà	牽牛花
plum flower	mooi fà	梅花
root	gàn	根
rose	mooi gwāi	玫瑰
sunflower	hēung yắt kwai	向日葵

IN THE COUNTRY

WATERSIDE 嬉水

Whether you are surfing on the rolling waves of the outlying islands, catching the crabs at the reservoirs, or swimming with the kids in the Conghua hot spring river near Guangzhou, you will find no lack of aquatic activities.

At the Beach 沙灘

Swimming at at beach with life guards and and shark nets is the safe option. In Hong Kong, the little red flag at the beach signals that it's not safe to go in the water.

Is it safe to swim here?
  hái nì dŏ yau súi ngòn chuen mā?   喺呢度游水安全嗎?

IN THE COUNTRY

awning	wǐng paang	泳棚
bath towel	dǎai mo gàn	大毛巾
bathing shed	sà tàan wǐng ngùk	沙灘泳屋
beach	sà tàan	沙灘
beach towel	sà tàan gàn	沙灘巾
boat	tḗng jái	艇仔
changing rooms	gàng yì sàt	更衣室
changing shed	wǐng paang	泳棚
clam digging	gwàt hín	掘蜆
current	hói lau	海流
ebb tide	súi tūi	水退
flood tide	súi jēung	水漲
goggles	wǒo ngǎan gēng	護眼鏡
lake	woo	湖
life buoy	gāu sàng hùen	救生圈
lifeguard	gāu sàng yuen	救生員
life jacket	gāu sàng yì	救生衣
renting a boat	jò tḗng	租艇
reservoir (Hong Kong)	súi tong	水塘
resevoir (China)	súi fōo	水庫
river	hoh	河
sails	faan	帆
sailboat	faan suen	帆船
sea	hói	海
shark net	fong sà mòng	防鯊網
shark warning flag	sà yue kei	鯊魚旗
speedboat	fāai tḗng	快艇
surfboard	wǎat báan	滑板
swimming cap	wǐng mǒ	泳帽
swimming suit	wǐng yì	泳衣
trunks	wǐng fōo	泳褲
wave	lǒng	浪
yacht	yau tḗng	遊艇

Aquatic Sports 水運

I like (surfing).
  ngőh jùng yī (wăat long)   我中意(滑浪)

Where can I rent/hire a/the ... please?
  chéng măn hái bìn dŏ   請問喺邊度
  hóh yí jò dó ...   可以租到 ...

aquatic sports	súi sēung wăn dŭng	水上運動
beach volleyball	sà tàan paai kau	沙灘排球
canoeing	dŭk mŭk jàu	獨木舟
diving	tīu súi	跳水
diving equipment	chim súi yŭng gūi	潛水用具
equipment	yŭng gūi	用具
fishing	dīu yúe	釣魚
flippers	wà haai	蛙鞋
jet ski	súi sēung dīn	水上電
	dàan chè	單車
rowing	chōi tếng	賽艇
rowing boat	pa tếng	扒艇
sailing	hong hói	航海
scuba diving	chim súi	潛水
snorkel	kàp hēi gwóon	吸氣管
surfing	wăat long	滑浪
swimming	yau súi	游水
swimming pool	yau súi chi	游水池

IN THE COUNTRY

SURFING

Surfing is not strictly allowed in Hong Kong, however you do find surfers holding their own at Big Wave Bay, Shek O.

synchronized swimming	súi sēung wán lūt chò	水上韻律操
water polo	súi kau	水球
water-skiing	wāat súi	滑水
windsurfing	wāat long fùng faan	滑浪風帆
yachting	yau téng chōi	遊艇賽

SPORTS & GAMES   康體

aerobics	wán lǔt chò	韻律操
archery	sē jīn	射箭
athletics	tái yǔk	體育
badminton	yǔe mo kau	羽毛球
baseball	páang kau	棒球
basketball	laam kau	籃球
billiards	tói bòh	檯波
boxing	kuen chōi	拳賽
bungee jumping	gò hùng dǎan tīu; bǎn jùe tīu	高空彈跳; 笨豬跳
car racing	chōi chè	賽車
chess	kéi	棋
Chinese chess	jēung kéi	象棋
cricket	báan kau	板球
cycling	cháai dàan chè	踩單車
equestrian	mǎ sǔt	馬術
fencing	gīm gǐk	劍擊
figure skating	fà sǐk lau bìng	花式溜冰
football	jùk kau	足球
gate ball	moon kau	門球
golf	gò yí fòo kau	高爾夫球
gymnastics	tái chò	體操
handball	sáu kau	手球
hockey	kùk gwān kau	曲棍球
hopscotch	tīu fèi gèi	跳飛機

horse riding	kei má	騎馬
indoor soccer	sàt nŏi jùk kau	室內足球
indoor sports	sàt nŏi wăn dŭng	室內運動
judo	yau dŏ	柔道
karate	hùng sáu dŏ	空手道
kite flying	fòng fùng jàng	放風箏
kung fu	gùng fòo	功夫
lawn bowls	chó děi gwán kau	草地滾球
Marathon	má làai chung	馬拉松
martial arts	mŏ sŭt	武術
mountain biking	yŭet yé dàan chè	越野單車
netball	mŏ báan laam kau;	無板籃球;
	nŭi jí tau kau	女子投球
polo	má kau	馬球
rollerskating	gwán jŭk lau bìng	滾軸溜冰
rugby	gāam láam kau	橄欖球
skateboarding	wăat báan	滑板
skiing	wăat sūet	滑雪
soccer	jùk kau	足球
softball	lui kau	壘球
sports	wăn dŭng	運動
squash	bìk kau	壁球
Sumo	yàt bóon sèung pōk	日本相撲
Tae Kwon Do	toi kuen dŏ	跆拳道
Tai Chi	tāai gĭk	太極
table tennis	bìng bàm bòh	乒乓波
ten-pin bowling	bó ling kau	保齡球
tennis	mŏng kau	網球
track & field	tin gĭng	田徑
trampoline	dăan chong	彈床
triathlon	sàam hong má làai chung	三項馬拉松
tug-of-war	băt hoh	拔河

volleyball	paai kau	排球
walkathon	bō hang wōot dūng	步行活動
weightlifting	gúi chúng	舉重
wrestling	sùt gōk	摔角

HEALTH 保健

In Hong Kong, it's quite easy to find a doctor any time from early morning to late evening, and there's always the emergency surgery in the public hospitals. Usually patients can be supplied immediately with prescribed medicines by their doctors. Most doctors can speak English, but there are some doctors practising traditional Chinese medicine who may not speak English. Unlike the doctors of Western medicine, these natural therapists usually prescribe mixtures of Chinese herbs, generally very strong and sometimes repulsive smelling, which can usually be bought in shops next door to the clinics.

In some bigger and more modern Cantonese cities in mainland China, you can still find a few doctors who speak English. But if you have to visit a doctor in a remote area, you'll need to take along an interpreter. You should also be prepared and carry a basic medical kit with any prescribed drugs you need. Avoid drinking tap water.

PLACES & REQUESTS 送診

Could you tell me where the ... is?

Chéng mǎn ... hái bìn dǒ ā?　　請問 ... 喺邊度呀?

Where's the nearest ...?	Chéng mǎn jūi kán gē ... hái bìn dǒ ā?	請問最近嘅 ... 喺邊度呀?
casualty ward	gàp jīng sàt	急症室
clinic	chán sóh	診所
dentist	nga yì sàng	牙醫生
doctor	yì sàng	醫生
hospital	yì yúen	醫院
nurse	wǒo sǐ	護士
operating theatre	sáu sūt sàt	手術室
pharmacy	yěuk fong	藥房

Please take me to a doctor.
  chéng dāai ngőh hūi tái yì sàng   請帶我去睇醫生

I've been injured.
  ngőh sáu jóh sèung   我受咗傷

I need an ambulance.
  ngőh yīu gīu gāu sèung chè   我要叫救傷車

Please call a doctor to room (number ...).
  chéng gīu yì sàng lei (... hő) fóng   請叫醫生嚟(... 號)房

I have to go to the casualty ward.
  ngőh yīu hūi yì yúen gàp jīng sàt   我要去醫院急症室

He/She needs first aid.
  kűi sùi yīu gàp gāu   佢需要急救

AT THE HOSPITAL/CLINIC   候診

I need a/an ...   ngőh sùi yīu   我需要
                      yàt wái ...   一位 ...

doctor   yì sàng   醫生
English-speaking   sìk góng yìng mán   識講英文
doctor   gē yì sàng   嘅醫生
female doctor   nűi yì sàng   女醫生
female nurse   nűi wőo sī   女護士
(English) interpreter (yìng mán) fàan yīk (英文)翻譯
male doctor   naam yì sàng   男醫生
male nurse   naam wőo sī   男護士

AT THE DOCTOR'S   閏問

(I'm) sick.
  (ngőh) yáu bēng   (我)有病

I'm not feeling well.
  ngőh m sùe fūk   我唔舒服

It hurts here.
  nì dő tūng   呢度痛

I have a fever.
  ngőh yáu fāat sìu   我有發燒

HEALTH

I've been vomiting.
　ngőh yấu ngáu tõ
我有嘔吐

I have a cough (and phlegm).
　ngőh yấu kàt sāu
　(tung maai yấu taam)
我有咳嗽
(同埋有痰)

I'm taking medication.
　ngőh sĭk gán yĕuk
我食緊藥

This is my usual medicine.
　ngőh ping si sĭk nì jĕk yĕuk
我平時食呢隻藥

I (don't) want a blood transfusion.
　ngőh (m) yīu sùe hūet
我(唔)要輸血

I don't want an operation.
　ngőh m yīu jŏ sáu sũt
我唔要做手術

Please use a new syringe.
　chéng yŭng sàn gē jàm
請用新嘅針

I have my own syringe.
　ngőh yấu jĭ géi gē jàm
我有自己嘅針

I feel (better/worse) now.
　ngőh yi gà gōk dàk
　(hó/chà) jóh dì
我而家覺得
(好/差)咗啲

How long before it heals?
　yīu géi női sìn jī hó fàan ā?
要幾耐先至好番呀?

AILMENTS　　徵兆

I can't sleep.	ngőh fān m jĕuk	我瞓唔着
I suffer from ...	ngőh ...	我 ...
I can't move my ...	ngőh gē ... m yùk dàk	我嘅 ... 唔郁得
I'm/I feel ...	ngőh ...	我 ...
breathless	hēi chúen	氣喘
very tired	hó gwõoi	好癐
tired (no concentration)	mő jìng san	冇精神
tired (no strength)	jàu sàn mő lĭk	週身冇力
weak (lethargic)	sàn tái hùi yĕuk	身體虛弱

THE DOCTOR MAY SAY ...

néi yáu màt yé sī ā?　　　　　你有苔嘢事呀？
  What's the matter?

yáu mó tũng ā?　　　　　　　有冇痛呀？
  Do you feel any pain?

bìn dõ tũng ā?　　　　　　　邊度痛呀？
  Where does it hurt?

néi yi gà gõk dàk dím ā?　　　你而家覺得點呀？
  How are you feeling?

ngõh tung néi ...　　我同你 ...　　I'll ...
  leung hũet ngāat　　量血壓　　check your
　　　　　　　　　　　　　　　　blood pressure
  bá mãk　　　　　　把脈　　　take your pulse
  tāam yĩt　　　　　探熱　　　take your
　　　　　　　　　　　　　　　temperature
  dá jàm　　　　　　打針　　　give you an
　　　　　　　　　　　　　　　injection

m gòi chui jóh dì sàam　　　唔該除咗啲衫
  Please get undressed.

sàm fòo kàp　　　　　　　　深呼吸
  Breathe deeply.

mãak dãai gõh háu　　　　　擘大個口
  Open your mouth.

sàn tiu léi chùt lei　　　　　伸條脷出嚟
  Stick out your tongue.

gám yéung tũng m tũng ā?　　咁樣痛唔痛呀？
  Does this hurt?

néi yáu mó fãat sìu ā?　　　　你有冇發燒呀？
  Do you have a temperature?

néi yí chin yáu gwóh　　　　你以前有過乜
màt yé bẽng ā?　　　　　　苔嘢病呀？
  What illnesses have you had in the past?

THE DOCTOR MAY SAY ...

géi sí hòi chí hǎi gám yéung ā? 幾時開始係咁樣呀?
How long have you been like this?

yí chin yǎu mǒ gám yéung ā? 以前有冇咁樣呀?
Have you had this before?

néi ping si yǎu mǒ sǐk yìn ā? 你平時有冇食煙呀?
Do you smoke?

néi ping si yǎu mǒ yám jáu ā? 你平時有冇飲酒呀?
Do you drink?

néi hǎi m hǎi yǎu sǐk   你係唔係有食
gán yěuk ā?   緊藥呀?
Are you on any medication?

néi yǎu mǒ dūi màt yế   你有冇對乜嘢
gwōh mán ā?   過敏呀?
Are you allergic to anything?

néi jǔng yǎu mǒ màt yế   你重有冇乜嘢
yīu mǎn ngốh ā?   要問我呀?
Do you have you anything more to ask me?

It's ...	nì dõ ...	呢度 ...
bleeding	chùt hūet	出血
broken	tửen jóh	斷咗
bruised	yúe jóh	瘀咗
dislocated	làt jóh gāau	甩咗骹
painful	hó tūng	好痛
sprained	náu sèung	扭傷
swollen	júng tūng	腫痛

I have (a/an) ...	ngốh ...	我 ...
altitude sickness	yǎu wāi gò jīng	有畏高症
appendicitis	yǎu maang	有盲
	chéung yim	腸炎
arthritis	yǎu gwàan jīt yim	有關節炎

HEALTH

English	Romanization	Chinese
asthma	yǎu hàau chúen	有哮喘
backache	yìu tūng	腰痛
been bitten by an insect	běi chung ngǎau	被蟲咬
been bitten by a dog	běi gáu ngǎau	被狗咬
breathing trouble	fòo kàp kwān naan	呼吸困難
burn	běi sìu sèung	被燒傷
cold	yǎu sèung fùng	有傷風
cold sweat	chùt lǎang hōn	出冷汗
constipated	bīn bēi	便秘
cramps	chàu gàn	抽筋
diabetes	yǎu tong nǐu běng	有糖尿病
diarrhoea	tǒ ngòh	肚痾
dizziness	tau wan	頭暈
food poisoning	sǐk mǎt jūng dǔk	食物中毒
hayfever	yǎu fà fán jīng	有花粉症
headache	tau tūng	頭痛
heart condition	yǎu sàm jǒng běng	有心臟病
hepatitis	yǎu gòn yim	有肝炎
high blood pressure	yǎu gò hüet ngāat	有高血壓
indigestion	sìu fà bàt leung	消化不良
inflammation	fāat yim	發炎
influenza	yǎu gám mǒ	有感冒
insomnia	sàt min	失眠
itch	han yěung	痕癢
lice	yǎu sāt	有虱
loss of appetite	sǐk jǎi	食滯
low blood pressure	yǎu dài hüet ngāat	有低血壓
malaria	yǎu yěuk jǎt	有瘧疾
migraine	yǎu pìn tau tūng	有偏頭痛
nervous breakdown	san gìng sùi yěuk	神經衰弱
neuralgia	san gìng tūng	神經痛
no appetite	mǒ wǎi háu	冇胃口

HEALTH

palpitations; high pulse rate	sàm tīu gàp chùk	心跳急促
pneumonia	fāi yim	肺炎
rheumatism	yấu fùng sàp	有風濕
runny nose	lau bēi súi	流鼻水
seasickness	wan suen lōng	暈船浪
skin lesion	pei fòo súen sèung	皮膚損傷
snoring problem	yấu bēi hon	有鼻鼾
sore throat	hau lung tūng	喉嚨痛
STD	yấu sīng bēng	有性病
stomach ache	tố tūng	肚痛
stomach ulcer	yấu wǎi kwóoi yeung	有胃潰瘍
sunstroke	jūng súe	中暑
tonsillitis	yấu bín to sīn yim	有扁桃腺炎
toothache	nga tūng	牙痛
travel sickness	wan lōng	暈浪
typhoid	yấu sèung hon	有傷寒
ulcer	yấu kwóoi yeung	有潰瘍

WOMEN'S HEALTH   婦科

Could I see a female doctor?
   ngốh yīu tái nűi yì sàng   我要睇女醫生

Could I see a gynaecologist?
   ngốh yīu tái főo fòh yì sàng   我要睇婦科醫生

I'm on the pill.
   ngốh sīk gán bēi yẳn yẻuk   我食緊避孕藥

I haven't had my period for (...) months.
   ngốh yí gìng (...) gōh yǔet   我已經(...)個月
   mố lei yǔet gìng   冇嚟月經

I'd like to have a pregnancy test.
   ngốh séung yīu yīm yẳn   我想要驗孕

I'm pregnant.
   ngốh waai jóh yẳn   我懷咗孕

legal abortion	hăp fāat lau cháan	合法流產
abortion	yan gùng lau cháan	人工流產
antenatal check-up	cháan chin gím cha	產前檢查
breast	yűe fong	乳房
breast feeding	wāi mő yűe	餵母乳
breast cancer	yűe ngaam	乳癌
caesarean birth	fáu fùk sàng cháan	剖腹生產
cervical cancer	jí gùng géng ngaam	子宮頸癌
cramps	gìng tūng	經痛
cystitis	pong gwòng yim	膀胱炎
fallopian tube	sùe lún gwóon	輸卵管
foetal movement	tòi dűng	胎動
gyneacologist	főo fòh yì sàng	婦科醫生
hormone	gìk sō;	激素;
	hőh yí mung	荷爾蒙
infertility	bàt yŭk	不育
lactation	bő yűe kei	哺乳期
menstruation	yűet gìng	月經
miscarriage	lau cháan	流產
morning-after pill	sĭ hău bĕi yăn yúen	事後避孕丸
pap smear	pāak sĭ to pín	柏氏塗片
	gím yĭn	檢驗

THE DOCTOR MAY SAY ...

néi hăi m hăi waai jóh yăn ā? 你係唔係懷嚟孕呀?
  Are you pregnant?

néi yi gà hăi m hăi gìng kei ā? 你而家係唔係經期呀?
  Do you have your period?

néi hăi m hăi sĭk gán bĕi 你唔係食緊避
yăn yúen ā? 孕丸呀?
  Are you on the pill?

sĕung chī gìng kei hăi géi si ā? 上次經期係幾時呀?
  When did you have your last period?

HEALTH

pelvic examination	fǒo fòh gím cha	婦科檢查
premature labour/birth	jó cháan	早產
premenstrual tension	gìng chin gán jèung	經前緊張
pregnant	waai yǎn	懷孕
stillbirth	séi tòi	死胎
ultrasound	chìu sìng bòh sō miu	超聲波掃描
uterus	jí gùng	子宮
vagina	yàm dǒ	陰道

ALLERGIES 過敏

I have a skin allergy.
ngǒh yǎu pei fòo gwōh mǎn 我有皮膚過敏

I'm allergic to ...	ngǒh dūi ... gwōh mǎn	我對 ... 過敏
antibiotics	kōng sàang sō	抗生素
aspirin	ā sǐ pàt ling	亞士匹靈
bee stings	mǎt fùng jàm chī	蜜蜂針刺
codeine	hóh dǒi yàn	可待因
dairy products	yǔe lōk sǐk mǎt	乳酪食物
food coloring	sǐk mǎt sìk sō	食物色素
iodine	dín	碘
lactose	yǔe tong	乳糖
meat	yǔk lǔi sǐk mǎt	肉類食物
MSG	měi jìng	味精
oranges	cháang	橙
penicillin	poon nei sài lam	盤尼西林
pollen	fà fán	花粉
wasp stings	wong fùng jàm chī	黃蜂針刺

ALTERNATIVE & FURTHER TREATMENTS 療法

acupuncture & cauterization	jàm gāu	針灸
blood transfusion	sùe hūet	輸血
blood test	yǐm hūet	驗血

hydrotherapy	súi liu fãat	水療法
immunisation	fong yĩk jūe sē	防疫注射
injection	dá jàm	打針
intensive care	sàm chīt jī liu	深切治療
massage	tùi na	推拿
physiotherapy	mãt léi jī liu	物理治療
radiotherapy	fòng sē dĩn liu	放射電療
reflexotherapy	fáan sē ngōn mòh jī liu	反射按摩治療
shiatsu	jí ngāat	指壓
X-ray	X-gwòng	X光
yoga	yue gà	瑜珈

AT THE CHEMIST   藥房

When you visit a doctor, the prescribed medicine is usually
provided. However there are some cases when the doctor is unable
to do so. It is then up to you to acquire the prescription from a
chemist. In Hong Kong, you can only get prescribed medicine
from a licenced chemist. An unlicensed chemist would only sell
common medicines or drugs like painkillers. Make sure you know
the correct dosage for your medication.

Do I need a prescription (for this)?
    (nì jēk yĕuk) yīu m yīu yì   (呢隻藥)要唔要醫
    sàng chúe fòng ā?   生處方呀?

I have a prescription.
    ngõh yãu yì sàng chúe fòng   我有醫生處方

HEALTH

Can I have a/an/ some ... please?	m gòi béi ngőh ...	唔該俾我 ...
antiseptic	sìu dŭk jài	消毒劑
aspirin	ā sī pàt ling	亞士匹靈
bandage	bàng dáai	繃帶
Band-aids	yĕuk súi gàau bō	藥水膠布
condom	bĕi yăn tō	避孕套
contraceptive	bĕi yăn yúen	避孕丸
cotton bud	min păang	棉棒
cough remedy	jí kàt yĕuk	止咳藥
cup of water	yàt bòoi súi	一杯水
eye drops	ngáan yĕuk súi	眼藥水
gauze	sà bō	紗布
insect repellent	chui chung jài	除蟲劑
iodine	dìn jáu	碘酒
laxative	hìng sē yĕuk	輕瀉藥
mercurochrome	hung yĕuk súi	紅藥水
painkiller	jí tūng yĕuk	止痛藥
seasickness pill	wan lőng yúen	暈浪丸
sleeping pill	ngòn min yĕuk	安眠藥
the pill	bĕi yăn yúen	避孕丸
thermometer	tăam yĭt jàm	探熱針
tiger balm	măan gàm yau	萬金油
tranquilliser	jàn jĭng jài	鎮靜劑
travel sickness pill	wan lőng yúen	暈浪丸
vaseline	fà sī líng	花士苓

PARTS OF THE BODY

各部器官

ankle	gēuk ngáan	腳眼
appendix	maang chéung	盲腸
arm	sáu bēi	手臂
back	bōoi jēk	背脊
beard	woo sò	鬍鬚

blood	hūet	血
bone	gwàt	骨
brain	nő	腦
breast	yűe fong	乳房
chest	hùng bő	胸部
ear	yí	耳
elbow	sáu jàang	手踭
eye	ngãan	眼
face	mĭn	面
faeces	dãai bĭn	大便
finger	sáu jí	手指
fingernail	jí gāap	指甲
foot	gēuk	腳
hair	tau fāat	頭髮
hand	sáu	手
head	tau	頭
heart	sàm jőng	心臟

THEY MAY SAY ...

mőoi chi gŏk fŭk (yàt) nàp
take (one) tablet of each
每次各服(一)粒

mőoi yàt fŭk (sàam/sēi) chī
take (three/four) times a day
每日服(三/四)次

fãan (chin/hǎu) fŭk yŭng
take before/after meal
飯(前/後)服用

mőoi yàt cha wǎan chūe (lĕung chī)
apply to the affected area (twice) a day
每日搽患處(兩次)

lam fān chin fŭk yŭng (yàt nàp)
take (1 tablet) before bedtime
臨瞓前服用(一粒)

chí yěuk hóh nang yắn jī kwān sǔi
This medicine may cause drowsiness.
此藥可能引致睏睡

HEALTH

hip	tuen bŏ	臀部
kidney	sān jŏng	腎臟
knee	sàt tau	膝頭
leg	dăai túi	大腿
lip	háu sun	口唇
liver	gòn jŏng	肝臟
lungs	fāi	肺
mouth	háu	口
muscle	gèi yŭk	肌肉
neck	géng	頸
nerve	san gìng	神經
nose	bĕi	鼻
palm	sáu jéung	手掌
rib	lăak gwàt	肋骨
saliva	háu súi	口水
shoulder	bōk tau	膊頭
skin	pei fòo	皮膚

spine	jēk jùi	脊椎
stomach	wăi	胃
sweat	hŏn	汗
teeth	nga	牙
throat	hau lung	喉嚨
thumb	mŏ jí	拇指
tongue	lĕi	脷
tonsils	bín to sīn	扁桃腺
urinate	síu bīn	小便
urine	nĭu	尿
vein	jĭng măk	靜脈
waist	yìu bŏ	腰部
wrist	sáu wóon	手腕

AT THE DENTIST 牙醫

Is there a dentist here?
   chéng mǎn nì dǒ yǎu mó
   nga yì sàng ā? 請問呢度有冇牙醫生呀?

My gum hurts.
   ngőh nga ngán tūng 我牙齦痛

Please (don't) give me an anaesthetic.
   chéng (m hó) yűng ma jūi yěuk 請(唔好)用麻醉藥

I have (a) ...	ngő ...	我 ...
cavity	yǎu jūe nga	有蛀牙
tooth decay	yǎu lāan nga	有爛牙
toothache	nga tūng	牙痛

Please have a	chéng něi tái yàt	請你睇一
look at my ...	tái ngőh gē ...	睇我嘅 ...
gum	nga ngán	牙齦
teeth	nga chí	牙齒

I (don't) want my	ngőh (m)	我(唔)
teeth to be ...	yīu ... nga	要 ... 牙
cleaned	sái	洗
extracted	tūet	脫
filled	bó	補

canine teeth	húen chí	犬齒
decayed tooth	jūe nga	蛀牙
dental floss	nga sīn	牙線
dentist	nga yì sàng	牙醫生
denture	gá nga	假牙
incisor	moon nga	門牙
jaw bone	nga chong	牙床
milk teeth	yűe chí	乳齒
molar	dǎai nga	大牙
roof of mouth	sěung ngǒk	上顎

teething	chùt nga	出牙
tooth	nga chí	牙齒
toothache	nga tūng	牙痛
tooth enamel	fāat long jàt	琺瑯質
tooth nerve	chí san gìng	齒神經
tooth root	nga gàn	牙根
wisdom tooth	jī wái chí	智慧齒

AT THE OPTOMETRIST 視光師

I'd like an eye test.
   ngőh yīu yĭm ngăan   我要驗眼

I want a pair of glasses.
   ngőh yīu yàt fōo ngăan gēng   我要一副眼鏡

I'm long/short sighted.
   ngőh yáu (yűen/găn) sī   我有(遠/近)視

artificial eye	yan jő ngăan	人造眼
astigmatism	sáan gwòng	散光
blind	maang ngăan	盲眼
cataract	bāak női jēung	白內障
contact lens	yán ying ngăan gēng	隱形眼鏡
eye	ngăan jìng	眼睛
eye drops	ngăan yěuk súi	眼藥水
eye test	yĭm ngăan	驗眼
eyebank	ngăan fōo	眼庫
glasses	ngăan gēng	眼鏡
glaucoma	lŭk női jēung	綠內障
ophthalmologist	ngăan fòh yì sàng	眼科醫生
optometrist	sī gwòng sì	視光師
pupil	tung húng	瞳孔
sunglasses	tāai yeung ngăan gēng	太陽眼鏡
tears	ngăan lŭi	眼淚
trachoma	sà ngăan	砂眼

SOME USEFUL PHRASES   應用詞句

I've been vaccinated.
  ngőh jūng jóh dáu   我種咗痘

I need a receipt (in English) for my health insurance.
  ngőh yīu yàt jèung (yűng yìng   我要一張(用英
  mán sé gē) sàu gűi sàn chíng gīn   文寫嘅)收據申請健
  hòng bó hím gàm   康保險金

I want my X-ray back.
  ngőh yīu lóh faan dì X-gwòng pín   我要攞番啲X-光片

I need a health certificate.
  ngőh yīu yàt jèung gīn hòng   我要一張健康
  jīng ming sùe   證明書

Can I travel ...?   ... hóh m hóh yí   ... 可唔可以
                                lűi hang ā?   旅行呀?

  tomorrow   tìng yàt   聽日
  in three days   sàam yàt női   三日內
  this week   nì gőh sìng kei női   呢個星期內

Some Useful Words 應用詞匯

accident	yī ngői	意外
acute	gàp sīng	急性
AIDS (Hong Kong)	ngōi jì bēng	愛滋病
AIDS (China)	ngăai jì bēng	艾滋病
to bleed	chùt hūet	出血
blood pressure	hūet ngàat	血壓
blood group	hūet ying	血型
cancer	ngaam	癌
chronic	măan sīng	慢性
consulting room	chán jīng sàt	診症室
first aid	gàp gāu	急救
health	gīn hòng	健康
history	bēng līk	病歷

hospital	yì yúen	醫院
inflammation	fāat yìm	發炎
influenza	lau hang sīng gám mō	流行性感冒
injection	dá jàm	打針
patient	bĕng yan	病人
Red Cross	hung sáp jī wóoi	紅十字會
side effects	fōo jōk yúng	副作用
surgeon	ngòi fòh yì sàng	外科醫生
swollen	hung júng	紅腫
symptoms	bĕng jìng	病徵
syringe	jàm túng	針筒
virus	bĕng dŭk	病毒
vitamin	wai tà mĭng	維他命

Traditional Chinese Health Practices 傳統中醫

把脈	bá māk	taking the pulse
大夫	dāai fòo	Chinese herbalist
跌打	dīt dá	Chinese bone setting
灸	gāu	cauterisation
虛	hùi	weak
針	jàm	acupuncture
指壓	jí ngāat	shiatsu

HERB EMPORIUM

A good place to purchase herbal medicines is Yue Hwa Chinese Products Emporium at the north-west corner of Nathan and Jordan Rds, just above Jordan MTR station. Before buying anything, explain your condition to a Chinese chemist and ask for a recommendation.

HEALTH

中藥	jùng yēuk	Chinese medicine
中醫	jùng yì	Chinese herbalist
甩骹	làt gāau	dislocated joint
涼茶	leung cha	herbal tea
萬金油	mǎan gàm yau	Tiger Balm ointment
按摩	ngōn mòh	massage
食療	sīk liu	diet therapy (herbal)
推拿	tùi na	massage
廿四味	yǎ sēi méi	Chinese herbal tea with 24 ingredients
穴道	yǔet dǒ	den; nerve spot

SPECIFIC NEEDS 特需

DISABLED TRAVELLERS 行動不便

In Hong Kong, visually impaired people always walk with a cane (red and white). Some public transport and major public buildings cater to disabled people.

Pedestrian crossings often use sound signals to indicate when it is safe to cross. A rapid, continuous pulse means to commence crossing. The change to a broken pattern indicates that is no longer safe.

Parks may also have facilities including toilets and pavement suitable for wheelchair access.

For emergencies, including fire, police and ambulance, dial 999, or fax 992 for the hearing impaired.

Is there any special service for disabled people?
yáu mó jùen wāi chaan jăt 有冇專為殘疾
yan sī gē dăk bĭt fŭk mó ā? 人士嘅特別服務呀？

I need assistance.
ngóh sùi yīu bòng mong 我需要幫忙

Is there wheelchair access?
gōh dŏ yáu mó lun yí tùng dŏ ā? 嗰度有冇輪椅通道呀？

Are guidedogs allowed in?
jún m jún dŏ maang 准唔准導盲
húen yăp hūi ā? 犬入去呀？

Is there a (guide) service for blind people?
yáu mó wāi maang yan gē 有冇為盲人嘅
(jí dŏ) fŭk mó ā? (指導)服務呀？

Can you please book a Rehabus/taxi for me (see page 222).
m gòi néi bòng ngóh děng 唔該你幫我訂
(fŭk hòng bà sí/dĭk sí) (復康巴士/的士)

Please speak louder/slower.
chéng néi gòng (dăai sèng/ 請你講(大聲/
măan) síu síu 慢)少少

219

SPECIFIC NEEDS

Does anyone here know English sign language?	nì dõ yấu mõ yan sìk yìng mán sáu yũe ā?	呢度有冇人識英文手語呀?
Does anyone here know how to lip read?	nì dõ yấu mõ yan sìk dũk sun sũt ā?	呢度有冇人識讀唇術呀?
I wear a hearing aid.	ngõh dāai jóh jõh tīng hēi	我戴咗助聽器

Where's the ... please?	chéng mãn ... hái bìn dõ ā?	請問 ... 喺邊度呀?
disabled toilet	chaan jãt yan sĩ chĩ sóh	殘疾人士廁所
elevator/lift	dĩn tài	電梯
wheelchair access	lun yí tùng dõ	輪椅通道
rehabilitation centre	fũk gĩn jùng sàm	復健中心

Please help me to ...	m gòi chéng bòng ngõh (...)	唔該請幫我(...)
cross the road	gwõh mã lõ	過馬路
get through the entrance gate	yãp dãai moon háu	入大門口
get through the rotary door	gwõh suen júen moon	過旋轉門
climb the steps	sẽung lau tài	上樓梯

Useful Terms 應用詞語

able-bodied	gĩn chuen yan sĩ	健全人士
artificial limbs	yĩ jì	義肢
blind	maang	盲
Braille	dím jĩ	點字
Braille library	dím jĩ to sùe gwóon	點字圖書館
cane	sáu jéung	手杖
Chinese sign language	jùng man sáu yũe	中文手語
colour blind	sìk maang	色盲
crutches	gwáai jéung	柺杖

deaf	lung	聾
disabled	chaan jàt	殘疾
	sī chī sóh	士廁所
elderly	ló nin yan	老年人
English sign language	yìng man sáu yűe	英文手語
guidedog	dò maang húen	導盲犬
handrails	foo sáu	扶手
hearing aid	jőh tīng hēi	助聽器
help phone	kau jőh dīn wá	求助電話
Paralympics	chaan jàt yan	殘疾人
	ngō wăn wóoi	奧運會
physical disability	yĕuk nang	弱能
quadriplegic	sēi jì tàan wŏon	四肢癱瘓
rehabilitation centre	fūk gĭn jùng sàm	復健中心
sign language	sáu yűe	手語
travelator	jĭ déng hang yan dō	自動行人道
wheelchair	lun yí	輪椅
wheelchair access	lun yí tùng dō	輪椅通道

Terms Particular to Mainland China

accessible facilities	mo jēung ngŏi	無障礙
	chīt sì	設施
aged/weak/sick/ disabled	ló yĕuk bēng chaan	老弱病殘
blind person	maang yan	盲人
Braille	maang man	盲文
deaf person	lung yan	聾人
disabled person	chaan jàt yan	殘疾人

Terms Particular to Hong Kong

In Hong Kong, it is more appropriate to use the following terms:

disabled person	chaan jàt yan sī	殘疾人士
hearing impaired	sàt chùng;	失聰;
	tīng gŏk sáu súen	聽覺受損

SPECIFIC NEEDS

less mobile	hang dūng bàt bīn	行動不便
mentally handicapped person	yẽuk nang yan sī	弱能人士
physically handicapped person	jì tái sèung chaan yan sī	肢體傷殘人士
visually impaired	sàt ming; sī gōk sǎu súen	失明; 視覺受損
wheelchair user	lun yí sí yǔng jé; lun yí yan sī	輪椅使用者; 輪椅人士

Disabled Access to Public Transport in Hong Kong 交通

Most of the MTR subway stations and KCR stations allow direct access to platforms through lifts, wheelchair aids, ramps, tactile guide paths and stairlifts. Some of them also provide call bells to get staff assistance. Induction loop intercom systems are also available at limited ticket offices for people with a hearing impairment.

The LRT, Light Rail Transit is fully accessible in all of the 57 road level stops. Reserved places are available inside vehicle compartments.

Most of the local buses have facilities to assist disabled passengers, but only a limited number of buses have the low-floor with ramps that allow wheelchair access. The Rehabus service provides a local transport network including a scheduled service and a dial-a-ride service.

PLEASE GIVE SEAT TO LESS MOBILE

The sign, 'Please give the seat to the less mobile', chéng yẽung jõh wái kàp sèung chaan yan sī is blue.

Ferries are a relatively accessible means of transport except for the hoverferries and those berthed alongside pontoons. Lower decks often have wheelchair space.

In order to improve the mobility of disabled people, the police have agreed to exercise discretion to allow taxi or car drivers to pick up and set down disabled passengers in restricted zones in some cases. Obtain the *Certificate for Picking Up or Setting Down of Disabled Taxi Passengers in Restricted Zones* before your ride.

call bell	kau jŏh dĭn ling	求助電鈴
direct access	jĭk jĭp tùng dŏ	直接通道
disabled passenger	séung chaan sing hāak	傷殘乘客
Easy Access Bus	yĭ dāap bà sí	易搭巴士
handrails	foo sáu	扶手
lift	dĭn tài	電梯
ramp	che lŏ; chē ló	斜路
Rehabus	fŭk hòng bà sí	復康巴士
stairlift	tài kàp sìng gōng gèi	梯級升降機
tactile guide paths	nàp dɐt man yán dŏ	凹凸紋引道
	yán lŏ jùen	引路磚
vertical lift	sui jĭk sìng gōng gèi	垂直升降機
wheelchair aid access	lun yí tùng dŏ	輪椅通道

GAY TRAVELLERS   同志

You can easily find some bars in the Lan Kwai Fong and Glenealy St area – both are close to Hong Kong Central. These areas are the best known gay and lesbian centres. There, you can also find more information. Try adult or larger bookshops for specific books and magazines.

In Hong Kong, some gay people call each other tung jī, meaning the person with same hobbies or interests; and the lesbians nűi tung jī, 'female comrade'. The words kāi dăi, denote a homosexual partner or 'gay boy'.

The gay and lesbian scenes still keep a very low profile. Among Chinese people, reactions generally fall under two extremes once you mention you are gay/lesbian. One would continue talking to you while the other may flee the scene and not respond.

Do you have any gay-related books/magazines?
    nì dŏ yắu mŏ tung sīng lűen   呢度有冇同性戀
    gē (sùe/jăap jī) ā?   嘅(書/雜誌)呀?

SPECIFIC NEEDS

Are we likely to be harassed here?
(lit: are we going to cause trouble by being here?)

ngőh děi hái nì dō wōoi m	我哋喺呢度會唔
wōoi yán hēi ma faan ā?	會引起麻煩呀?

Where are the gay hangouts?

dì gèi ló dòh sō hái bìn dō ā?	啲基佬多數喺邊度呀?

Is there a/an ... near by?	nì dō fŏo gán	呢度附近
	yáu mŏ ... ā?	有冇 ... 呀?
adult bookshop	sìng yan sùe dìm	成人書店
bar	jáu bà	酒吧
gay bar	gèi bà	基吧
gay street/district	tung jĭ wŏot	同志活
	dŭng kùi	動區
club	wŏoi sóh	會所
gay (col)	gèi;	基;
	gèi ló	基佬
homosexual	tung sīng lűen	同性戀
lesbian	nűi tung sīng lűen	女同性戀
nightclub	yĕ júng wòoi	夜總會

TRAVELLING WITH A FAMILY   闔府

I'm travelling with my family.

ngőh tung ngőh ngùk kéi	我同我屋企
yan yàt chai lűi hang	人一齊旅行

We're travelling with (one/two/three) kid(s).

ngőh děi tung (yàt/léung/sàam)	我哋同(一/兩/三)
gŏh sài lŏ jái yàt chai lűi hang	個細路仔一齊旅行

We want to (sit/stay) together.

ngőh děi yìu tung maai yàt	我哋要同埋一
chai (chóh/jŭe)	齊(坐/住)

Are there facilities for (babies/children)?

yáu mŏ (yìng yi; yì tung)	有冇(嬰兒; 兒童)
gē chīt bĕi ā?	嘅設備呀?

Are there other (families/children) ...?
　　... jŭng yáu mő kei tà　　　　　... 重有冇其他
　　(gà tìng; yì tung) ā?　　　　　(家庭; 兒童)呀?

Will you provide childcare service during the ...
　　... kei gàan néi dĕi yáu mő tai　　... 期間你哋有冇提
　　gùng tōk yi fūk mő ā?　　　　　供托兒服務呀?

Is there a child-minding　... yáu mő tōk　　　... 有冇托
service (in this) ...?　　　yi fūk mő ā?　　　兒服務呀?

church	nì gàan gāau tóng	呢間教堂
hotel	nì gàan jáu dìm	呢間酒店
here	nì dõ	呢度
conference	wőoi yí	會議
meeting	wőoi yí	會議
cocktail party	gàai méi jáu wóoi	雞尾酒會
shopping centre	kāu màt	購物

I need a babysitter ...　　... ngőh yìu wán　　　... 我要搵
　　　　　　　　　　gőh bó mő　　　　個褓姆

from 10 am to	gàm yàt sǎp	今日十
6 pm today	dím dō lūk dím	點到六點
next week	hǎ gőh sìng kei	下個星期
now	yi gà	而家
tonight	gàm mǎan	今晚
tomorrow	tìng yàt	聽日

Can you provide a (French/English)-speaking babysitter?
　　hóh m hóh yí tai gùng yàt gőh　　可唔可以提供一個
　　sìk góng (fāat/yìng) mán　　　識講(法/英)文
　　gē bó mő ā?　　　　　　　嘅褓姆呀?

How much is it?
　　géi dòh chín ā?　　　　　　幾多錢呀?

Where's the childcare room please?
　　chéng màn tōk yi sàt　　　　請問托兒室
　　hái bìn dõ ā?　　　　　　　喺邊度呀?

May I put my ... here?		
ngốh hóh m hóh yí fōng		我可唔可以放
ngốh gē ... hái nì dố ā?		我嘅 ... 喺呢度呀?

Do you have any	néi dẽi yấu mő	你哋有冇
... for the kids?	... béi sāi lố jái ā?	... 俾細路仔呀?
baby carriages	yìng yi láam	嬰兒籃
capsules	sáu tai yìng yi láam	手提嬰兒籃
computer games	dĭn nő yau hēi gèi	電腦遊戲機
playpens	yau hēi chong	遊戲床
pushers/strollers	sáu tùi chè	手推車
puzzles(wooden blocks)	jìk mŭk	積木
toys	wőon gŭi	玩具
TV games	dĭn sĩ yau hēi gèi	電視遊戲機

Can you add an	m gòi hái fong	唔該喺
extra ... to the room?	gàan gà dòh jèung ...	房間加多張 ...
bed	chong	床
cot	yŭk yìng chong	育嬰床
high chair	gò dāng	高凳
playpen	yấu hēi chong	遊戲床

I need a car with a (baby/child) seat.	
ngốh sùi yīu yấu maai (yìng yi; yi tung) jőh wái gē chè	我需要有埋(嬰兒; 兒童)座位嘅車

Do you hire out family cars?	
yấu mő gà ting chè chùt jò ā?	有冇家庭車出租呀?

Does this car have a child seat?	
nì gā chè yấu mő yi tung jőh wái ā?	呢架車有冇兒童座位呀?

Is it safe for (babies/children)?	
(yìng yi; yi tung) ngòn chuen m ngòn chuen gā?	(嬰兒; 兒童)安全唔安全㗎?

Are there any children's activities here?	
nì dő yấu mő yi tung wőot dŭng jīt mŭk ā?	呢度有冇兒童活動節目呀?

Is it suitable for all ages?
hǎi m hǎi ngàam sāai
sóh yǎu nin ling gā?
係唔係啱哂
所有年齡㗎?

Is it suitable for the whole family?
hǎi m hǎi ngàam sāai chuen gà ā?
係唔係啱哂全家呀?

Is there a family discount?
yǎu mő gà ting yàu dői
jīt kāu ā?
有冇家庭優待
折扣呀?

Are children allowed to join?
jún m jún yi tung chàam gà ā?
准唔准兒童參加呀?

Is there a children's menu?
yǎu mő yi tung chàan páai ā?
有冇兒童餐牌呀?

What time is the children's program on?
yi tung jīt mǔk géi dím
jùng hòi chí ā?
兒童節目幾點
鐘開始呀?

Is there a playground around here?
nì dõ fõo gǎn yǎu mő
yi tung yǎu lők cheung ā?
呢度附近有冇
兒童遊樂場呀?

Where can I buy (milk powder) please?
chéng màn bìn dõ hőh
yǐ mǎai dó (nǎai fán) ā?
請問邊度可
以買到(奶粉)呀?

baby food	yìng yi sĩk bán	兒童食品
baby powder	yìng yi sóng sàn fán	嬰兒爽身粉
baby soap	yìng yi faan gáan	嬰兒番梘
babysitter	bó mő	褓姆
baby chair	yìng yi dāng	嬰兒凳
baby's bottle	nǎai jùn	奶樽
bib	wai júi	圍咀
casual child care centre	lam sĩ tõk yi sóh	臨時托兒所
children's video	yi tung lǔk yíng dáai	兒童錄影帶
child care centre	tõk yi sóh	托兒所
computer games	dĩn nő yau hēi	電腦遊戲
cot	yǔk yìng chong	育嬰床

SPECIFIC NEEDS

crayons	lăap bàt	蠟筆
disposable nappies	jí nĭu pín	紙尿片
drawing material	kwóoi to yŭng gŭi	繪圖用具
dummy	năai júi	奶咀
feeding bottle	năai jùn	奶樽
milk	ngau năai	牛奶
milk powder	năai fán	奶粉
nappy	nĭu pín	尿片
nappy rash cream	yìng yí sàp chán gò	嬰兒濕疹膏
playground	yi tung yăui lŏk cheung	兒童遊樂場
powdered milk	năai fán	奶粉
pram	yìng yi sáu tùi chè	嬰兒手推車
soy milk	dāu năai	豆奶
talcum powder	sóng sàn fán	爽身粉
teat	năai júi	奶咀
toy	wŏon gŭi	玩具

EDUCATION   教育

Hong Kong has ideal personnel, materials, facilities and the appropriate environment for learning Cantonese, Mandarin and other languages. There are many study options available at universities and other language institutes.

I want to study (Cantonese).
　　ngőh séung dŭk (gwóng dùng wá)　我想讀(廣東話)

I want to select this subject.
　　ngőh séung súen sàu nì yàt fòh　我想選修呢一科

What qualifications do I need?
　　sùi yīu yăui màt yé jì gāak ā?　需要有乜嘢資格呀?

I want to apply for a (scholarship).
　　ngőh séung sàn chíng　我想申請
　　(jŭng hŏk gàm)　(獎學金)

When does school begin?
　　hŏk hăau géi si hòi fōh ā?　學校幾時開課呀?

When do holidays begin?
  géi si hòi chí fōng gā ā? 幾時開始放假呀?

How many units do I need?
  sùi yīu sàu géi dòh gōh
  hŏk fàn ā? 需要修幾多個
學分呀?

How many lessons per week?
  yàt gōh sìng kei yáu géi
  dòh jīt fòh ā? 一個星期有幾
多節課呀?

assignment	jāap jōk	習作
auditor (unenrolled student)	pong tīng sàng	旁聽生
boarder	gēi sùk sàng	寄宿生
certificate	jīng sùe	證書
department	hŏk hāi	學系
diploma	man pang	文憑
examination	háau sī	考試
exchange student	gàau wŏon hŏk sàng	交換學生
faculty	hŏk yúen	學院
... fee	... fài	... 費
foreign student	ngŏi gwōk hŏk sàng	外國學生
high school	gò jùng	高中
international school	gwōk jāi hŏk hāau	國際學校
language school	yúe yin hŏk hāau	語言學校
lesson	góng fòh	講課
lecturer	góng sì	講師
scholarship	jéung hŏk gàm	獎學金
school	hŏk hāau	學校
school holiday	hŏk hāau gā kei	學校假期
semester	hŏk kei	學期
short course	dúen kei fòh ching	短期課程
summer course	hà gwāi fòh ching	夏季課程
term	hŏk kei	學期
tutor	jōh gàau	助教
university	dàai hŏk	大學

SPECIFIC NEEDS

MID-TERM ACCOMMODATION 居住

This section is for those looking for long or mid-term accommodation, including those looking into dormitories and school boarding. Students intending to board should submit their application in advance. Rooms are in high demand, even for short term accommodation. Most universities in China give priority to and supply better facilities for foreign students.

In Hong Kong, long term tenants normally have to pay all the management fees, maintenance, electricity, water, gas and telephone. Some may even have to pay the rates too.

I'm looking for accomodation that is close to a ...	ngốh yīu wán gōh kán ... gē jūe sùk	我要搵 個近 ... 嘅住宿
bus stop	bà sí jām	巴士站
subway station	děi tīt jām	地鐵站
school	hŏk hāau	學校
train station	fóh chè jām	火車站
university	dāai hŏk	大學

Is it furnished?
yấu mố lin maai gà sì ā? 有冇連埋傢俬呀?

Do I have to pay for the ...?
ngốh yīu m yīu béi ... ā? 我要唔要俾 ... 呀?

Does it include ...?
hăi m hăi bàau maai ... ā? 係唔係包埋 ... 呀?

Do I need to sign a contract?
yīu m yīu chìm hăp tung ā? 要唔要簽合同呀?

How much is the ...?	... dāai yēuk yīu géi dòh chín ā?	... 大約要 幾多錢呀?
deposit	bó jīng gàm	保證金
handling charge	sáu jūk fai	手續費
management fee	gwóon léi fai	管理費
rates	chàai héung	差餉
telephone	dĭn wá fai	電話費

I intend to stay for ...	ngőh wōoi jūe ...	我會住 ...
three months	sàam gōh yŭet	三個月
half a year	bōon nin	半年
a school term	yàt gōh hŏk kei	一個學期
two semesters	léung gōh hŏk kei	兩個學期
a year	yàt nin	一年

How much notice do I have to give before leaving?

jáu jì chin yīu géi nŏi tùng jì ā?	走之前要幾耐 通知呀?

Where can I buy/rent the ...?

bìn dŏ hóh yî (măai/jò) dó ... ā?	邊度可以(買/租) 到 ... 呀?

How do I pay the rent?

ngőh dím yéung béi jò gàm ā?	我點樣俾租金呀?

I'll send it by mail.

ngőh wōoi gēi béi néi	我會寄俾你

Can I use the ...?	ngőh hóh m hóh yî yūng ... ā?	我可唔 可以用 ... 呀?
dishwasher	sái wóon gèi	洗碗機
electrical appliances	dīn hēi yūng gèi	電器用具
fax	chuen jàn gèi	傳真機
furniture	gà sì	傢俬
kitchen	chue fóng	廚房
microwave	mei bòh lo	微波爐
telephone	dīn wá	電話
TV	dīn sī	電視
video recorder	lŭk yíng gèi	錄影機
washing machine	sái yì gèi	洗衣機
refrigerator	sūet gwăi	雪櫃

ON BUSINESS   商務

The well known official trade fair CECF, Chinese Export Commodities Fair is held in Guangzhou twice a year, in April (Spring Session) and October (Autumn Session). The Hong Kong Convention and Exhibition Centre is one of the most highly regarded conference centres in the world. The ceremony commemorating returning Hong Kong to China was held there.

Useful Terms 應用詞語

conference	tó lŭn wóoi	討論會
congress	dŏi bíu dăai wóoi	代表大會
convention	wŏoi yí	會議
delegation	dŏi bíu tuen	代表團
exhibition	jín lăam wóoi	展覽會
Exposition	bōk lăam wóoi	博覽會
Fair	gàau yĭk wóoi	交易會
representative	dŏi bíu	代表
trade exhibition	sèung bán jín	商品展
	lăam wóoi	覽會

The Chinese Export Commodities Fair (CECF)

jùng gwōk chùt háu sèung	中國出口商
bán gàau yĭk wóoi	品交易會

Where's a/the	chéng măn ...	請問 ...
... please?	hái bìn dŏ ā?	喺邊度呀?
ATM	jĭ dŭng tai fóon gèi	自動提款機
business card	jĭ dŭng yàn	自動印
printing machine	ming pín gèi	名片機
business centre	sèung mŏ jùng sàm	商務中心
fax machine	chuen jàn gèi	傳真機
photocopier	yíng yàn gèi	影印機

I'm one of the members/representatives.

ngőh hăi (sing yuen/	我係(成員/
dŏi bíu) jì yàt	代表)之一

SPECIFIC NEEDS

I need to use a (telephone).
ngóh séung yǔng (dīn wá)
我想用(電話)

I want to send a (parcel) to ...
ngóh yīu sūng gōh
(bàau gwóh) hūi ...
我要送個
(包裹)去 ...

I have an appointment with ...
ngóh yēuk jóh ...
我約咗 ...

I need an (English/French) interpreter.
ngóh yīu yàt wái (yìng/fáat)
mán chuen yīk
我要一位(英/法)
文傳譯

Here is my business card.
nì jèung hǎi ngóh ming pín
呢張係我名片

CHINESE EXPORT COMMODITIES FAIR		
Spring Session	chùn gàau wóoi	春交會
Autumn Session	chàu gàau wóoi	秋交會

Useful Words 應用詞匯

agent	dōi léi	代理
business	sàng yī	生意
business card	ming pín	名片
business lunch	gùng jök ńg chàan	工作午餐
buyer	mǎai gà	買家
cargo	fòh màt	貨物
Chamber of Commerce	sèung wóoi	商會
client	gōo hāak	顧客
colleague	tung sī	同事
company	gùng sì	公司
computer	dīn nó	電腦
corporation	fàat yan	法人
customer	gōo hāak	顧客

SPECIFIC NEEDS

demonstration	sī fãan	示範
distributor	fàn sìu sèung	分銷商
e mail	dĩn yau	電郵
fax	chuen jàn	傳真
internet	wõo luen mõng	互聯網
internet connection	sèung mõng	上網
laptop	sáu tai dĩn nõ	手提電腦
loss	kwài súen	虧損
manager	gìng lẽi	經理
market	sí cheung	市場
marketing	sí cheung sìu sãu	市場銷售
meeting	wõoi yĩ	會議
profit	ying lẽi	盈利
proposal	gãi wãak sùe	計劃書
royalty	jùen lẽi fãi	專利費
sales promotion	tùi sìu	推銷
sales point	mãai dím	賣點
strike	bã gùng	罷工
trademark	jũe chãak sèung bìu	註冊商標
union	gùng wóoi	工會

ON TOUR   團隊

We're in the same group.

| ngõh dẽi hãi tung maai | 我哋係同埋 |
| yàt gõh tuen | 一個團 |

I'm a member of the ...	ngõh hãi ... gē sing yuen	我係 ... 嘅成員
band	ngõk dúi	樂隊
basketball team	laam kau dúi	籃球隊
choir	hãp chēung tuen	合唱團
delegation	dõi bíu tuen	代表團
football team	jùk kau dúi	足球隊
troupe	gòh mõ tuen	歌舞團
orchestra	gàau héung ngõk tuen	交響樂團

SPECIFIC NEEDS

We're here	ngốh dẽi lei nì	我哋嚟呢
for a/an ...	dõ chàam gà ...	度參加 ...
competition	béi chōi	比賽
conference	tó lŭn wóoi	討論會
exchange student	gàau wŏon hŏk	交換學
scheme	sàang gāi wăak	生計劃
meeting	wóoi yí	會議
performance	bíu yín	表演
trade fair	sèung bán gàau	商品交
	yĭk wóoi	易會

We're here for ...	ngốh dẽi lei nì dõ ...	我哋嚟呢度 ...
shopping	chói kāu fōh măt	採購貨物
short term study	dúen kei hŏk jăap	短期學習
sightseeing	gwòon gwòng	觀光
study	hŏk jăap	學習
training	său fân	受訓

Please speak	chéng nếi tung	請你同
with our ...	ngốh dẽi gē ... góng	我哋嘅 ... 講
coach	gāau lĭn	教練
conductor	jí fài	指揮
director	dõ yín	導演
group leader	tuen jéung	團長
manager	gìng léi	經理
spokesperson	fāat yin yan	發言人
teacher	lố sì	老師

Useful Words 應用詞匯

dress rehearsal	chòi paai	綵排
free time	jĭ yau si gāan	自由時間
group member	tuen yuen	團員
guide	dõ yau	導遊
press conference	gēi jé jìu dõi wóoi	記者招待會
local guide (HK)	dõ yau	導遊

SPECIFIC NEEDS

local guide (China)	dēi pooi	地陪
manager	gìng léi	經理
rehearsal	paai yín	排演
sightseeing	gwòon gwòng	觀光
student group	hŏk sàng tuen	學生團
study group	hŏk jăap tuen	學習團
tour leader	lĭng dúi	領隊
tourist	yau hāak	遊客
tourist bus	lūi yau chè	旅遊車

Sightseeing Tours 觀光

You can book most local tours through travel agents and hotel service desks.

Where can I book a tour?
bìn dŏ hóh yĭ yūe dĕng
lūi hang tuen ā?

邊度可以預訂
旅行團呀?

Do you organise (English-speaking) group tours?
néi dēi yău mŏ băan (góng yìng
mán gē) lūi hang tuen ā?

你哋有冇辦(講英
文嘅)旅行團呀?

What's the departure time?
géi dím jùng chùt fāat ā?

幾點鐘出發呀?

Where's the pick-up point?
hái bìn dŏ jăap hăp ā?

喺邊度集合呀?

I'm with this group.
ngóh tung maai nì gŏh tuen gē

我同埋呢個團嘅

I've lost my group.
ngóh jáu sàt jóh ngóh gē tuen

我走失咗我嘅團

Have you seen a group of (Australians)?
chéng mǎn yău mŏ gìn dó yàt
gŏh (ngò jàu) tuen ā?

請問有冇見到一
個(澳洲)團呀?

How long will we stop for?
ngóh dēi wōoi ting lau géi nŏi ā?

我哋會停留幾耐呀?

What time do I have to be back?

ngőh yīu géi dím jùng
jì chin fàan lei ā?

我要幾點鐘
之前番嚟呀?

I don't want too many shopping stops.

ngőh m séung ngòn paai gām
dòh mǎai yế gē si gāan

我唔想安排咁
多買嘢嘅時間

I want to buy some (Chinese herbal medicine/handicrafts).

ngőh séung mǎai dì (jùng
yẻuk/sáu gùng ngǎi bán)

我想買啲(中
藥/手工藝品)

FILM, TV & MEDIA   傳媒

Can we film here?

hái nì dỏ hóh m hóh yí
pāak sīp ā?

喺呢度可唔可以
拍攝呀?

Who should we ask for permission to film here?

wán bìn gōh sàn chíng pāak
sīp húi hóh ā?

搵邊個申請拍
攝許可呀?

We're making a ...	ngőh dẻi pāak sīp gán ...	我哋拍攝緊 ...
commercial	gwóng gō pín	廣告片
documentary	gēi lǔk pín	記錄片
film	dĭn yíng	電影
report	bō dỏ	報導
TV series	dĭn sĭ lin jǔk kēk	電視連續劇

We're conducting an interview.

ngőh dẻi jỏ gán chói fóng

我哋做緊採訪

Does anyone here speak English?

nì dỏ yấu mỏ yan sìk góng
yìng mán ā?

呢度有冇人識講
英文呀?

I need (10) temporary extras to help.

ngőh yīu (sẳp) gōh lam si yín
yuen bòng sáu

我要(十)個臨時演
員幫手

SPECIFIC NEEDS

Useful Words

actor	yín yuen	演員
antenna	tìn sīn	天線
broadcasting	gwóng bōh	廣播
camera	sīp yíng gèi	攝影機
commentary	pong sŭt	旁述
commentator	pong sŭt yuen	旁述員
correspondent	dāk pāai yuen	特派員
costume	fŭk sìk	服飾
current affairs	si sĭ	時事
director	dō yín	導演
equipment	hēi choi	器材
to film	pāak sīp	拍攝
film crew	sīp yíng dúi	攝影隊
information	jì sūn	資訊
interview (report)	chói fóng	採訪
journalist	gēi jé	記者
lighting	dàng gwòng	燈光
live transmission	yĭn cheung jĭk bōh	現場直播
local news	bóon dēi sàn mán	本地新聞
make-up	fā jòng	化妝
master tape	mŏ dáai	母帶
media	chuen mooi	傳媒
news	sàn mán	新聞
on air	gwóng bōh jùng	廣播中
the press	sàn man gāai	新聞界
press conference	gēi jé jìu dŏi wóoi	記者招待會
recording (audio)	lŭk yàm	錄音
recording (video)	lŭk yíng	錄影
reporter	bō dŏ yuen	報導員
script	kĕk bóon	劇本
satellite	wăi sìng	衛星
simulcast	luen bōh	聯播

SPECIFIC NEEDS

sound	yàm héung	音響
subtitle	jì mǒk	字幕
transmission	júen bōh	轉播
viewer	gwòon jūng	觀眾
world news	sāi gāai sàn mán	世界新聞

PILGRIMAGE & RELIGION   信徒

The world's largest outdoor seated bronze statue, the Tian-Tan Buddha, tìn tan dāai fàt is located next to the Po-Lin Monastery (bó lìn jí, the'precious lotus temple'), in Hong Kong.

In Hong Kong and Macau, refer to the telephone directories or Yellow Pages first for church locations.

The TSPM, Three-Self Patriotic Movement churches are the officially registered worship areas in China open to the public. In major cities, there are other foreign language places of worship, run by foreigners for foreigners. It is advisable to check the time and location of the service before you go.

What's your religion?
    néi sūn màt yé gāau ā?   你信乜嘢教呀?

I'm (a) ...	ngǒh hǎi ... to	我信 ... 徒
Buddhist	fàt gāau	佛教
Catholic	tìn júe gāau	天主教
Christian	gèi dùk	基督
Confucian	húng gāau	孔教
Hindu	yān dǒ gāau	印度教
Jewish	yau tāai gāau	猶太教
Muslim	yì sì laan gāau;	伊斯蘭教;
	wooi gāau	回教
Orthodox	dùng jīng gāau	東正教
Protestant	sàn gāau	新教
Taoist	dǒ gāau	道教

SPECIFIC NEEDS

I believe (in God).	ngőh sūn (san)	我信(神)
I don't believe (in fate)	ngőh m sūn (mǐng wǎn)	我唔信 (命運)
I'm not religious.	ngőh m sūn gāau	我唔信教
I'm an atheist.	ngőh hǎi mo san lǚn jé	我信無神 論者

Do you go to the church/mass?
nếi yẩu mő hūi (lẩi bāai tong/mǒng nei sāat) ā? 你有冇去(禮拜 堂/望彌撒)呀?

Is there a quiet room for praying (in the/this) ... ?	hái ... yẩu mő jǐng sàt béi yan kei tò ā?	喺 ... 有冇 靜室俾 人祈禱呀?
airport	gèi cheung	機場
church	nì gàn gāau tóng	呢間教堂
here	nì dō	呢度
hospital	nì gàn yì yúen	呢間醫院
building	nì dūng dāai hǎ	呢棟大廈

Some Useful Words 應用詞匯

agnosticism	bàt hóh jì lǚn	不可知論
ancestor worship	bāai jó sìn	拜祖先
atheism	mo san lǚn	無神論
Buddhist temple	fāt jí	佛寺
Bible	sīng gìng	聖經
cathedral	dāai gāau tóng; jōh tong	大教堂; 座堂
church	lẩi bāai tong	禮拜堂
Christ	gèi dùk	基督
Confucian temple	húng mǐu	孔廟
Creed	sun gìng	信經
Dalai Lama	dāat lāai là ma	達賴喇嘛
Dhyana temple	sim yúen	禪院
fate	mǐng wǎn	命運

God	san	神
Koran	góo laan gìng	古蘭經
mass	nei sāat	彌撒
materialism	wai mắt lŭn	唯物論
meditation	mắk séung	默想
monastery	sàu dŏ yúen	修道院
mosque	chìng jàn jí	清真寺
offering	fūng hīn	奉獻
pagoda	tāap	塔
to pray	kei tó	祈禱
shrine	chi tóng	祠堂
sermon	góng dŏ	講道
Sunday service/ worship	júe yắt sung bāai	主日崇拜
Sunday school	júe yắt hŏk	主日學
Taoist temple	dŏ gwōon; gùng	道觀; 宮
temple	míu/jí	廟/寺
worship	sung bāai	崇拜
Yoga	yue gà	瑜珈

Attending A Funeral 喪禮

When attending a funeral in Hong Kong, you can order wreaths from florists. Alternatively, giving the relatives of the deceased some money, referred to as bāak gàm, in a special white envelope (never use red in funeral affairs) is also quite acceptable. Mourners are normally dressed in plain black, white or dark colours. Once again, pink and red, which symbolise happiness, are not appropriate. Ask the funeral directors in advance if you don't know what's appropriate in certain circumstances.

I'd like to order a wreath.
ngőh yīu dĕng gōh fà hùen　　　我要訂個花圈
Please send this wreath to (this address).
chéng sūng gōh fà hùen　　　請送個花圈
hūi (nì gōh dĕi jí)　　　　　　去(呢個地址)

SPECIFIC NEEDS

attending a funeral	sūng bān	送殯
condolences	dīu yín	弔唁
mourning for parent	sáu hāau	守孝
sending a wreath	sūng fā hùen	送花圈
rest in peace (RIP)	ngòn sìk	安息
rest in the Lord	sìk lo gwài júe	息勞歸主
burial	tó jōng	土葬
cemetery	fan cheung	墳場
coffin	gwòon múk	棺木
cremation	fóh jōng	火葬
funeral director	bān yi gwóon	殯儀館
funeral rites	sòng lái	喪禮
funeral service	chùt bān	出殯
funeral wreath	fā hùen	花圈
funeral parlor	bān yi gwóon	殯儀館
grave	fan mó	墳墓
mortuary	lím fong	殮房
mourning	ngòi dó	哀悼
overnight vigil	sáu ling	守靈
tombstone	mó bèi	墓碑

TIMES, DATES & FESTIVALS

時令

TELLING THE TIME

報時

Telling the time in Cantonese is quite easy once you've mastered the numbers (see page 255). Just try to remember a few key words.

(two) hour/s	(léung gōh) jùng tau	(兩個)鐘頭
... o'clock	... dím;	... 點;
	... dím jùng	... 點鐘
half past ...	... dím bōon	... 點半
minute	fàn	分
second	mǐu	秒

What time is it now?
   yi gà hǎi géi dím jùng ā?　　而家係幾點鐘呀?

It's now ...	yi gà hǎi ...	而家係 ...
8.00	bāat dím jùng	八點鐘
10.20	sǎp dím yǐ sǎp fàn	十點二十分
2.30	léung dím bōon;	兩點半;
	léung dím sàam sǎp fàn	兩點三十分
11.45	sǎp yàt dím sēi	十一點四
	sǎp ng̊ fàn	十五分

The common units for telling the time in Cantonese are jǐ (a five-minute sector of time) and gwàt (a quarter of an hour).

five minutes (one five-minute section)	yàt gōh jǐ	一個字
ten minutes two five-minute sections)	léung gōh jǐ	兩個字
one quarter	yàt gōh gwàt	一個骨
three quarters	sàam gōh gwàt	三個骨

9.05	gáu dím ling ńg fàn;	九點零五分;
	gáu dím yàt gōh jī	九點一個字
7.45	chàt dím sēi sǎp ńg fàn	七點四十五分
	chàt dím gáu gōh jī	七點九個字
	chàt dím sàam gōh gwàt	七點三個骨

When you want to specify morning or afternoon, say the appropriate phrase before the time.

in the morning	sěung ńg	上午
noon	jùng ńg;	中午;
	ngāan jāu	晏晝
in the afternoon	hǎ ńg	下午
in the evening	mǎan sěung	晚上
midnight	bōon yé	半夜

7.10 am	sěung ńg chàt dím sǎp fàn	上午七點十分
12.00 noon	jùng ńg sǎp yī dím	中午十二點
3.15 pm	hǎ ńg sàam dím yàt gōh gwàt	下午三點一個骨
8.30 pm	mǎan sěung bāat dím bōon	晚上八點半
12.00 midnight	bōon yé sǎp yī dím	半夜十二點
Summer Time	hǎ lǐng si gāan	夏令時間

DAYS OF THE WEEK   星期

Use the numbers 1-6 plus sìng kei to form the words Monday to Saturday. Sunday is an exception.

Sunday	sìng kei yǎt	星期日
Monday	sìng kei yàt	星期一
Tuesday	sìng kei yī	星期二
Wednesday	sìng kei sàam	星期三
Thursday	sìng kei sēi	星期四

Friday	sìng kei ńg	星期五
Saturday	sìng kei lŭk	星期六
today	gàm yàt	今日
yesterday	kam yàt	噚日 the day
before yesterday	chìn yàt	前日
two days before yesterday	dǎai chìn yàt	大前日
tomorrow	tìng yàt	聽日
the day after tomorrow	hǎu yàt	後日
two days after tomorrow	dǎai hǎu yàt	大後日
tonight	gàm màan	今晚
last night	kam mǎan	噚晚
tomorrow evening	tìng màan	聽晚
week	sìng kei	星期
this week	nì gōh sìng kei	呢個星期
last week	sěung gōh sìng kei	上個星期
next week	hǎ gōh sìng kei	下個星期
one week	yàt gōh sìng kei	一個星期
fortnight	léung gōh sìng kei	兩個星期
four weeks	sēi gōh sìng kei	四個星期

See you (3 pm) next Monday.

| hǎ sìng kei yàt hǎ ńg | 下星期一下午 |
| (sàam) dím jùng gīn | (三)點鐘見 |

MONTHS   月份

Months in Cantonese are easy, put the numbers 1 – 12 in front of the word month, yŭet:

January	yàt yŭet	一月
February	yǐ yŭet	二月
March	sàam yŭet	三月
April	sēi yŭet	四月
May	ńg yŭet	五月

TIMES, DATES & FESTIVALS

June	lŭk yŭet	六月
July	chàt yŭet	七月
August	bāat yŭet	八月
September	gáu yŭet	九月
October	săp yŭet	十月
November	săp yàt yŭet	十一月
December	săp yĭ yŭet	十二月
lunar January	jìng yŭet	正月
leap year	yŭn nin	閏年
leap month (lunar calendar)	yŭn yŭet	閏月
leap February	yŭn yĭ yŭet	閏二月
this month	nì gōh yŭet	呢個月
last month	sĕung gōh yŭet	上個月
next month	hă gōh yŭet	下個月

SEASONS   季節

spring	chùn gwāi	春季
summer	hă gwāi	夏季
autumn	chàu gwāi	秋季
winter	dùng gwāi	冬季
seasons	gwāi jīt	季節
rainy season	yŭe gwāi	雨季

(See page 179)

LEAP MONTH

The leap year of the existing Gregorian calendar occurs every fourth year, when February has an 'extra' day. In the lunar calendar, there are seven leap years in a 19-year cycle; with an extra month within each leap year. The placement of these months differs each time and is calculated by astrologists using orbiting paths of the Earth. Using this system, a person who was born in leap February in 1947 will meet their first birthday in the leap February 2004.

DATES 日期

Simply use yăt or hŏ (col) after the numbers.

... day	... yăt; ... hŏ	... 日; ... 號
the 1st	yàt yăt; yàt hŏ	一日; 一號
the 24th	yĭ săp sēi yăt; yĭ săp sēi hŏ	二十四日; 二十四號

What date is it today?
gàm yăt hăi géi si ā? 今日係幾時呀?

Is it a holiday today?
gàm yăt hăi m hăi gā kei ā? 今日係唔係假期呀?

To express dates of the year, the order is year-month-day.

25 December
săp yĭ yŭet yĭ săp nğ yăt 十二月二十五日

Tuesday, 1 July, 1997
yàt gáu gáu chàt nin chàt 一九九七年七
yŭet yàt yăt sìng kei yĭ 月一日星期二

Today is 14 Feb, Valentine's Day.
gàm yăt hăi yĭ yŭet săp sēi 今日係二月十四
yăt ching yan jĭt 日情人節

I was born in ... (year) ... (month) ... (day).
ngőh hái ... nin ... yŭet 我喺 ... 年 ... 月
... yăt chùt sāi ... 日出世

In colloquial speech, sometimes the last word 'day', yăt, is left unsaid.

| 15 August | bāat yŭet săp nğ | 八月十五 |
| 7 July | chàt yŭet chàt | 七月七 |

SOME USEFUL WORDS 應用詞匯

now	yi gà; yì gà	而家
this morning	gàm jìu	今朝
today	gàm yàt	今日
this afternoon	gàm yàt hǎng	今日下午
tonight	gàm màan	今晚
this week	nì gōh sìng kei	呢個星期
this month	nì gōh yùet	呢個月
this year	gàm nín	今年

Past 過去

just now	jīng wǎ;	正話;
	tau sìn	頭先
(30) minutes ago	(sàam sǎp) fàn	(三十)分
	jùng chin	鐘前
last night	kam mǎan	噚晚
yesterday afternoon	kam yàt hǎng	噚日下午
yesterday	kam yàt	噚日
yesterday morning	kam yàt jìu	噚日朝
day before yesterday	chin yàt	前日
two days before yesterday	dǎai chin yàt	大前日
(four) days ago	(sēi) yàt chin	(四)日前
last week	sěung gōh sìng kei	上個星期
last month	sěung gōh yùet	上個月
last year	gǎu nín	舊年

TIMES, DATES & FESTIVALS

DID YOU KNOW ...	The lunar calendar, also called the agricultural calendar, is the calendar related to daily farming, fishery and living in general. It indicates the tides, and times for sowing and harvesting. A lunar month is the period from one new moon to the next, averaging only 29.53 days.

Future 未來

a while	yàt jăn gàan	一陣間
in (20) minutes	(yĭ sãp) fàn jùng hãu	(二十)分鐘後
tonight	gàm màan	今晚
tomorrow morning	tìng jìu	聽朝
tomorrow	tìng yàt	聽日
tomorrow afternoon	tìng yàt hã ńg	聽日下午
tomorrow night	tìng màan	聽晚
day after tomorrow	hãu yàt	後日
two days after tomorrow	dãai hãu yàt	大後日
within (24) hours	(yĭ sãp sēi) síu si nõi	(二十四)小時內
within (three) days	(sàam) yàt nõi	(三)日內
(three) days later	(sàam) yàt hãu	(三)日後
next week	hã gōh sìng kei	下個星期
next month	hã gōh yũet	下個月
next year	ming nín	明年

Others 雜項

after ...	... jì hãu	... 之後
always	gìng seung	經常
before ...	... jì chin	... 之前
century	sāi géi	世紀
day	yàt	日
early	jó	早
everyday	mõoi yàt	每日
forever	wĩng yũen	永遠
from ... to ...	yau ... dõ ...	由 ... 到 ...
never	chung loi mő	從來冇
not yet	mẽi dàk	未得
on time	jún si	準時
past	gwōh hũi	過去
present	yĩn jõi	現在

recently	jūi gān	最近
still	jūng hāi	重係
sometimes	yáu si	有時
soon	yàt jān	一陣
sunrise	yàt chùt	日出
sunset	yàt lōk	日落
late	chi dō	遲到
until	dō	到
year	nin	年

FESTIVALS & HOLIDAYS 節期

The Chinese New Year is the most celebrated festival for the Cantonese. In Hong Kong and Macau, Christmas and Easter holidays are celebrated enthusiastically too. Of course, Valentine's Day, Father's Day, Mother's Day and International May Day are also in everyone's calendar.

bank holidays	ngan hong gā kei	銀行假期
Children's Day	yi tung jīt	兒童節
Christmas	sīng dāan jīt	聖誕節
Easter	fūk wŏot jīt	復活節
Father's Day	fŏo chàn jīt	父親節
festivals	jīt yāt	節日
Good Friday	sáu nǎan jīt	受難節
holidays	gā kei	假期
May Day	lo dŭng jīt	勞動節
Mother's Day	mŏ chàn jīt	母親節
New Year holidays	sàn nin gā kei; chùn jīt	新年假期; 春節
public holidays	gùng jūng gā kei	公眾假期
traditional festivals	chuen túng jīt yāt	傳統節日
Valentine's Day	ching yan jīt	情人節

TRADITIONAL FESTIVALS 傳統節慶

Chinese New Year, nung lĭk sàn nin or chùn jĭt, Lunar New Year, is the most important festival in the year. The most popular New Year greeting is gùng héi fàat choi, meaning 'I hope that you gain lots of money'. A special New Year's Eve free market nin sìu sí cheung, is held every year in different suburbs in Hong Kong.

拜年	bāai nin	giving New Year greetings
髮菜	fàat chôi	hair-like weed
瓜子	gwà jí	dried watermelon seed
煎堆	jìn dùi	deep-fried sweet sesame ball
利是	lĕi sĭ	lucky money sealed in red envelopes
蘿蔔糕	loh bāak gò	steamed radish cake
年宵市場	nin sìu sí cheung	New Year's Eve free market
年糕	nin gò	steamed sweet sticky rice cake
新年快樂	sàn nin fàai lŏk	Happy New Year!
桃花	to fà	peach blossoms (bring good luck throughout the year)
油角	yau gók	deep-fried assorted dumplings

HAIR-LIKE WEED

Dried oysters with hair-like weed ho sí fàat chôi is a popular dish during the Chinese New Year period. The phrase ho sí (dried oysters) sounds like the phrase for 'good business', hó sĭ, and fàat chôi, hair-like weed, sounds like 'get wealthy', fàat choi.

Qing Ming
    chìng míng   清明
    this festival, chìng míng, which literally means clear and bright, is held on the 4th or 5th of April. In the lunar calendar, it is the date which indicates springtime growth. Together with chung yéung, these are the two special days when the Chinese people sweep and tidy up their ancestors' tombs.

| 拜山 | bāai sàan | paying tribute to a relative's grave |
| 掃墓 | sō mŏ | sweeping the grave |

Dragon Boat Festival or Iris Festival
    dùen ńg   端午
    this is a day to celebrate a poet wàt yuen, who lived in the 4th century BC, during the Warring Kingdoms in the country of chóh. It takes place on the 5th of May in the lunar calendar (late May to June in the solar calendar). The dumplings are thrown into the river for the fish to eat. It is a sacrificial offering so they will not eat the body of their beloved poet, who threw himself into the river. Another deterrance is the loud drumming of the dragon boats which is supposed to scare the fish away.

| 粽 | júng | wrapped dumpling |
| 龍船 | lung suen | dragon boat |

DID YOU KNOW ...

Lucky money, or red envelope lēi sī or ngāat sūi chin is a monetary New Year gift given by any married people to youngsters and senior managers to junior employees in business. Children receive lēi sī (which phonetically sounds like 'good for business', lēi sī) when they greet their eldery relatives for the New Year.

Maidens' Festival
    chàt jĭk; hàt háau   七夕; 乞巧
    the double-seven (7th of lunar July) festival is the day for young
    ladies to pray to the Spinster Maid, or jìk nűi (Vega, a star) to
    beg for delicate skills. The Spinster Maid and her lover, the
    Cowboy, or ngau long, (Altair) are only allowed to meet on
    the eve of this day. In their story, birds form a bridge across the
    Milky Way between the lovers, allowing them to meet.

Mid-Autumn Festival
    jùng chàu   中秋
    the Autumn Moon Festival, or Lantern Festival, occurs on
    the full moon evening in lunar August. On this day everyone
    eats the sweet moon cakes. Some areas still hold the lantern
    parade, especially for the children's entertainment.

月餅   yŭet béng   moon cakes
花燈   fà dàng   decorated lanterns

Chong Yang Festival
    chung yéung; chung gáu   重陽; 重九
    the double-nine (9th of lunar September) festival is the day
    for hiking and the sweeping of tombs.

CHINESE DYNASTIES   歷朝
When travelling around it is often necessary to have an
understanding of the major periods of Chinese history. The
following list is a brief outline of the Chinese dynasties from which
Chinese art, archaeology, architecture and literature have evolved.

先史   Pre-history   (Before 2205 BC)
夏   Xia   2205 BC - 1766 BC   hâ
商   Shang   1766 BC - 1123 BC   sèung
周   Zhou   1122 BC - 249 BC   jàu
春秋   Chunqiu   722 BC - 480 BC   chùn chàu
戰國   Warring Kingdoms   403 BC - 221 BC   jìn gwŏk

秦	Qin	221 BC - 207 BC	chun
西漢	Western Han	206 BC - AD 7	sài hōn
東漢	Eastern Han	25 - 220	dùng hōn
三國	Three Kingdoms	220 - 265	sàam gwōk
晉	Jin	265 - 317	jūn
南朝	Southern Dynasties	317 - 589	naam chiu
北朝	Northern Dynasties	386 - 581	bàk chiu
隋	Sui	590 - 618	chui
唐	Tang	618 - 906	tong
五代	Five Dynasties	907 - 960	ng̃ dòi
北宋	Northern Song	960 - 1126	bàk sūng
南宋	Southern Song	1127 - 1279	naam sūng
元	Yuan	1260 - 1368	yuen
明	Ming	1368 - 1644	ming
清	Qing	1644 - 1912	chìng

NUMBERS & AMOUNTS 數碼

CARDINAL NUMBERS 數目

The simplest way to make long numbers is to disregard the units of tens, hundreds and thousands, and use only the numbers from zero to nine. That means that for the number of 3388, instead of sàam chìn sàam bāak bāat sāp bāat (three thousand three hundred eighty eight) you may just use sàam sàam bāat bāat (three, three, eight, eight).

0	ling	零
1	yàt	一
2	yī (or léung)	二 (兩)
3	sàam	三
4	sēi	四
5	nǵ	五
6	lūk	六
7	chàt	七
8	bāat	八
9	gáu	九
10	sāp	十
11	sāp yàt	十一
12	sāp yī	十二
13	sāp sàam	十三
14	sāp sēi	十四
15	sāp nǵ	十五
16	sāp lūk	十六
17	sāp chàt	十七
18	sāp bāat	十八
19	sāp gáu	十九
20	yī sāp	二十
21	yī sāp yàt	二十一
22	yī sāp yī	二十二
23	yī sāp sàam	二十三

NUMBERS & AMOUNTS

29	yī sǎp gáu	二十九
30	sàam sǎp	三十
36	sàam sǎp lǔk	三十六
39	sàam sǎp gáu	三十九
40	sēi sǎp	四十
50	ng̃ sǎp	五十
60	lǔk sǎp	六十
70	chàt sǎp	七十
80	bāat sǎp	八十
90	gáu sǎp	九十
99	gáu sǎp gáu	九十九
100	yàt bāak	一百
101	yàt bāak ling yàt	一百零一
109	yàt bāak ling gáu	一百零九
110	yàt bāak yàt sǎp	一百一十
113	yàt bāak yàt sǎp sàam	一百一十三
120	yàt bāak yī sǎp	一百二十
190	yàt bāak gáu sǎp	一百九十
200	yī bāak	二百
347	sàam bāak sēi sǎp chàt	三百四十七
999	gáu bāak gáu sǎp gáu	九百九十九
1000	yàt chìn	一千
1001	yàt chìn ling yàt	一千零一
9416	gáu chìn sēi bāak yàt sǎp lǔk	九千四百一十六
10,000	yàt mǎan	一萬
100,000	sǎp mǎan	十萬
112,000	sǎp yàt mǎan yī chìn	十一萬二千
1,000,000	yàt bāak mǎan	一百萬
1,230,000	yàt bāak yī sǎp sàam mǎan	一百二十三萬
10,000,000	yàt chìn mǎan	一千萬
100,000,000	yàt yìk	一億

Another method of saying two is léung, which only applies to single unit or classified units; and is used only in quantities.

two	léung	兩
20,000	léung māan	兩萬
two sheets of paper	léung jèung jí	兩張紙
two cups of tea	léung bòoi cha	兩杯茶
twice	léung chī	兩次

Measure Words 量詞

Measure words (classifiers, or counters) are normally necessary between the numbers and countable nouns. There are hundreds of measure words, most of which refer to the noun's shape or appearance. The most common one is gōh, means 'a piece'; but it can also apply to people as well.

a basket	lung	籠
a bottle	jùn	樽
flat shape	jèung	張
long shape	tiu	條
pair	dūi	對

(two) baskets of	(léung) lung chà	(兩)籠叉
barbecue pork bun	sìu bàau	燒飽
a cup of tea	yàt bòoi cha	一杯茶
three people	sàam gōh yan	三個人

NUMBERS & AMOUNTS

DID YOU KNOW ... Westerners use the unit of a thousand to count larger numbers, but traditionally the Chinese use the māan, or a ten-thousand unit. Hence, a hundred thousand becomes sǎp māan, or ten ten-thousands.

Decimal Point 小數

decimal point	dím	點
0.0023	ling dím ling ling	零點零零
	yī sàam	二三
3.1416	sàam dím yàt sēi	三點一四
	yàt lǔk	一六
25.4	yī sǎp ńg dím sēi	二十五點四

Minus 負數

Put the word fõo in front of the figure to make it negative.

minus	fõo	負
-273.15	fõo yī chàt sàam	負二七三
	dím yàt ńg	點一五

Fractions 分數

Unlike the Western way of looking at a fraction, that is, as one on three for a third, the Chinese see it as 'three parts one'. So to say a fraction, you should first say the denominator (in this case, three), followed by fãn jì, then the numerator (one).

1/3	sàam fãn jì yàt	三分之一
22/7	chàt fãn jì yī sǎp yī	七分之二十二

In the case of a mixed fraction, you first say the whole number, which in this case is thirteen, then add the word yàu, then the rest will follow the above rule.

13¹/₄	sǎp sàam yàu sēi	十三又四
	fãn jì yàt	分之一

Percentage 百分比

Simply add the numbers after the word 'percent', bāak fãn jì

10%	bāak fãn jì sǎp	百分之十
36.7%	bāak fãn jì sàam sǎp	百分之三十
	lǔk dím chàt	六點七
-20%	fõo bāak fãn jì yī sǎp	負百分之二十

When talking about a discount, the number applies to the amount paid rather than the amount being taken off. For example, instead of saying 15% off, the Cantonese say 85%.

10% discount = 90%	gáu jīt	九折
15% discount = 85%	bāat ńg jīt	八五折

ORDINAL NUMBERS 數序

Simply add the dāi before the numbers.

1st	dāi yàt	第一
2nd	dāi yī	第二
9th	dāi gáu	第九
23rd	dāi yī sāp sàam	第二十三
the last	dāi mèi	第尾
the last one	mèi yàt	尾一
the second last	mèi yí	尾二
1st place, champion	gwōon gwàn	冠軍
2nd place	ā gwàn	亞軍
3rd place	gwāi gwàn	季軍
the last place	dīn gwàn	殿軍

UNITS 單位

Besides the Metric System, the traditional Chinese System is also very common in daily life, especially in the local markets.

Metric System 公制

kilometre	gùng léi	公里
metre	gùng chēk;	公尺;
	máí	米
centimetre	gùng fàn	公分
kilogram	gùng gàn	公斤
gram	hàk	克
litre	gùng sìng	公升

My height is (182) cm.
  ngőh sàn gò (yàt bāak bāat   我身高(一百八
  sǎp yǐ) gùng fàn   十二)公分

Other Systems 雜制

yard	mǎ	碼
foot	yìng chēk	英呎
inch	yìng chūen	英吋
pound	bōng	磅
ounce	ngòn sí	安士
square foot	fòng chēk	方呎
the Chinese catty	gàn	斤
the Chinese tael	léung	兩

3 catties equal 4 pounds.
  sàam gàn dáng yùe sēi bōng   三斤等於四磅

16 taels equal a catty.
  sǎp lùk léung dáng yùe yàt gàn   十六兩等於一斤

AMOUNTS   銀碼

dollar (for)	yuen	元
dollar (gen)	màn	文
dollar (col)	gōh	個
ten cents (for)	gōk	角
ten cents (gen & col)	ho jí	毫子
a cent (for)	fàn	分
a cent (gen & col)	sìn	仙
half dollar	bōon	半
US dollar	měi gàm	美金
Australian dollar	ngōu yuen	澳元
Hong Kong dollar	góng bǎi	港幣
Renminbi	yan man bǎi	人民幣

Formal

US$24.60
  méi yuen yǐ sǎp sēi 美元二十四
  yuen lǔk gōk 元六角

HK$1.38
  góng bǎi yàt yuen sàam 港幣一元三
  gōk bāat fàn 角八分

RMB1.50
  yan man bǎi yàt yuen ńg gōk 人民幣一元五角

General

US$24.60
  méi gàm yǐ sǎp sēi màn lǔk ho 美金二十四文六毫

HK$1.38
  góng bǎi yàt màn sàam 港幣一文三
  ho bāat sìn 毫八仙

RMB1.50
  yan man bǎi yàt màn ńg ho 人民幣一文五毫

Colloquial

US$24.60
  méi gàm yǎ sēi gōh lǔk 美金廿四個六

HK$1.38
  góng bǎi yàt g ōh sàam ho bāat 港幣一個三毫八

RMB1.50
  yan man bǎi gōh bōon 人民幣個半

SOME USEFUL WORDS 應用詞匯

3 quarters	sàam gōh gwàt	三個骨
a lot/much	hó dòh	好多
a pair	yàt dūi	一對
a quarter	yàt gōh gwàt	一個骨
about	dǎai yēuk	大約
add	gà	加

amount	ngan mǎ	銀碼
to calculate	gāi sō	計數
to count	só	數
divide	chui	除
double	sèung pőoi	雙倍
few	hó síu	好少
first time	dǎi yàt chī	第一次
half	yàt bōon	一半
half price	bōon gā	半價
How many?	géi dòh?	幾多?
How much?	géi dòh chín?	幾多錢?
less	síu dì	少啲
more	dòh dì	多啲
multiply	sing	乘
number	sō mŭk	數目
none	mő	冇
once	yàt chī	一次
some	yàt dì	一啲
subtract	gáam	減
triple	sàam pőoi	三倍
twice	léung chī	兩次

EMERGENCIES 應急

In Hong Kong, the phone number 999 gáu gáu gáu, serves all emergencies. While in Macau, 333 is for the police and 3300 for an ambulance. The Public Security Bureau (PSB) gùng ngòn is China's police force, and their foreign affairs departments, ngŏi sĭ fòh, take care of affairs of foreigners, including applications for visa extension. Check the telephone number of your embassy or consulate in case of an emergency.

In case of an emergency, the most common word expression used is gāu měng ā! literally meaning 'save my life', or 'Help!'.

Help!	gāu měng ā!	救命呀!
Fire!	fóh jùk ā!	火燭呀!
indecent assault	fèi lái ā!	非禮呀!
Thief!	chéung yé ā!	搶嘢呀!
Catch him!	jùk jŭe kŭi!	捉住佢!

CAUTION 示警

Be careful!	yàn jŭe!	因住!
Danger!	ngai hím!	危險!
Go away!	jáu hòi!	走開!
Stop!	ting dài!	停低!
Watch out!	tái jŭe!	睇住!

REPORTING AN ACCIDENT 告急

There has been an accident!
góh dŏ fàat sàng yī ngŏi
咽度發生意外

There has been a collision!
góh dŏ jŏng chè
咽度撞車

There's a fight.
góh dŏ yáu yan dá gàau
咽度有人打交

Someone has been injured.
yáu yan sáu jóh sèung
有人受咗傷

VICTIM 受害

I've been injured.
ngőh sáu jóh sèung   我受咗傷

I've been raped.
ngőh béi yan keung gàan   我被人強奸

I've been robbed.
ngőh béi yan dá gīp   我被人打劫

I've lost my ...
ngőh m gīn jóh ngőh gē ...   我唔見咗我嘅 ...

Someone took my ...	yáu yan lóh	有人攞
	jóh ngőh gē ...	咗我嘅 ...
bag	dói	袋
camera	yíng séung gèi	影相機
credit card	sūn yűng kàat	信用卡
handbag	sáu dói	手袋
luggage	hang léi	行李
money	chín	錢
passport	wőo jīu	護照
travellers' cheques	lűi hang jì pīu	旅行支票
wallet	ngan bàau	銀包
watch	sáu bìu	手錶

EMERGENCY CALLS 急召

Call the ambulance!
gīu gāu sèung chè!   叫救傷車!

Call a doctor!
gīu yì sàng!   叫醫生!

Call the fire brigade!
gīu sìu fong gúk!   叫消防局!

Call the police! (Hong Kong)
gīu gíng chàat!   叫警察!

Call the police! (China)
gīu gùng ngòn!   叫公安!

MEDICAL ATTENTION 急救

He/She needs a doctor.
yīu tung kűi gīu yì sàng 要同佢叫醫生

He/She needs first aid.
yīu tung kűi gàp gāu 要同佢急救

He/She needs to go to a hospital.
yīu sūng kűi hūi yì yúen 要送佢去醫院

He/She needs mouth to mouth resuscitation.
yīu tung kűi jǒ yan gùng fōo kàp 要同佢做人工呼吸

My blood group is (A/B/O/AB) Positive/Negative.
ngőh hūet ying hǎi (jīng/fōo) 我血型係(正/負)
(A/B/O/AB) ying (A/B/O/AB)型

burns	sìu sèung	燒傷
critical condition	ching fōng ngai tői	情況危殆
high fever	gò yīt	高熱
stretcher	dàam gá	擔架
unconscious	bàt síng yan sǐ	不省人事

DEALING WITH THE POLICE 報警

I want to report an offence.
ngőh yīu bō ngòn 我要報案

Can anyone speak English?
yǎu mő yan sìk góng yìng mán ā? 有冇人識講英文呀?

Do you understand?
néi ming m ming bǎak ā? 你明唔明白呀?

I understand.
ngőh ming bǎak 我明白

I don't understand.
ngőh m ming bǎak 我唔明白

I don't speak Cantonese.
ngőh m sìk góng gwóng dùng wá 我唔識講廣東話

EMERGENCIES

I want to an (English) interpreter.
ngőh yīu (yìng)
mán chuen yĭk

我要(英)
文傳譯

I did not do this/that.
ngőh mő jŏ dō (nì/góh) yĕung

我冇做到(呢/嗰)樣

Not me!
m hăi ngőh

唔係我

I'm innocent.
ngőh hăi chìng băak mo jŭi

我係清白無罪

Could I make a phone call?
ngőh hőh m hőh yĭ dá
gōh dĭn wá ā?

我可唔可以打個
電話呀?

I wish to contact my ...	ngőh yīu tung ngőh gē ... luen lōk	我要同我嘅 ... 聯絡
consulate	lĭng sí gwóon	領事館
embassy	dăai sī gwóon	大使館
family	gà yan	家人
friend	pang yău	朋友
lawyer	lŭt sì	律師

Useful Terms

to accuse	hūng gō	控告
to arrest	kùi bŏ	拘捕
court	fāat ting	法廷
crime	jŭi ngōn	罪案
defendant	bĕi gō	被告
detention	kùi lau	拘留
deportation	dăi gāai chùt gíng	遞解出境
evidence	jīng gūi	證據
eyewitness	mŭk gìk jīng yan	目擊證人
a fine (penalty)	fãt fóon	罰款
plaintiff	yuen gō	原告
police car	gíng chè	警車

THE POLICE MAY SAY ...

néi yìn jŏi béi kùi bŏ 你現在被拘捕
You have been arrested.

chéng néi tung ngŏh dĕi 請你同我哋
faan hūi chàai gwōon 番去差館
Please come with us to the police station.

chéng néi béi ngŏh	請你俾我	Please show
tái néi gē ...	睇你嘅 ...	me your ...
chè paai	車牌	driver's licence
sàn fán jīng	身份證	identity card
wŏo jìu	護照	passport
gùng jŏk jīng	工作證	work permit

néi gīu màt yĕ méng ā? 你叫乜嘢名呀?
What's your name?

néi yi gà jŭe hái bìn dŏ ā? 你而家住喺邊度呀?
Where are you staying?

néi hái bìn dŏ lei gā? 你喺邊度嚟㗎?
Where do you come from?

ngŏh yīu gŏ néi ...	我要告你 ...	You will be charged with ...
mo paai gā sái	無牌駕駛	driving without a valid driver's licence
jūi jáu gā chè	醉酒駕車	drink driving
chìu chùk gā sái	超速駕駛	exceeding the speed limit
wai lǎi pàak chè	違例泊車	illegal parking
chong dūk	藏毒	illegal possession of drugs
chong hāai	藏械	illegal possession of weapons
fèi fāat gùi lau	非法居留	illegal residence

police officer	gíng gwòon	警官
prosecution	jí hūng	指控
rape	keung gàan	強奸
smuggle	jáu sì	走私
summons	chuen pīu	傳票
theft	tàu sīt	偷竊
a thief	chāak	賊
warning	gíng gō	警告
witness	jīng yan	證人

Useful Phrases 應用詞句

Hurry up!
fāai dì! 快啲!

Could you help me please?
hóh m hóh yí chéng néi
bóng sáu ā? 可唔可以請你
幫手呀?

Don't move!
máai yùk! 咪郁!

Hands up!
gúi gò sáu! 舉高手!

I'm lost.
ngőh dōng sàt lŏ 我蕩失路

I am terribly sorry.
ngőh hó dũi m jũe 我好對唔住

Where's the toilet please?
chéng mān chī sóh hái bìn dō ā? 請問廁所喺邊度呀?

lack of evidence
jīng gūi bàt jùk 證據不足

| DID YOU KNOW ... | ngau yŭk gòn, literally means a dried beef slice, an unofficial terms of the illegal parking or traffic fine ticket in Hong Kong. |

EMERGENCIES

A

able (to be)	hóh nang	可能
aboard	sing dāap	乘搭
about	dáai yēuk	大約
above	sěung mīn	上面
accept	jip sǎu	接受
account (bank)	wōo háu	戶口
acrobatic	jǎap gěi	雜技
across	waang gwóh	橫過
actor	yín yuen	演員
address	dēi jí	地址
to admire	jāan séung	讚賞
admission fee	yǎp cheung fâi	入場費
to admit	jūn yǎp	進入
adult	dāai yan	大人
advantage	yàu sái	優勢
advice	gīn yí	建議
to advise	hūen gō	勸告
aerogram	hong hùng	航空
	yau gáan	郵柬
aeroplane	fèi gèi	飛機
afraid	pā	怕
after	jì hāu	之後
afternoon	ngāan jāu	晏晝
again	jōi chī	再次
age	nin ling	年齡
agency	dōi léi	代理
agree	tung yī	同意

I agree.
ngǒh tung yī
我同意

I don't agree.
ngǒh m tung yī
我唔同意

agriculture	nung ngǎi	農藝
ahead	chin mīn	前面
aid (help)	bòng mong	幫忙

AIDS	ngōi jì bēng	愛滋病
air	hùng hēi	空氣
air-conditioned	hùng tiu	空調
airport	gèi cheung	機場
airport tax	gèi cheung sūi	機場稅
alarm clock	nāau jùng	鬧鐘
alcohol	jáu jìng	酒精
allergy	gwōh mán	過敏
allow	jún húi	准許
alone	dàan dúk	單獨
already	yǐ gìng	已經
always	gìng seung	經常
amateur	yīp yue	業餘
amount	ngan mǎ	銀碼
and	tung maai	同埋
angry	nàu	嬲
animals	dǔng mǎt	動物
anniversary	jàu nin	周年
	gēi nǐm	紀念
annoying	kwàn yǔu	困擾
annual	mǒoi nin	每年
answer	wooi dáap	回答
antinuclear	fáan hǎt	反核
antiques	góo dúng	古董
antiseptic	sìu dúk	消毒
appetizer	chàan chin	餐前
	síu sǐk	小食
appointment	yūe yěuk	預約
to argue	bìn lūn	辯論
arm	sáu bēi	手臂
arrivals	dō dāat	到達
to arrive	dō	到
art	ngǎi sùt	藝術
art gallery	měi sùt gwóon	美術館
arts	man ngǎi	文藝
ashtray	yìn fòoi gòng	煙灰缸
to ask	mān	問
aspirin	ā sǐ pàt	亞士匹
	ling	靈
assault	mǒ yǔk	侮辱

asthma	hàau chuén	哮喘
attention	jūe yī	注意
atlas	dēi to	地圖
ATM	jí dūng tai fóon gèi	自動提款機
automatic	jí dūng	自動
autumn	chàu gwāi	秋季
average	ping gwàn	平均
awful	hòh pā dìk	可怕的

B

baby	yìng yi	嬰兒
baby food	yìng yi sīk bán	嬰兒食品
baby powder	yìng yi sóng sàn fán	嬰兒爽身粉
babysitter	bó mō	褓姆
backpacker	bōoi nong hāak	背囊客
bad	m hó	唔好
bag	dói	袋
baggage	hang léi	行李
baggage claim	tai chúi hang léi chūe	提取行李處
bakery	mīn bàau pó	麵包舖
ball	bòh	波
bamboo	jūk	竹
band	ngŏk dúi	樂隊
bandage	bàng dáai	繃帶
bank	ngan hong	銀行
bar	jáu bà	酒吧
barber	fei fāat pó	飛髮舖
basket	láam	籃
bathroom	chùng leung fóng	沖涼房
battery	dīn chi	電池
beach	sà tàan	沙灘
bear	hung	熊
beautiful	lēng	靚

because	yàn wāi	因為
bed, double	sèung yan chong	雙人床
bedroom	sūi fóng	睡房
bed, single	dàan yan chong	單人床
beer	bè jáu	啤酒
before	jì chin	之前
beggar	hàt yì	乞兒
to begin	hòi chí	開始
behind	hāu bīn	後便
below	hă bīn	下便
beside	jàk bìn	側便
best	jūi hó	最好
better	gāng hó	更好
between	jì gàan	之間
bib	wai júi	圍咀
bicycle	dàan chè	單車
big	dāai	大
bill	dàan	單
binoculars	mŏng yŭen gèng	望遠鏡
bird	jēuk nĭu	雀鳥
birth certificate	chùt sāi jí	出世紙
birthday	sàang yàt	生日
bitter	fóo	苦
black	hāk	黑
black market	hāk sí	黑市
black and white	hāk bāak	黑白
blanket	jìn	氈
to bleed	lau hūet	流血
to bless	jùk fūk	祝福
Bless you	jùk nĕi	祝你
blind	maang	盲
blood	hūet	血

blue	laam sìk	藍色
boarding pass	dàng gèi jīng	登機證
boat	suen	船
body	sàn tái	身體
bone	gwàt	骨
book	sùe	書
booking	yûe yêuk	預約
bookshop	sùe dìm	書店
boot (shoes)	hèuh	靴
bored	mõon	悶
boring	mố yán	冇癮
borrow	jē	借
boss	bòh sí	波士
bottle opener	hòi ping hēi	開瓶器
bottom	dái	底

Bottoms up!
gòn bòoi!
干杯!

box	hãp	盒
boyfriend	naam pang yáu	男朋友
bra	hùng wai	胸圍
brake	sàat chè	煞車
brave	yũng gám	勇敢
bread	mĭn bàau	麵包
breakfast	jó chàan	早餐
breast	yûe fong	乳房
to breathe	fòo kàp	呼吸
bridge	kiu	橋
bright	gwòng	光
to bring	lìng	拎
brother	hìng dãi	兄弟
brown	fè sìk	啡色
bruise	yúe sèung	瘀傷
brush	chàat	刷
Buddhism	fàt gàau	佛教
budget	yûe sūen	預算
bus terminal	bà sí júng jãam	巴士總站
bus stop	bà sí jãam	巴士站

bus (in China)	gùng gũng hēi chè	公共汽車
bus (in Hong Kong)	bà sí	巴士
business	yìp mõ	業務
business class	sèung mõ hāak wái	商務客位
business hour	ying yìp si gàan	營業時間
businessman	sèung yan	商人
busy	mong	忙
but	bàt gwõh	不過
butter	ngau yau	牛油
butterfly	woo dĩp	蝴蝶
button	náu	鈕
buy	mãai	買

I'd like to buy ...
ngõh yìu mãai ...
我要買 ...

Where can I buy a ticket?
bìn dõ hóh yí mãai dó fèi ã?
邊度可以買到飛呀?

cake	sài béng	西餅
calculator	gài sõ gèi	計數機
calendar	yàt lĩk	日曆
camellia	cha fà	茶花
camera	ying séung gèi	影相機
can (to be able to)	hóh yí	可以

I can do it.
ngõh hóh yí jõ
我可以做

I can't do it.
ngõh m hóh yí jõ
我唔可以做

a can	gwōon táu	罐頭
can opener	gwōon tau dò	罐頭刀
to cancel	chúi sìu	取消
candle	lāap jùk	蠟燭
cannot	m hóh yí	唔可以
capital	sáu dò	首都
car	chè	車
car park	ting chè cheung	停車場
card	kàat	卡
to care (about)	gwàan sàm	關心
to care (for someone)	gwàan waai	關懷
Careful!	yàn jǔe!	
		因住!
Carnival	gà nin wa	嘉年華
cash	yín gàm	現金
cashier	chùt nǎap	出納
cassette	kà sìk	卡式
	lǔk yàm dáai	錄音帶
casual dress	bǐn jòng	便裝
cat	màau	貓
cathedral	dǎai gāau tóng	大教堂
Catholic	tìn júe gāau	天主教
caves	dǔng yǔet	洞穴
CD	lui se díp	鐳射碟
to celebrate	hìng jùk	慶祝
certificate	jìng sùe	證書
chair	dàng	凳
champagne	hèung bàn	香檳
chance	gèi wǒoi	機會
change	wǒon	換
changing room	gàng yì sàt	更衣室
cheap	peng	平
check-in	dàng gēi sáu jùk	登記手續

check-out (hotel)	tūi fóng	退房
chef	chue sì	廚師
chemist	yěuk jài sì	藥劑師
cheque	jì pīu	支票
cherries	chè lei jí	車厘子
cherry blossom	yìng fà	櫻花
chess	kéi	棋
chewing gum	hèung háu gàau	香口膠
children	sǎi lǒ gòh	細路哥
China	jùng gwōk	中國
chocolate	jùe gòo lìk	朱古力
to choose	súen jǎak	選擇
chopsticks	fāai jí	筷子
Christian	gèi dùk to	基督徒
Christmas	sìng dāan jít	聖誕節
chrys-anthemum	gùk fà	菊花
church	gāau tóng	教堂
church	lǎi bāai tong	禮拜堂
cicada	sim	蟬
cigar	sūet gà	雪茄
cigarette	yìn jái	煙仔
cinema	hèi yúen	戲院
circus	mǎ hèi	馬戲
citizenship	gùng man	公民
city	sìng sí	城市
city centre	sí jùng sàm	市中心
clean	chìng gìt	清潔
cleaning	dá sō	打掃
client	hāak wǒo	客戶
cliff	yuen ngaai	懸崖
climb	pàan dàng	攀登
cloakroom	yì mó gàan	衣帽間
clock	si jùng	時鐘
close	gwàan bāi	關閉
clothing	yì fǔk	衣服
cloud	wan	雲
cloudy	yàm tìn	陰天

D

coach (training)	gāau lĭn	教練
coach (bus)	dāai hāak chè	大客車
coat	ngŏi tō	外套
cocaine	hóh kà yàn	可卡因
cocktail party	gài mĕi	雞尾
	jáu wóoi	酒會
cocoa	gùk góo	谷咕
coffee	gā fè	咖啡
a cold	sèung fùng	傷風
cold (adj)	dūng	凍
cold water	dūng súi	凍水
collect call	dūi fòng	對方
	fŏo fóon	付款
colour	chói sìk	彩色
comb	sòh	梳
to come	loi	來
comedy	héi kĕk	喜劇
comfortable	sùe fŭk	舒服
community	sĕ kwàn	社群
company	gùng sì	公司
compass	jí naam jàm	指南針
computer	dĭn nŏ	電腦
concert	yàm ngŏk	音樂
	wóoi	會
condoms	bĕi yĭn tō	避孕套
to confirm	kŏk yĭng	確認

Congratulations!
gùng hĕi!
恭喜

conservative	bò sáu	保守
constipation	bĭn bĕi	便秘
consulate	lĭng sí	領事
contact lenses	yán yìng	隱形
	ngăan géng	眼鏡
contraception	bĕi yĭn	避孕
contract	hăp tung	合同
to cook	júe	煮
coolie	gòo lèi	咕喱
copy, a	fŏo bóon	副本

coriander	yuen sài	芫茜
corn	sùk mĕi	粟米
to cost	fà fài	花費

How much does it cost to go to ...?
hūi ... yīu géi dòh chín ā?
去 ... 要幾多錢呀?

It costs a lot.
dò géi dòh chín gā
都幾多錢㗎

cotton	min	棉
cough	kàt	咳
to count	só	數
coupon	yàu dŏi gūen	優待券
cow	ngau	牛
crafts	sáu ngăi	手藝
crazy	chì sīn	黐線
credit card	sūn yŭng	信用
	kàat	卡
cricket	báan kau	板球
cuddle	yúng pŏ	擁抱
cup	bòoi	杯
cupboard	bòoi gwăi	杯櫃
curry	gā lèi	咖哩
customs	hói gwàan	海關
customs declaration	hói gwàan	海關
	sàn bò dàan	申報單
to cut	jín	剪
cyclone	suen fùng	旋風
cystitis	pong gwòng	膀胱
	yim	炎

D

Daddy	ba bà	爸爸
daily	mŏoi yàt	每日
dairy products	yŭe lŏk	乳酪
	jai bán	製品
dancing	tiu mŏ	跳舞
dangerous	ngai hím	危險
dark	hàk ngàm	黑暗

D

D I C T I O N A R Y

D

date of birth	chùt sàng	出生
	nìn yūet yàt	年月日
daughter	nűi	女
day	yàt	日
dead	séi	死
deaf	lung	聾
to decide	kűet dîng	決定
deck (of cards)	pè páai	啤牌
deck (of ship)	gāap bán	甲板
deep	sàm	深
deer	lúk	鹿
deforestation	fàt lam	伐林
degree (level)	ching dô	程度
delay	chi	遲
delicious	hó sĩk	好食
democracy	man júe	民主
demonstration	sī fãan	示範
dental floss	nga sĩn	牙線
dentist	nga yì	牙醫
to deny	fáu yíng	否認
deodorant	chui chãu jài	除臭劑
department store	bāak fòh gùng sì	百貨公司
departure	chùt fāat	出發
deposit (bank)	chuen fóon	存款
desert	sà mõk	沙漠
dessert	tìm dím	甜點
destination	mõk dīk dēi	目的地
diabetic	tong lĩu bēng	糖尿病
diarrhoea	tõ ngòh	肚痾
diary	yàt gēi	日記
dictionary	jī dĩn	字典
diesel	yau jà	油渣
different	m tung	唔同
difficult	kwān naan	困難
dinner	mãan chàan	晚餐
direction	fòng hèung	方向
directory	dĩn wá bó	電話簿

dirty	wòo jò	污糟
disabled	sèung chaan	傷殘
disadvantage	bàt lēi	不利
discount	jīt kàu	折扣
discover	fāat yín	發現
discrimination	kei sĩ	歧視
disease	jàt bēng	疾病
disk	díp	碟
distilled water	jìng lãu súi	蒸餾水
diving	tìu súi	跳水
divorced	lei fàn	離婚
dizzy	tau wan	頭暈
to do	jõ	做

What are you doing?
néi jõ gán màt yế ā?
你做緊乜嘢呀?

I didn't do it.
ngőh mő jõ dō
我有做到

doctor	yì sàng	醫生
dog	gáu	狗
dolls	gùng jái	公仔
door	moon	門
double bed	sèung yan chong	雙人床
double	sèung pőoi	雙倍
down	hã bĩn	下便
dozen	dà	打
dream	mũng	夢
dress	tõ jòng	套裝
dress shop	si jòng gùng sì	時裝公司
drink	yám	飲
driver	sì gèi	司機
driving licence	chè paai	車牌
drug (medical)	yẽuk	藥
drug (recreational)	dũk bán	毒品

drug addiction	dŭk yán	毒癮
drug dealer	dŭk fáan	毒販
drums	góo	鼓
drunk	yám júi	飲醉
dummy (baby's)	náai júi	奶咀
durian	lau lìn	榴槤
dust	chan ngàai	塵埃

E

e-mail	dĭn yau	電郵
each	mŏei yàt gŏh	每一個
ear	yĭ	耳
early	jó	早
Earth	dĕi kau	地球
earthquake	dĕi jàn	地震
east	dùng	東
Easter	fŭk wŏot jĭt	復活節
easy	yung yĭ	容易
to eat	sĭk	食
economy class	gìng jài wài	經濟位
editor	pìn chàp	編輯
education	găau yŭk	教育
elections	súen gúi	選舉
electricity	dĭn lĭk	電力
elevator	sìng gŏng gèi	升降機
embarrassed	naan hàm	難堪
embarass-ment	naan wai ching	難為情
embassy	dăai sĭ gwóon	大使館
emergency	gán gàp	緊急
employee	gōo yuen	僱員
employer	gōo júe	僱主
empty	hùng	空
end	yuen	完
energy	nang lĭk	能力
engagement	dĭng fàn	訂婚
engine	gèi hēi	機器

English	yìng mán	英文
to enjoy (oneself)	hòi sàm	開心
enough	gāu	夠
entertainment	yue lŏk	娛樂
entrance	yăp háu	入口
envelope	sūn fùng	信封
environment	waan gíng	環境
epileptic	făat yeung dīu	發羊吊
equal	sèung dáng	相等
ethnic	man jŭk	民族
Europe	ngàu jàu	歐洲
every day	mŏei yàt	每日
excellent	yàu yŭet dīk	優越的
exchange	jáau wŏon	找換
exchange rate	wŏoi lŭt	匯率
exciting	hìng fán	興奮

Excuse me.
dŭi m jŭe
對唔住

exhibition	jín lăam	展覽
exit	chùt háu	出口
expensive	gwāi	貴
experience	gìng yĭm	經驗
eye	ngáan	眼

F

face	mĭn	面
factory	gùng chóng	工廠
faint	wan dài	暈低
family	gà ting	家庭
famous	chùt méng	出名
fan	fùng sīn	風扇

Fantastic!
jìng chói!
精采!

far away	yǘen	遠
farm	nung cheung	農場
farmer	nung man	農民
fashion	lau hang	流行
fast(adj)	fäai	快
fat	fei	肥
father	fồo chàn	父親
fax	chuen jàn	傳真
fear	pā	怕
fee	fai yǜng	費用
feeding bottle	nǎai jùn	奶樽
to feel	gám gók	感覺
feeling	gám sǎu	感受
female	nǚi sìng	女性
festival	jit yàt	節日
fever	fàat sìu	發燒
few	síu	少
fiance	mēi fàn fòo	未婚夫
fiancee	mēi fàn chài	未婚妻
fiction	chòng jòk	創作
	síu süet	小説
to fill	chùng mǒon	充滿
film (negatives)	dái pín	底片
film (cinema)	dǐn yíng	電影
film (for camera)	fèi lám	菲林
films (movies)	yíng pín	影片
fine weather	ching tìn	晴天
finger	sáu jí	手指
Fire!	**fóh jùk ā!**	**火燭呀!**
fire	fóh	火
first aid	gàp gàu	急救
first aid box	gàp gàu sèung	急救箱
first class	tau dáng	頭等

first	dǎi yàt	第一
fish	yúe	魚
fishing	dìu yúe	釣魚
fit	sìk hăp	適合
flag	kei	旗
flight number	hồ bàan gèi	號班機
floating restaurant	hói sìn fóng	海鮮舫
flower	fà	花
a fly	wòo yìng	烏蠅
fog	mồ	霧
food street	sĭk gàai	食街
food poisoning	sĭk màt jùng dǔk	食物中毒
foot	gèuk	腳
football (soccer)	jùk kau	足球
footpath	síu gìng	小徑
foreign country	ngồi gwòk	外國
foreigner	ngồi gwòk yan	外國人
forest	sàm lam	森林
forever	wíng yǘen	永遠
to forget	mong gèi	忘記
to forgive	fòon sùe	寬恕
formula	gùng sìk	公式
fountain	pàn chuen	噴泉
free	jĩ yau	自由
free of charge	mín fài	免費
freeze	dūng gĭt	凍結
fresh	sàn sìn	新鮮
friend	pang yǎu	朋友
front of, in	chin bǐn	前便
frozen foods	gàp dūng sĭk màt	急凍食物
fruit	sàang gwóh	生果
full	mồon	滿
funny	yǎu chūi	有趣

| fuse | fòoi sí | 灰土 |
| future | jèung lòi | 將來 |

G

gallery	wá lóng	畫廊
to gamble	dó bŏk	賭博
game	yàu hēi	遊戲
garden	fà yúen	花園
gas cartridge	hēi túng	氣筒
gate	dàng gèi	登機
(boarding)	jăap háu	閘口
gay	gèi	基
gay bar	gèi bà	基吧
gene	gèi yàn	基因

Get out!
chùt hūi
出去!

Get lost!
jáu hòi!
走開!

girl	nŭi jái	女仔
girlfriend	nŭi pàng yáu	女朋友
give	béi	俾

Could you give me ...?
hóh m hóh yí béi ... ngŏh?
可唔可以俾 ... 我?

give way	yèung lŏ	讓路
glasses	ngăan géng	眼鏡
gloves	sáu tō	手套
go	hūi	去
go straight ahead	yàt jĭk hūi	一直去
goal (soccer)	lùng mòon	龍門
goalkeeper	sáu lùng mòon	守龍門
goat	sàan yèung	山羊
God	sàn	神

| gold | gàm | 金 |
| good | hó | 好 |

Good luck.
hó wăn
好運

Goodbye.
jòi gĭn
再見

Goodnight.
jó táu
早啾

government	jìng fŏo	政府
grand father	jó fŏo	祖父
grand mother	jó mŏ	祖母
grass	chó	草
It's great!	jàn hăi hó lā	真係好喇
greedy	tàam sàm	貪心
green	lŭk	綠
grey	fòoi sìk	灰色
grocery store	jăap fòh pó	雜貨舖
guess	góo	估
guest	yàn hāak	人客
guesthouse	bàn gwóon	賓館
guide (person)	dŏ yàu	導遊
guidebook	lŭi yàu jí nàam	旅遊指南
guide dog	dŏ màang húen	導盲犬
guilty feeling	nŏi gàu	內疚
guitar	gìt tà	結他
gun	chèung	槍

H

hail	bìng bŏk	冰雹
hair	tàu fāat	頭髮
hairbrush	sòh	梳
hairdresser	mĕi fāat sì	美髮師

half	yàt bōon	一半
hallucination	wàan gōk	幻覺
hammer	chui jái	鎚仔
hand	sáu	手
handbag	sáu dói	手袋
hand made	sáu gùng	手工
handkerchief	sáu gàn	手巾
handsome	yìng jūn	英俊

Happy Birthday!
sàang yàt fàai lòk
生日快樂

happy	hòi sàm	開心
harbour	góng háu	港口
hard/soft	ngáang/yún	硬/軟
to have	yáu	有

Do you have ...?
néi yáu mó ...?
你有冇 ...?

I have ...
ngóh yáu ...
我有 ...

hayfever	fà fán jìng	花粉症
he/him	kúi	佢
head	tau	頭
headache	tau tũng	頭痛
to heal	jĩ liu	治療
health	gĩn hòng	健康
to hear	tèng	聽
heart	sàm	心
heat	yĩt	熱
heater	nũen lo	暖爐
heavy	chúng	重

Hello.
hà lóh
哈囉

help	bòng mong	幫忙
herbs	chó yèuk	草藥
here	nì dõ	呢度

hero	yìng hung	英雄
heroin	hói lòk yìng	海洛英
to hide	yán chong	隱藏
hi-fi	sàn lĩk sùng	身歷聲
high	gò	高
highway	gùng lõ	公路
hill	sàan gòng	山崗
to hire	jò yũng	租用
historical sites	góo jĩk	古跡
to hitchhike	dāap sũn fùng chè	搭順風車
HIV positive	HIV dāai kwán jé	HIV帶菌者
hobbies	hìng chūi	興趣
holiday	gã kei	假期
home	ngùk kéi	屋企
homesick	sì hèung bēng	思鄉病
homosexual	tung sìng lũen	同性戀
honest	sìng sàt	誠實
honey	màt tong	蜜糖
honeymoon	màt yũet	蜜月
Hong Kong	hèung góng	香港
hope	hèi mõng	希望
horse	mã	馬
horrible	hóh pā	可怕
horseracing	páau mã	跑馬
hospital	yì yúen	醫院
hot (taste)	lāat	辣
hot/cold	yĩt/dũng	熱/凍

It's hot today.
gàm yàt hó yĩt
今日好熱

I'm hot.
ngóh hó yĩt
我好熱

hotel	jái dìm	酒店
hour	jùng tau	鐘頭
housewife	júe fóo	主婦

278

I

How are you?
néi hó mā?
你好嗎?

How many?
géi dòh ā?
幾多呀?

How much?
géi dòh chín ā?
幾多錢呀?

How?
dím ā?
點呀?

human rights | yan kuen | 人權
humour | yàu mǎk | 幽默
hungry | ngòh | 餓

Hurry up!
fàai dì!
快啲!

hurt | sèung hói | 傷害
husband(col) | lố gùng | 老公
husband | jèung fòo | 丈夫
hut | síu ngùk | 小屋

I

I/me | ngőh | 我
ice | sūet | 雪
identification card | sàn fán jìng | 身份證
if | yue gwóh | 如果
ill | bēng | 病
illegal | fèi fàat | 非法
immediately | jìk hàk | 即刻
Immigration | yǎp gíng | 入境
  sĭ mǒ | 事務
important | jǔng yìu | 重要
not important | m jǔng yìu | 唔重要

impossible | mő hóh nang | 冇可能
to improve | gói leung | 改良

in front of ...
... chin bǐn
... 前便

included | lin maai | 連埋
increase | jàng gà | 增加
income tax | yǎp sìk sūi | 入息稅
incompre-hensible | naan ming | 難明
indicator | jí bìu | 指標
indigestion | sìu fǎ | 消化
  bàt leung | 不良
industry | gùng yǐp | 工業
indoor | sàt női | 室內
infant | yìng yi | 嬰兒
inflation | tùng fòh | 通貨
  paang jèung | 膨漲
influenza | lau hang sìng | 流行性
  gám mố | 感冒
information | jì sùn | 資訊
injection | dá jàm | 打針
injure | sǎu sèung | 受傷
insect repellent | sàat chung jài | 殺蟲劑
inside | lői bǐn | 裡便
to insist | júe jèung | 主張
to insure | bó hím | 保險
intelligent | chùng ming | 聰明
interest (hobby) | hìng chùi | 興趣
internet | wőo luen mőng | 互聯網
internet cafe | mőng lòk gà fè | 網絡咖啡
interpreter | chuen yǐk | 傳譯
interval | bòon cheung | 半場
  yàu sìk | 休息
interview | mĭn taam | 面談
to invite | yìu chíng | 邀請

invoice	fàat pîu	發票
island	dó	島
itch	han yěung	痕癢
itinerary	hang ching bíu	行程 表

J

jail	gàam yŭk	監獄
jar	jùn	樽
jaw	ngŏk	顎
jealous	dō gěi	妒忌
jeans	ngau jái fòo	牛仔褲
jeep	gàt pó chè	吉普車
job	gùng jŏk	工作
jockey	ke sì	騎師
jogging	woon bŏ páau	緩步跑
joke	sīu wá	笑話
journey	lúi ching	旅程
juice	gwóh jàp	果汁
jump	tīu	跳
junk (boat)	faan suen	帆船

K

karaoke	kà làai O K	卡拉 O K
key	sóh si	鎖匙
keyboard	gĭn poon	鍵盤
kick	těk	踢
to kill	sāat hŏi	殺害
kind	yan chi	仁慈
kiosk	síu sĭk dìm	小食店
kiss	mǎn	吻
kitchen	chue fóng	廚房
kitten (cat)	màau jái	貓仔
knapsack	bōoi nong	背囊
know	jì dò	知道
kung fu	gùng fòo	功夫
kitchen	chue fóng	廚房
kitten (cat)	màau jái	貓仔

| knapsack | bōoi nong | 背囊 |
| to know | jì dō | 知道 |

L

lake	woo	湖
land	tó děi	土地
landmark	děi bìu	地標
landscape	yuen gíng	園景
landslide	sàan bàng	山崩
languages	yŭe yin	語言
large	dǎai	大
last	jūi hāu	最後
last (col)	dăi mèi	第尾
last night	kam màan	禽晚
late	chi dō	遲到
laundry	sái yì pó	洗衣舖
law	fàat lŭt	法律
lawyer	lŭt sì	律師
lazy	lǎan	懶
leader	lǐng dŏ	領導
leaf	sŭe yǐp	樹葉
to learn	hŏk jǎap	學習
left	jóh bìn	左便
left luggage	hang léi wai sàt	行李 遺失
leg	túi	腿
lemon	ning mùng	檸檬
less	síu	少
letter	sūn	信
library	to sùe gwóon	圖書館
licence	paai jìu	牌照
lie, a	góng dǎai wǎ	講大話
light (bright)	gwòng	光
lighter	dá fóh gèi	打火機
lightning	sím dǐn	閃電
like	jùng yì	中意
little	síu	小
lock	sóh	鎖
long	cheung	長

Long time no see.
hó nòi mố gīn
好耐冇見

to lose	wai sàt	遺失
lotus	hoh fà	荷花
loud	dãai sèng	大聲
love	ngói	愛
lover	ngói yan	愛人
low	dài	低
lucky	hó chói	好彩
luggage	hang léi	行李
lunch	ng̃ chàan	午餐

M

machine	gèi hēi	機器
magazine	jãap jì	雜誌
mail	yau jìng	郵政
mailbox	yau sèung	郵箱
main road	dãai lõ	大路
to make	jõ	做
make-up	fà jòng	化妝
malt sugar	mãk nga tóng	麥芽糖
manager	gìng léi	經理
manners	lái mãau	禮貌
many	hó dòh	好多
map	dẽi to	地圖
maple	fùng	楓
market	sí cheung	市場
to marry	gìt fàn	結婚
massage	ngòn mòh	按摩
matches	fóh chaai	火柴

It doesn't matter.
m gán yìu
唔緊要

What's the matter?
màt yế sĩ ã?
乜嘢事呀?

mattress	chong jĩn	床墊

maybe	wãak jé	或者
mayor	sí jéung	市長
to meet	gìn mĩn	見面
medicine	yểuk	藥
melody	suen lút	旋律
melon	mãt gwà	蜜瓜
member	wóoi yuen	會員
menu	chòi dàan	菜單

Merry Chirstmas.
sīng dãan fāai lõk
聖誕快樂

message	sūn sìk	訊息
midnight	bōon yé	半夜
migraine	pìn tau tūng	偏頭痛
mind	sì séung	思想
to mind	jūe yī	注意
minute	fàn jùng	分鐘

Just a minute.
yàt jãn
一陣

mirror	gēng	鏡
mistake	chõh ng̃	錯誤
mobile phone	dãai gòh dãai	大哥大
modem	tiu jãi gáai	調制解
	tiu hēi	調器
modern	mòh dàng	摩登
money exchange	jáau wõon dìm	找換店
monkey	mã làu	馬騮
moon	yũet	月
mother	mố chàn	母親
mountain	sàan	山
mountain bike	pàan sàan dàan chè	攀山單車
mountain range	sàan mãk	山脈
mouse	lõ súe	老鼠
mouth	háu	口
movie	dĩn yíng	電影

mud	nai	泥
mum	mà mi	媽咪
museum	bōk mæt gwóon	博物館
music	yàm ngŏk	音樂

N

nail clippers	jí găap kím	指甲鉗
name	sīng ming	姓名
nappy	nĭu pín	尿片
nationality	gwōk jĭk	國籍
nausea	jōk ngáu	作嘔
near	kán	近
nearby	fóo gän	附近
to need	sùi yīu	需要
needle	jàm	針
never	chung loi mŏ	從來冇
New Year's Day	sàn nin	新年
New Year's Eve	chui jĭk	除夕
next month	hă gŏh yuet	下個月
no	bàt	不

No smoking.
bàt jún kàp yìn
不准吸煙

No entry.
bàt jún sái yăp
不准駛入

No parking.
bàt jún pāak chè
不准泊車

No waiting.
bàt jún ting chè dáng hău
不准停車等候

noisy	cho	嘈
none	mŏ	冇
noon	ngāan jāu	晏晝

north	bàk	北
now	yi gà	而家
number	hŏ mǎ	號碼

O

obvious	ming hín	明顯
o'clock	jùng tau	鐘頭
occupation	jĭk yĭp	職業
ocean	hói yeung	海洋
October	săp yuĕt	十月
octopus	bāat jáau yue	八爪魚
Octopus Card	bāat dăat tùng	八達通
office	băan gùng sàt	辦公室
often	gìng seung	經常
oil	yau	油
OK	dĭm	掂
old friend	lŏ yáu	老友
olive	gāam lăam	橄欖
omelette	ngàm lĭt	奄列
on	jŏi sĕung	在上
on sale	dăai gáam gā	大減價
on time	jún si	準時
once	yàt chī	一次

One way only.
dàan ching lŏ
單程路

onion	yeung chùng	洋蔥
open	hòi	開
opera	gòh kĕk	歌劇
operator	jĭp sîn sàng	接線生
opposite	sèung fáan	相反
or	wăak jé	或者
oral exam	háu sĭ	口試
orange	cháang	橙
orange juice	cháang jàp	橙汁
orchid	laan fà	蘭花
to order	mĭng lĭng	命令
to order (a meal)	dím (chôi)	點(菜)

ordinary	pó tùng	普通
to organise	jó jìk	組織
orgasm	sĭng gò chiu	性高潮
original	yuen jòng	原裝
outside	ngŏi mĭn	外面
overdose	yéuk jài	藥劑
	gwŏh lēung	過量
overdue	gwōh kei	過期
ox tail soup	ngau méi	牛尾
	tòng	湯
oxygen	yéung hēi	氧氣
oyster	ho	蠔
oyster sauce	ho yau	蠔油
ozone layer	chāu yéung	臭氧
	chang	層

P

pacifier (dummy)	năai júi	奶咀
package (deal)	bàau maai sāai	包埋晒
a packet (of cigarettes)	yàt bàau (yìn jái)	一包 (煙仔)
padlock	sóh tau	鎖頭
pain	tūng	痛
painkiller	jí tūng yéuk	止痛藥
to paint	yau chàt	油漆
painter	wá gà	畫家
painting (art)	kwóoi wá ngǎi sùt	繪畫藝術
paintings	kwóoi wá	繪畫
palace	gùng dĭn	宮殿
palm	jùng lúi	棕櫚
panda	hung màau	熊貓
paper	jí	紙
Paralympics	chaan jàt yan ngŏ wăn wóoi	殘疾人奧運會
parcel	bàau gwóh	包裹
a park	gùng yúen	公園
parking	dŏi hāak	代客

service	pāak chè	泊車
parrot	yìng mŏ	鸚鵡
partner	pāak dŏng	拍檔
partnership	hăp fóh	合伙
	gwàan hăi	關係
party	jŭi wŏoi	聚會
party (political)	jìng dóng	政黨
pass	hăp gāak	合格
passport	wŏo jĭu	護照
passport number	wŏo jĭu hŏ mă	護照號碼
past	gwōh hūi	過去
path	síu gĭng	小徑
patient (adj)	yán nŏi	忍耐
to pay	jì fŏo	支付
pea sprouts	dău miu	豆苗
peace	woh ping	和平
peach	tó	桃
peacock	húng jĕuk	孔雀
peak	sàan déng	山頂
peanuts	fā sàng	花生
pear	bè léi	啤梨
peas	dáu	豆
pedestrian	hang yan	行人
pencil	yuen bàt	鉛筆
penguin	kéi ngŏh	企鵝
peninsula	bòon dó	半島
penis	yàm gĭng	陰莖
penknife	dò jái	刀仔
pensioner	său woon	受援
	jŏh yan sĭ	助人士
peony	măau dàan	牡丹
people	yan	人
perfume	hèung súi	香水
personal	sì yan	私人
personality	gŏh sìng	個性
petrol	dĭn yau	電油
petrol station	gà yau jăam	加油站
pharmacy	yéuk fong	藥房
phonebook	dĭn wá bó	電話簿

phonecard	dīn wá kàat	電話卡
photo	sēung pín	相片
a piece	yàt gĭn	一件
pig	jùe	豬
pigeon	bǎak gāp	白鴿
pill	yĕuk yúen	藥丸
the Pill	háu fúk běi yǎn yúen	口服避孕丸
pillow	jám tau	枕頭
pillowcase	jám tau tō	枕頭套
ping-pong	bìng bàm kau	乒乓球
pipe	yìn dáu	煙斗
pizza	yĭ dǎai lěi sìu béng	意大利燒餅
place of birth	chùt sàng děi	出生地
plate	dĭp	碟

Please.
chèng
請□

plug	chāap sò táu	插蘇頭
plum	móoi	梅
plum sauce	mooi jí jēung	梅子醬
police station	gíng chúe	警署
policeman (in Hong Kong)	gíng chāat	警察
policeman (in China)	gùng ngòn	公安
pollution	wòo yĭm	污染
pomelo	yáu	柚
pool (swimming)	wǐng chi	泳池
poplar	bǎak yeung sūe	白揚樹
popular music	lau hang yàm ngŏk	流行音樂
pork	jùe yŭk	豬肉
port	góng háu	港口
post office	yau gúk	郵局
postcard	ming sūn pín	明信片

postman	yau chàai	郵差
pot	wóo	壺
potato	sue jái	薯仔
pottery	to hěi	陶器
poverty	kūet fǎt	缺乏
power	nang lĭk	能力
pram	yìng yi chè	嬰兒車
to pray	kei tó	祈禱
pregnant	waai yǎn	懷孕
prejudice	pìn gĭn	偏見
pre-menstrual tension	gìng chin gán jèung	經前緊張
to prepare	jún běi	準備
pretty	lēng	靚
price	gã chin	價錢
printed matter	yàn chāat bán	印刷品
profit	lěi yĭk	利益
to protect	bó wŏo	保護
public square	dǎai dàat déi	大笪地
public telephone	gùng jūng dīn wá	公眾電話
public toilet	gùng chĭ	公廁
pudding	bō dìn	布甸
to pull	làai	拉
pump	bàm	泵
punch(drink)	bàn jǐ	賓治
puncture	gàt chùen	拮穿
to punish	jàak fǎt	責罰
pure	sun jīng	純正
purple	jí sìk	紫色
to push	tùi	推
to put	fōng	放

Q

qualifications	jì gàak	資格
quality	jàt lěung	質量
quantity	sŏ lěung	數量
quarantine	gím yĭk	檢疫
question	mǎn tai	問題

queue	paai dúi	排隊
quick	fāai	快
quiet	jĭng	靜
quota	pūi ngáak	配額

R

race (breed)	júng jŭk	種族
race (sport)	béi chōi	比賽
racing bike	béi chōi yŭng	比賽用
	dàan chè	單車
racism	júng jŭk	種族
	kei sĭ	歧視
racquet	kau páak	球拍
radiator (car)	súi sèung	水箱
radio	sàu yàm gèi	收音機
railway	fóh chè jăam	火車站
station		
rain	yŭe	雨
rainbow	chói hung	彩虹
raincoat	yŭe yì	雨衣
rainy season	yŭe gwâi	雨季
rape	keung gàan	強奸
rare	hón yáu	罕有
rash	sín	癬生
raw	sàang	生
razor	tāi dò	剃刀
reading	tái sùe	睇書
real estate	déi cháan dôi	地產代
agent	léi sèung	理商
reaction	fáan yìng	反應
reason	léi yau	理由
receipt	sàu gūi	收據
to receive	jip sáu	接受
recently	jùi gán	最近
to recommend	tùi jìn	推薦
red	hung sìk	紅色
Red Cross	hung sǎp	紅十
	jĭ wóoi	字會
reference	chàam háau	參考
refugee	nǎan man	難民

refund	tūi chín	退錢
registration	dàng gēi	登記
relationship	gwàan hǎi	關係
relatives	chàn chìk	親戚
religion	jùng gàau	宗教
to remember	gēi dàk	記得
to rent	jò	租
to repair	sàu jíng	修整
to repeat	chung fùk	重複
to reply	wooi fùk	回覆
reservation	yŭe dĕng	預訂
respect	jùen gĭng	尊敬
restricted	găm kùi	禁區
area		
rickshaw	chè jái	車仔
right (correct)	jĭng kōk	正確
right	yǎu bìn	右便
rights	kuen lěi	權利
to risk	fùng hím	風險
river	hoh	河
road	dô lô	道路
to rob	chéung gíp	搶劫
rock	ngaam sĕk	岩石
romantic	lõng măan	浪漫
	hēi sìk	氣息
room	fong gàan	房間
root	gàn	根
rope	sing sōk	繩索
round	yuen	圓
to run	jáu	走

S

sad	sèung sàm	傷心
safe	ngòn chuen	安全
scared	gèng	驚
scarves	wai gàn	圍巾
scientist	fòh hŏk gà	科學家
scissors	gàau jín	較剪
sea	hói	海
seasons	gwāi jìt	季節

seatbelt	ngòn chuen dáai	安全帶
second (place)	dǎi yǐ	第二
seconds (time)	míu	秒
secret	bēi màt	秘密
secretary	bēi sùe	秘書
section	fàn dǔen	分段
to see	tái	睇

We'll see!
chi dì sìn
遲啲先

I see. (understand)
ngőh ming
我明

See you later.
chi dì gìn
遲啲見

See you tomorrow.
tìng yàt gìn
聽日見

to sew	fung	縫
sex (m/f)	sĭng bĭt	性別
sexy	sĭng gám	性感
shame	cháu	醜
shirt	sùt sàam	恤衫
shoes	haai	鞋
shop	pō táu	舖頭
short	dúen	短
show	jín sĭ	展示
shower (bath)	fà sá chùng sàn	花酒沖身
shower (rain)	jàau yǔe	驟雨
signature	chìm méng	簽名
silk	sì	絲
silver	ngan	銀
single	dàan dŭk	單獨
single (person)	dàan sàn	單身

to sit	chŏh	坐
size	chēk mǎ	尺碼
skirt	kwan	裙
sky	tìn hùng	天空
sleepy	ngǎan fàn	眼瞓
small	sǎi	細
to smell	man	聞

Smells nice.
hó hèung
好香

to smile	mei sĭu	微笑
to smoke	sĭk yìn	食煙
son	jái	仔
sorry	dūi m jŭe	對唔住

Sounds great!
tèng lei géi hó bòh!
聽嚟幾好喎!

south	naam	南
souvenir	gēi nĭm bán	紀念品
space	hùng gàan	空間
to speak	góng wǎ	講話
special	dàk bĭt	特別
speed	chùk dŏ	速度
spoon	chi gàng	匙羹
spring (season)	chùn gwàai	春季
square	sēi fòng	四方
stamp	yau pīu	郵票
star	sìng	星
stone	sěk tau	石頭
stop	ting	停
storm	bŏ fùng yǔe	暴風雨
stupid	yue chún	愚蠢
sugar	tong	糖
summer	hǎ gwài	夏季
sun	yàt táu	日頭
sunblock cream	tàai yeung yau	太陽油
sunglasses	tàai yeung ngǎan géng	太陽眼鏡

sunrise	yàt chùt	日出
sunset	yàt lòk	日落
swamp	jíu jǎak	沼澤
syringe	jàm túng	針筒

T

table	tói	檯
tall	gò	高
tampons	min tíu wǎi sàng gàn	棉條衛生巾
tasty	hó sǐk	好食
Taoism	dò gāau	道教
Taoist temple	gùng	宮
Taoist temple	dò gwòon	道觀
taro	wǒo táu	芋頭
tax	sūi	稅
taxi	dìk sí	的士
taxi stand	dìk sí jǎam	的士站
tea	cha	茶
tea with milk	nǎai cha	奶茶
tea pot	cha wóo	茶壺
tea spoon	cha gàng	茶羹
teacher	gāau sì	教師
team work	tuen dǔi gùng jòk	團隊工作
telegram	dìn bò	電報
telephone	dìn wá	電話
telephone booth	dìn wá ting	電話亭
telephone card	dìn wá kàat	電話卡
telephone number	dìn wá hǒ mǎ	電話號碼
temperature	wàn dò	溫度
temple	míu	廟
tenant	jǔe wǒo	住戶

Thank you.
dòh jě
多謝

theatre	kěk yúen	劇院
thin	bòk	薄
to think	séung	想
thirsty	háu hòt	口渴
throat	hau lung	喉嚨
thunder	lui	雷
ticket office	sǎu pìu chūe	售票處
tide	chiu jìk	潮汐
tie	léng tàai	領呔
tiger	fóo	虎
time table	si gāan bíu	時間表
tip (gratuity)	tìp sí	貼士
tired	gwǒoi	瘤
tissues	jí gàn	紙巾
tonight	gàm màan	今晚
toast	dòh sí	多士
toaster	dòh sí lo	多士爐
tobacco	yìn sì	菸絲
today	gàm yàt	今日
toilet	chī sóh	廁所
toilet paper	chī jí	廁紙
tomato	fàan ké	番茄
tomorrow	tìng yàt	聽日
toothache	nga tūng	牙痛
toothbrush	nga cháat	牙刷
toothpaste	nga gò	牙膏
torch	sáu dǐn túng	手電筒
tourist	yau hǎak	遊客
tourist information centre	yau hǎak jì sūn jùng sàm	遊客資訊中心
toys	wǒon gǔi	玩具
trademark	sèung bìu	商標
traffic jam	sàk chè	塞車
traffic signals	gàau tùng dàng	交通燈
train	fóh chè	火車
train station	fóh chè jǎam	火車站
tram stop	dǐn chè jǎam	電車站
tramways	dǐn chè	電車

transit	jūen dāap	轉搭
translation	faan yĭk	翻譯
travel	lŭi hang	旅行
travel agency	lŭi hang sé	旅行社
travellers' cheque	lŭi hang jì pīu	旅行 支票
tray	poon	盤
tree	sŭe	樹
triple	sàam pŏoi	三倍
tripod	sàam gēuk gá	三腳架
trousers	fōo	褲
trout	jùn yúe	鱒魚
true	jàn sàt	真實
trust	sūn lăai	信賴
truth	jàn léi	真理
Tuesday	sìng kei yĭ	星期二

Turn left.
jūen jóh
轉左

Turn right.
jūen yàu
轉右

twice	léung chi	兩次
typhoon	gŭi fùng	颱風
tyre	chè tàai	車胎

umbrella	jè	遮
uncle	sùk sùk	叔叔
to understand	ming bàak	明白
underwear	nŏi yĭ	內衣
umemployed	sàt yĭp	失業
unions	gùng wóoi	工會
university	dăai hŏk	大學
up	sĕung bīn	上便
urgent	gán gàp	緊急
useful	yŭu yŭng	有用

vacation	gā kei	假期
vaccination	fong yĭk jūe sĕ	防疫 注射
valley	sàan gùk	山谷
valuables	gwāi jŭng màt bán	貴重 物品
van	síu bà	小巴
vanilla	wăn nèi ná	雲呢拿
vaseline	fā sĭ líng	花士苓
vegetarian	sō sĭk jé	素食者

I'm vegetarian.
ngŏh hăi sĭk sō gē
我係食素嘅

view	gíng jí	景緻
village	hèung chùen	鄉村
VIP	gwāi bàn	貴賓
virus	bĕng dŭk	病毒
visa	chìm jĭng	簽證
to visit	fóng mǎn	訪問
voice	sìng yàm	聲音

to wait	dáng hău	等候
waiter	fóh gēi	伙記
waiter (female)	síu jé	小姐
to walk	haang	行
to want	yīu	要
warm	nŭen	暖
washing powder	sái yì fán	洗衣粉
washing machine	sái yì gèi	洗衣機
a watch	sáu bìu	手錶
water	súi	水
waterfall	bŭk bō	瀑布
wave	lŏng	浪

way	dõ lõ	道路

Please tell me the way to ...
m gòi wǎ ngőh jì hūi ... gē lõ
唔該話我知去 ... 嘅路

Which way?
bìn tiu lõ ā?
邊條路呀?

way out	chùt háu	出口
we/us	ngőh děi	我哋
weak	yűen yěuk	軟弱
to wear	chùen jěuk	穿著
wedding	gīt fàn	結婚
wedding party	fàn yīn	婚宴
week	sìng kei	星期

Welcome.
fòon ying
歡迎

well, a	jéng	井
well, (adj)	hó	好
west	sài	西
western style restaurant	sài chàan tèng	西餐廳
Western food	sài chàan	西餐
wet	sàp	濕
wet towel	sàp mo gàn	濕毛巾

What?
màt yế ā?
乜嘢呀?

What is he saying?
kűi gòng màt yế ā?
佢講乜嘢呀?

What time is it?
géi dím jùng ā?
幾點鐘呀?

| wheelchair | lun yí | 輪椅 |

When?
géi sí ā?
幾時呀?

When does it leave?
kűi géi sí lei hòi ā?
佢幾時離開呀?

Where?
bìn dõ ā?
邊度呀?

Where is the bank?
ngan hong hái bìn dõ ā?
銀行喺邊度呀?

| white | bãak | 白 |

Why?
dím gáai ā?
點解呀?

wife (col)	lõ poh	老婆
wife	tāai táai	太太
wild animal	yế sàng dűng màt	野生動物
willow	yeung láu	楊柳
to win	yeng	贏
wind	fùng	風
window	chèung	窗
wine	po to jáu	葡萄酒
winter	dùng gwài	冬季
wise	chùng ming	聰明
to wish	jùk yűen	祝願
with	tung maai	同埋
wool	mo	毛
work	gùng jòk	工作
world	sài gāai	世界
worried	dàam sàm	擔心
to write	sé	寫
writing brush	mo bàt	毛筆
wrong	chöh	錯

I'm wrong.
ngőh chöh jóh
我錯咗

Y

| year | nin | 年 |
| yellow | wong sìk | 黃色 |

Yes.
hāi
係

yesterday	kam yàt	噚日
yoghurt	sùen nǎai	酸奶
you	néi	你
young	hāu sàang	後生
younger brother	dai dái	弟弟
younger brother (col)	sāi ló	細佬

younger sister	mooi móoi	妹妹
younger sister (col)	sāi móoi	細妹
youth hostel	chìng nin sùk sē	青年宿舍

Z

zebra crossing	bàan mǎ sìn	斑馬線
zero	ling	零
zipper	làai lín	拉錬
zone	dēi kùi	地區
zoo	dūng màt yuen	動物園

In this dictionary we have listed the Cantonese transliterations alphabetically. Please note that there are no entries under vowels.

B

ba bà	爸爸	Daddy
bà sí jǎam	巴士站	bus stop
bà sí	巴士	bus (in Hong Kong)
bàau gwóh	包裹	parcel
bàk	北	north
bàn gwóon	賓館	guesthouse
bàt gwòh	不過	but
bàt jún kàp yìn 不准吸煙 No smoking.		
bàt jún pàak chè 不准泊車 No parking.		
bàt jún sái yǎp 不准駛入 No entry.		
bàt	不	no
bǎak	白	white
bēi mǎt	秘密	secret
bè jáu	啤酒	beer
běi	鼻	nose
bēi yǎn	避孕	contraception
bēi yǎn tō	避孕套	condoms
běng dǔk	病毒	virus
běng	病	ill
béi	俾	to give
béng gòn	餅干	biscuit
bìn dǒ ǎ? 邊度呀? Where?		

bìng bàm kau	乒乓球	ping-pong
bìng bǒk	冰雹	hail
bǐn jòng	便裝	casual dress
bìn lǔn	辯論	to argue
bó fèi	補飛	upgrade ticket
bō jí	報紙	newspaper
bōoi jěk	背脊	back (body)
bōoi nong	背囊	knapsack
bōoi nong hāak	背囊客	backpacker
bōon yé	半夜	midnight
bòh sí	波士	boss
bòh	波	ball
bòng mong	幫忙	help
bòoi	杯	cup
bòoi gwǎi	杯櫃	cupboard
bō fùng yǔe	暴風雨	storm
bǒk	薄	thin
bǔk bō	瀑布	waterfall

C

cha	茶	tea
chàn chìk	親戚	relatives
chàu gwǎi	秋季	autumn
cháu	醜	shame
chan ngàai	塵埃	dust
chěk má	尺碼	size
chè	車	car
chè lei jí	車厘子	cherries
chè paai	車牌	driving licence
cheung	長	long
chèung	槍	gun
chéung gìp	搶劫	to rob

chi dì gīn
遲啲見
See you later.

chi dì sìn
遲啲先
We'll see!

chi dō	遲到	late
chi gàng	匙羹	spoon
chi	遲	delay
chī jí	廁紙	toilet paper
chì sīn	黐線	crazy
chìm jìng	簽証	visa
chìm méng	簽名	signature
chìng gīt	清潔	clean
chìng nin	青年	youth hostel
sùk sē	宿舍	

chèng
請
Please.

... chin bǐn	... 前便	in front of ...
chin mǐn	前面	ahead
ching dō	程度	degree (level)
ching tìn	晴天	fine weather
chiu jīk	潮汐	tide
cho	嘈	noisy
chó yèuk	草藥	herbs
chǒh	坐	to sit
chōh	錯	wrong/ mistake/ fault
chōi dàan	菜單	menu
chói hung	彩虹	rainbow
chói sìk	彩色	colour
chói sìk fèi lám	彩色 菲林	colour film
chong jín	床墊	mattress
chǔng	重	heavy

chùng leung fóng	沖涼 房	bathroom
chùng ming	聰明	intelligent/ wise
chùng mŏon	充滿	to fill
chùt fāat	出發	departure
chùt háu	出口	exit/way out

chùt hŭi
出去
Get out!

chùt méng	出名	famous
chùt nǎap	出納	cashier
chùt sāi jí	出世紙	birth certificate
chùt sàng děi	出生地	place of birth
chùt sàng nin yǔet yàt	出生年 月日	date of birth
chúi siu	取消	to cancel
chuen jèuk	穿著	wear
chue fóng	廚房	kitchen
chue sì	廚師	chef
chuen fóon	存款	deposit (bank)
chuen yīk	傳譯	interpreter
chui jīk	除夕	New Year's Eve
chung fùk	重複	to repeat
chung loi mŏ	從來有	never

D

dá fóh gèi	打火機	lighter
dá ma jèuk	打麻雀	mah jong (to play)
dá sŏ	打掃	cleaning
dāng	凳	chair
dà	打	dozen
dàan ching lŏ	單程路	one way only

dàan dŭk	單獨	alone/single	
dàan	單	bill	
dài	低	low	
dàng gēi	登記	registration	
dàng gēi sáu jūk	登記 手續	check-in	
dàng gèi jāap háu	登機 閘口	gate (boarding)	
dàng gèi jīng	登機証	boarding pass	
dăai	大	big/large	
dăai gáam gā	大減價	on sale	
dăai gòh dăai	大哥大	mobile phone	
dăai hŏk	大學	university	
dăai lŏ	大路	main road	
dăai sèng	大聲	loud	
dăai sī gwóon	大使館	embassy	
dăai yàt	第一	number one	
dăai yan	大人	adult	
dăai yēuk	大約	about	
dăi mèi	第尾	last (col)	
dăi yàt	第一	first	
dăk bīt	特別	special	
dái	底	bottom	
dáng hāu	等候	wait	
dai dái	弟弟	younger brother	
dĕi bīu	地標	landmark	
dĕi jí	地址	address	
dĕi kau	地球	Earth	
dĕi to	地圖	map	
dĭk sí	的士	taxi	
dīm	掂	OK	
dīn bō	電報	telegram	
dīn lĭk	電力	electricity	
dīn nŏ	電腦	computer	
dīn wá	電話	telephone	
dīn wá bó	電話簿	directory	

dĭn yau	電油	petrol	
dĭn yíng	電影	movie	
dím (chòi)	點(菜)	to order (a meal)	
dím ā? 點呀?		How?	
dím gáai ā? 點解呀?		Why?	
dó bŏk	賭博	to gamble	
dò gēi	妒忌	jealous	
dŏ	到	to arrive	
dŏ dăat	到達	arrivals	
dŏ gāau	道教	Taoism	
dŏ lŏ	道路	road/way	
dŏ yau	導遊	guide (person)	
dói	袋	bag	
dūi fòng fŏo fóon	對方 付款	collect call	
dūi m jŭe 對唔住		Excuse me; Sorry.	
dūng	凍	cold (adj)	
dūng súi	凍水	cold water	
dùng gwāi	冬季	winter	
dùng	東	east	
dŭk bán	毒品	drug (recreational)	
dŭk fáan	毒販	drug dealer	
dŭk se	毒蛇	poisonious snake	
dŭng màt yuen	動物 園	zoo	
dúen	短	short	

F

fāai dì!
快啲!
Hurry up!

fāai jí	筷子	chopsticks
fāai	快	fast (adj)/ quick
fāai	快	
fāat gwōk	法國	France
fāat lŭt	法律	law
fāat sìu	發燒	fever
fāat yeung dīu	發羊吊	epileptic
fāi yŭng	費用	fee
fā	花	flower
fā fāi	花費	to cost
fā fán jīng	花粉症	hayfever
fā yúen	花園	garden
fāan gáan	番梘	soap
fāan yĭk	翻譯	translation
fān jùng	分鐘	minute
fāt gāau	佛教	Buddhism
fáu yĭng	否認	to deny
fèi fāat pó	飛髮舖	barber
fèi fāat	非法	illegal
fèi gèi	飛機	aeroplane
fèi lám	菲林	film (for camera)
fei	肥	fat
fòng hēung	方向	direction
fòo kàp	呼吸	to breathe
fòoi sí	灰土	fuse
fòoi sìk	灰色	grey
fòon sūe	寬恕	to forgive

fòon ying
歡迎
Welcome.

fǒo chàn	父親	father
fǒo gǎn	附近	nearby
fóh chè jāam	火車站	railway station

fóh jùk ā!
火燭呀!
Fire!

fóh chè	火車	train
fóh gēi	伙記	waiter
fóh	火	fire
fóng mǎn	訪問	to visit
fóo	苦	bitter
fong gàan	房間	room
fong yĭk	防疫	vaccination
jūe sě	看注	
fùng hím	風險	risk
fùng sīn	風扇	fan
fŭk mŏ	服務	service
fŭk wŏot jĭt	復活節	Easter
fung	縫	to sew

G

gā chin	價錢	price
gā kei	假期	holiday/ vacation
gāap bán	甲板	deck (of ship)
gāau yŭk	教育	education
gāi sŏ gèi	計數機	calculator
gām kùi	禁區	restricted area
gāng hó	更好	better
gāu	夠	enough
gā ting	家庭	family
gàam yŭk	監獄	jail
gāi yŭk	雞肉	chicken
gàm	金	gold
gàm màan	今晚	tonight

gàm yåt	今日	today
gàng yì sàt	更衣室	changing room
gàp gàu	急救	first aid
gám gòk	感覺	to feel
gám såu	感受	feeling
gán gåp	緊急	emergency/urgent
gèi dàk	記得	to remember
gèi hõ	記號	mark
gèuk	腳	foot
gèi cheung	機場	airport
gèi hèi	機器	engine/machine
gèi wõoi	機會	chance
gèi	基	gay
gèng	驚	scared

géi dòh ā?
幾多呀?
How many?

géi dòh chín ā?
幾多錢呀?
How much?

géi sí ā?
幾時呀?
When?

géng	頸	neck
gìn mìn	見面	to meet
gìn yí	建議	advice
gìt fàn	結婚	to marry/wedding
gìt tà	結他	guitar
gìng jāi wái	經濟位	economy class
gìng léi	經理	manager
gìng seung	經常	always/often
gìng yìm	經驗	experience

gín hòng sīk māt	健康食物	health foods
gín hòng	健康	health
gín sàn sàt	健身室	gym
gím yīk	檢疫	quarantine
gíng chāat	警察	policeman (in Hong Kong)
gíng chúe	警署	police station
gò	高	high/tall
gòo lèi	咕喱	coolie
gói leung	改良	to improve
góng dãai wã	講大話	a lie
góng háu	港口	harbour/port
góng wã	講話	to speak
góo jìk	古跡	historical sites
góo	估	guess
góo	鼓	drums
goh gòh	哥哥	elder brother
gùk fà	菊花	chrysanthemum
gùng chì	公廁	public toilet
gùng fòo	功夫	kung fu
gùng gũng hèi chè	公共汽車	bus (in China)

gùng hèi!
恭喜
Congratulations!

gùng jòk	工作	job/work
gùng ngòn	公安	policeman (in China)
gùng wõoi	工會	unions
gùng yúen	公園	a park
gũi fùng	颶風	typhoon
gwāi	貴	expensive
gwāi jit	季節	seasons
gwāi jũng	貴重	valuables
māt bán	物品	

gwàan bāi	關閉	close
gwàan sàm	關心	to care (about)
gwàan waai	關懷	to care (for someone)
gwōh hūi	過去	past
gwōh kei	過期	overdue
gwōh màn	過敏	allergy
gwōk jīk	國籍	nationality
gwōon táu	罐頭	a can
gwòon gwòng	觀光	sightseeing
gwóoi	癐	tired
gwóh yan	果仁	nuts

H

hāak wǒo	客戶	client
hàk	黑	black

hà lóh
哈囉
Hello.

hàk bǎak	黑白	black and white
hàk ngām	黑暗	dark
hàk sí	黑市	black market
hàt yì	乞兒	beggar
hǎ bǐn	下便	below/ down
hǎ gwāi	夏季	summer

hǎi
係
Yes.

hǎp fóh	合伙	partnership
gwàan hǎi	關係	
hǎp tung	合同	contract
hǎp	盒	box
hāu bǐn	後便	behind

hāu sàang	後生	young
háu	口	mouth
háu hōt	口渴	thirsty
haang	行	walk
hang ching bíu	行程表	itinerary
hang léi	行李	baggage/ luggage
hang yan	行人	pedestrian
hau lung	喉嚨	throat
hēi yúen	戲院	cinema
hèi mǒng	希望	hope
hèung chùen	鄉村	village
hèung góng	香港	Hong Kong
hìng dǎi	兄弟	brother
HIV dāai kwán jè	**HIV** 帶菌者	HIV positive
hó chói	好彩	lucky
hó dòh	好多	many
hó hèung	好香	smells nice
hó nǒi	好耐	long time
mǒ gīn	冇見	no see
hó sǐk	好食	delicious/ tasty

hó wǎn
好運
Good luck.

hó	好	good/nice/ well(adj)
hòi	開	to open
hòi chí	開始	to begin
hòi sàm	開心	happy/ to enjoy (oneself)
hō mǎ	號碼	number
hǒk jǎap	學習	to learn
hóh kà yàn	可卡因	cocaine
hóh nang	可能	able(to be)

J

hóh pā dìk	可怕的	awful/horrible
hóh yí	可以	can (to be able)
hói	海	sea
hói gwàan	海關	customs
hói lǒk yìng*	海洛英	heroin
hói yeung	海洋	ocean
hón yǎu	罕有	rare
hoh fà	荷花	lotus
hoh	河	river
hūen gō	勸告	to advise
hūet	血	blood
hūi	去	to go
hùng	空	empty
hùng gàan	空間	space
hùng hēi	空氣	air
hùng tiu	空調	air-conditioned
hung	熊	bear
hung màau	熊貓	panda
hung sìk	紅色	red

J

jāak fǎt	責罰	to punish
jāan séung	讚賞	to admire
jàk bìn	側便	beside
jàm túng	針筒	syringe

jàn hǎi hó lā!
真係好喇!
It's great!

jàn léi	真理	truth
jàn sàt	真實	true
jǎap fòh pó	雜貨舖	grocery store
jǎap jì	雜誌	magazine
jǎt běng	疾病	disease
jáau wǒon dìm	找換店	money exchange

jáau wǒon	找換	exchange
jái dīm	酒店	hotel
jái	仔	son
jám tau	枕頭	pillow

jáu hòi!
走開!
Get lost!

jáu jìng	酒精	alcohol
jáu long	酒廊	lounge
jáu	走	to run
jē	借	to borrow
jè	遮	umbrella
jèung loi	將來	future
jěung fòo	丈太	husband
jí	紙	paper
jí naam jàm	指南針	compass
jí tūng yěuk	止痛藥	painkiller
jìng fóo	政府	government
jìng kōk	正確	right (correct)
jìp sǎu	接受	to accept/receive
jìt yǎt	節日	festival
jì chin	之前	before
jì dó	知道	to know
jì fòo	支付	pay
jì gàan	之間	between
jì hǎu	之後	after
jì pīu	支票	cheque
jì sūn	資訊	information
jìk hàk	即刻	immediately
jìk yǐp	職業	occupation
jìn	氈	blanket
jín	剪	to cut

jìng chói!
精采!
Fantastic!

jìng làu súi	蒸餾水	distilled water
jì dín	字典	dictionary
jì dūng tai fóon gèi	自動提款機	ATM
jì liu	治療	to heal
jì yau	自油	free
jìng	靜	quiet
jó	早	early
jó chàan	早餐	breakfast
jó fōo	祖父	grand father
jó jìk	組織	to organise
jó mó	祖母	grand mother
jó táu 早唞 Goodnight.		
jōi chí	再次	again
jōi gīn 再見 Goodbye.		
jōk ngáu	作嘔	nausea
jò	租	rent
jŏ	做	to do/make
jōi sĕung	在上	on
jóh bìn	左便	left
jūe yī	注意	attention/to mind
jūen dāap	轉搭	transit
jūen jóh	轉左	turn left
jūen yàu	轉右	turn right
jùi gahn	最近	recently
jūi hāu	最後	last
jūi hó	最好	best
jūn yăp	進入	to admit/enter
jùe bó	珠寶	jewellery

jùe gòu lìk	朱古力	chocolate
jùen gīng	尊敬	respect
jùen yìp	專業	profession
jùk	竹	bamboo
jùk kau	足球	football (soccer)
jùk yŭen	祝願	to wish
jùng gàau	宗教	religion
jùng gwōk	中國	China
jùng gwōk cha	中國茶	Chinese tea
jùng lŭi	棕櫚	palm
jùng tau	鐘頭	hour
jùng yì	中意	like
jūe sùk	住宿	accommodation
jŭe wŏo	住戶	tenant
júe	煮	to cook
júe fŏo	主婦	housewife
júe jèung	主張	to insist
jún bĕi	準備	to prepare
jún húi	准許	to allow
júng jùk kei sĭ	種族 歧視	racism
jŭng yìu	重要	important

K

kàat	卡	card
kàt	咳	cough
kán	近	near
kam yāt	噚日	yesterday
kei sĭ	歧視	discrimination
kei	旗	flag
keung gàan	強奸	rape
kiu	橋	bridge
kōk yĭng	確認	to confirm
kŭi	佢	he/him
kuen lĕi	權利	rights
kwān naan	困難	difficult

kwān yí	困擾	annoying

L

lǎan	懶	lazy
lǎi mǎau	禮貌	manners
lāap jùk	蠟燭	candle
làai	拉	to pull
lǎat jìu jēung	辣椒醬	chilli sauce
lǎat jìu	辣椒	chilli
lǎat	辣	hot (taste)
laam sìk	藍色	blue
lau hang	流行	fashion
lau hūet	流血	to bleed
léi yau	理由口	reason
léung chi	兩次	twice
lēng	靚	beautiful/ pretty
lēi yìk	利益	profit
léng tàai	領呔	tie
líng dǒ	領導	leader
líng sí	領事	consulate
lìng	拎	to bring
lim gā	廉價	budget accomodation
jūe sùk	住宿	
lin maai	連埋	included
ling	零	zero
lǒ gùng	老公	husband (col)
lǒ poh	老婆	wife (col)
lǒ ying	露營	camp
loi wooi fèi	來回飛	return ticket
loi	來	to come
lūi bǐn	便	inside
lūi ching	旅程	journey
lūi hang	旅行	travel
lūk	綠	green
lūk cha	綠茶	green tea
lūk yūet	六月	June
lui	雷	thunder
lung	聾	deaf

M

lung moon	龍門	goal (soccer)

m gán yīu	唔緊要	
It doesn't matter.		
m hó	唔好	bad/not good
m hóh yí	唔可以	cannot
m jùng yī	唔中意	to hate
m júng yīu	唔重要	not important
m tung	唔同	different
mǎ	馬	horse
mǎ hèi	馬戲	circus
mǎ làu	馬騮	monkey
mǎai	買	buy
mǎan chàan	晚餐	dinner
mǎn	吻	kiss
mà mi	媽咪	mum
màau	貓	cat
màau jái	貓仔	kitten (cat)
màn	蚊	mosquito
màt yě ā?	乜嘢呀？	
What?		
màt yě sǐ ā?	乜嘢事呀？	
What's the matter?		
mǎan jí gíp	萬字夾	clips
mǎn	問	to ask
mǎn tai	問題	question
mǎt	襪	socks
mǎt yūet	蜜月	honeymoon
maang	盲	blind
man	聞	to smell
man jǔk	民族	ethnic
man júe	民主	democracy

man ngāi	文藝	arts
mei sīu	微笑	to smile
mĭn fàai	免費	free of charge
mĭn	面	face
mĭn bàau	麵包	bread
míu	廟	temple
min tíu wăi	棉條衛	tampons
sàng gàn	生巾	
min	棉	cotton
ming bàak	明白	to understand
mŏ	冇	none
mŏ chàn	母親	mother
mŏ hóh nang	冇可能	impossible
mŏ yán	冇癮	boring
mŏ yĕ	冇嘢	nothing
mŏoi nin	每年	annual
mŏoi yàt gŏh	每一個	each
mŏoi yàt	每日	daily
mŏon	滿	full
mŏ	霧	fog
mŏk dìk dĕi	目的地	destination
mŏon	悶	bored
moh gòo	蘑菇	mushroom
mong	忙	busy
mong gēi	忘記	to forget
moon	門	door
mŭng	夢	dream

N

năai yau	奶油	cream
nàu	嬲	angry
náu	鈕	button
naam pang yău	男朋友	boyfriend
naam	南	south
naan hàm	難堪	embarassed
naan wai ching	難為情	embarassment

| nang lĭk | 能力 | power/energy |
| néi | 你 | you |

néi hó mă?
你好嗎?
How are you?

néi yău mŏ ...?
你有冇 ...?
Do you have ...?

ng chàan	午餐	lunch
nga cháat	牙刷	toothbrush
nga gò	牙膏	toothpaste
nga tūng	牙痛	toothache
nga yì	牙醫	dentist
ngăan	眼	eye
ngăan jāu	晏晝	noon/afternoon
ngăang/yŭen	硬/軟	hard/soft
ngăi sŭt	藝術	art
ngaam	癌	cancer
ngai hím	危險	dangerous
ngan	銀	silver
ngan hong	銀行	bank
ngan mă	銀碼	amount
ngau	牛	cow
ngau jái fòo	牛仔褲	jeans
ngau yŭk	牛肉	beef
ngŏh	我	I/me

ngŏh chōh jóh
我錯咗
I'm wrong.

| ngŏh dĕi | 我哋 | we/us |

ngŏh hóh yĭ jŏ
我可以做
I can do it.

ngŏh m hóh yĭ jŏ
我唔可以做
I can't do it.

ngốh m tung yī 我唔同意 I don't agree.		
ngốh tung yī 我同意 I agree.		
ngốh yắu ... 我有 ... I have ...		
ngồi	愛	love
ngồi jì bĕng	愛滋病	AIDS
ngồi yan	愛人	lover
ngòn chuen	安全	safe
ngòn chuen dáai	安全帶	seatbelt
ngồh	餓	hungry
ngồi gwōk yan	外國人	foreigner
ngồi mĩn	外面	outside
ngõk	顎	jaw
ngùk kéi	屋企	home
nì đồ	呢度	here
nĩu pín	尿片	nappy
nin	年	year
nin ling	年齡	age
nin nin yắu gàm yắt 年年有今日 Many happy returns!		
nố	腦	brain
nối yì	內衣	underwear
nửen	暖	warm
nửen lo	暖爐	heater
nửi	女	daughter/ female
nửi jái	女仔	girl
nửi pang yắu	女朋友	girlfriend
nửi sĩng	女性	female

nung cheung	農場	farm
nung man	農民	farmer

P

pā	怕	afraid/fear
pāak dōng	拍檔	partner
pàan dàng	攀登	to climb
paai dúi	排隊	queue
paai jiu	牌照	licence
pang yắu	朋友	friend
pè páai	啤牌	deck (of cards)
péi	皮	leather
peng	平	cheap
ping gwàn	平均	average
pó tùng	普通	ordinary
pống	蚌	clam
pō táu	舖頭	shop

S

sāat hỗi	殺害	to kill
sāi	細	small
sāi gāai	世界	world
sāi géi	世紀	century
sāi lồ gòh	細路哥	children
sà mồk	沙漠	desert
sàan	山	mountain
sàan bàng	山崩	landslide
sàan gòng	山崗	hill
sàan gùk	山谷	valley
sàan lồ	山路	mountain path/track
sàan mằk	山脈	mountain range
sàang gwóh	生果	fruit
sàang yắt	生日	birthday

sàang yất fàai lŏk	生日快樂	Happy Birthday!
sài	西	west
sàk chè	塞車	traffic jam
sàm	心	heart
sàm	深	deep
sàm lam	森林	forest
sàn fán jìng	身份證	identification card
sàn mán	新聞	news
sàn nin	新年	New Year's Day
sàn sìn	新鮮	fresh
sàn tái	身體	body
sàp	濕	wet
sàt nŏi	室內	indoor
sàt yĭp	失業	unemployed
sàu gũi	收據	receipt
sàu yàm gèi	收音機	radio
sãu sèung	受傷	to injure
sái sáu gàan	洗手間	toilet
sáu dò	首都	capital
sáu	手	hand
sáu gùng	手工	handmade
san	神	God
se	蛇	snake
sé	寫	to write
sé kwàn	社群	community
sèung pín	相片	photo
sèung dáng	相等	equal
sèung fáan	相反	opposite
sèung fùng	傷風	a cold
sèung sàm	傷心	sad
sèung bĭn	上便	up
sèung mĭn	上面	above
séi	死	dead
séung	想	to think
si gàan bíu	時間表	timetable
si jùng	時鐘	clock
sĩ jùng sàm	市中心	city centre
sĩ cheung	市場	market
sìng bĩt	性別	sex (m/f)
sìng gám	性感	sexy
sìng gò chiu	性高潮	orgasm
sìng ming	姓名	name
sìu wá	笑話	joke
sì hèung bĕng	思鄉病	homesick
sì	絲	silk
sìn gwóh jàp	鮮果汁	fresh juice
sìng	星	star
sìng gòng gèi	升降機	elevator
sìng yàm	聲音	voice
sĩ dòh*	士多	a store
sĩk	食	to eat
sĩk gàai	食街	food street
sĩk mãt	食物	food
	中毒	poisoning
jùng dŭk		
sĩk yìn	食煙	to smoke
sím dĩn	閃電	lightning
sín	癬	rash
síu gĭng	小徑	footpath
síu lŏ	小跟	path
síu	少	few/less
síu	小	little/small
sing dàap	乘搭	aboard
sing sãt	誠實	honest
sing sí	城市	city
só	數	to count
sō mŭk	數目	number
sō sĩk gwóon	素食館	vegetarian restaurant
sō sĩk jé	素食者	vegetarian
sòh	梳	comb/ hairbrush
sòng lái	喪禮	funeral
sóh	鎖	lock
sóh si	鎖匙	key

sūet	雪	ice/snow
sūet gà	雪茄	cigar
sūn	信	letter
sūn lǎai	信賴	trust
sūn sìk	訊息	message
sùe fùk	舒服	comfortable
sùi yìu	需要	to need
sùk sùk	叔叔	uncle
sùt sàam	恤衫	shirt
sǔe	樹	tree
sǔi fóng	睡房	bedroom
sǔen jǎak	選擇	to choose
súi	水	water
suen	船	boat
suen fùng	旋風	cyclone
sun jìng	純正	pure

T

tāai táai	太太	wife
tāi dò	剃刀	razor
tàam sàm	貪心	greedy
tái	睇	to see
tai chúi hang lěi chūe	提取行李處	baggage claim
tau	頭	head
tau fàat	頭髮	hair
tau tūng	頭痛	headache
tau wan	頭暈	dizzy
tēk	踢	to kick
tèng	聽	to hear

tèng lei géi hó bōh
聽嚟幾好喎
Sounds great.

tìu	跳	to jump
tìu mǒ	跳舞	dancing
tìn hùng	天空	sky
ting	停	stop
tìng yàt	聽日	tomorrow

tìng yàt gīn
聽日見
See you tomorrow.

tó děi	土地	land
tói	檯	table
tong lǐu bēng	糖尿病	diabetic
tūi chín	退錢	refund
tūi fóng	退房	check-out (hotel)
tūng	痛	pain
túi	腿	leg
tùi	推	to push
tùi jìn	推薦	to recommend
tung maai	同埋	and/with
tung sìng lǔen	同性戀	homosexual
tung yì	同意	to agree

W

wǎai jóh	壞咗	faulty
wǎak jé	或者	maybe/or
wǎn dǔng	運動	sport
waan gíng	環境	environment
waang gwōh	橫過	across
wai sàt	遺失	to lose
wan	雲	cloud
wǐng yǔen	永遠	forever
wòo jò	污糟	dirty
wǒo háu	戶口	account (bank)
wǒo luen mǒng	互聯網	internet
wǒo jǐu	護照	passport
wǒo jǐu hò mǎ	護照號碼	passport number
wǒo sǐ	護士	nurse
wǒoi lút	匯率	exchange rate

woh ping	和平	peace
woo	湖	lake
wooi fùk	回覆	to reply

Y

yáu chūi	有趣	funny
yáu yūng	有用	useful
yáu	有	to have
yàm gīng	陰莖	penis
yàm ngŏk	音樂	music

yàn jŭe
因住!
Careful!

yàn wái	因為	because
yàt bāak	一柏	a hundred
yàt bàau	一包	a packet (of
(yìn jái)	(煙仔)	cigarettes)
yàt bōon	一半	half
yàt chì	一次	once

yàt faan fùng sŭn!
一帆風順!
Bon voyage!

yàt gìn	一件	a piece

yàt jăn
一陣
Just a minute.

yàt jĭk hūi	一直去	go straight ahead
yàu dŏi gŭen	優待券	coupon
yàu mâk	幽默	humour
yàu sāi	優勢	advantage
yàu yŭet dĭk	優越的	excellent
yă bìn	右便	right
yăp gíng	入境	Immigration
sĭ mŏ	事務	

yăp háu	入口	entrance
yàt	日	day
yàt chùt	日出	sunrise
yàt lŏk	日落	sunset
yàt táu	日頭	sun
yàu yĭk	右翼	right-wing
yám	飲	to drink
yám jūi	飲醉	drunk
yán chong	隱藏	to hide
yan chi	仁慈	kind
yan hāak	人客	guest
yan	人	people
yau chàt	油漆	to paint
yau hāak	遊客	tourist
yau jĭng	郵政	mail
yau pìu	郵票	stamp
yau	油	oil
yĕ sàng	野生	wild animal
dŭng màt	動物	
yĕung hĕi	氧氣	oxygen
yĕuk	藥	drug (medical)
yĕuk jài	藥劑	overdose
gwŏh lĕung	過量	
yĕung lŏ	讓路	give way
yeng	贏	to win
yi gà	而家	now
yĭ	耳	ear
yĭ fàn	已婚	married
yĭ gìng	已經	already
yìu	要	want
yì fŭk	衣服	clothing
yì mó gàan	衣帽間	cloakroom
yì sàng	醫生	doctor
yì yúen	醫院	hospital
yìn fòoi gòng	煙灰缸	ashtray
yìn jái	煙仔	cigarette
yìn sì	菸絲	tobacco
yìng fà	櫻花	cherry blossom

yìng hung	英雄	hero
yìng jūn	英俊	handsome
yìng mán	英文	English
yìng yi	嬰兒	baby/infant
yìu chíng	邀請	to invite
yĭn dŏi	現代	modern
yĭn gàm	現金	cash
yĭp mŏ	業務	business
yĭt/dūng	熱/凍	hot/cold
yíng séung gèi	影相機	camera
yim	鹽	salt
ying dĕi	營地	campsite
yŭe	雨	rain
yŭe fong	乳房	breast
yŭe gwāi	雨季	rainy season
yŭe yì	雨衣	raincoat
yŭe yin	語言	languages

yŭen yĕuk	軟弱	weak
yŭen	遠	far away
yŭng gám	勇敢	brave
yŭe dĕng	預訂	reservation
yŭe sūen	預算	budget
yŭe yēuk	預約	appointment /booking
yŭet	月	moon
yŭk lūi	肉類	meat
yúe	魚	fish
yue chún	愚蠢	stupid
yue lŏk	娛樂	entertainment
yuen	完	end
yuen gíng	園景	landscape
yuen jòng	原裝	original
yuen ngaai	懸崖	cliff
yung yĭ	容易	easy

CANTONESE FINDER

Phrasebooks

L onely Planet phrasebooks are packed with essential words and phrases to help travellers communicate with the locals. With colour tabs for quick reference, an extensive vocabulary and use of script, these handy pocket-sized language guides cover day-to-day travel situations.

- handy pocket-sized books
- easy to understand Pronunciation chapter
- clear & comprehensive Grammar chapter
- romanisation alongside script to allow ease of pronunciation
- script throughout so users can point to phrases for every situation
- full of cultural information and tips for the traveller

'...vital for a real DIY spirit and attitude in language learning'

– Backpacker

'the phrasebooks have good cultural backgrounders and offer solid advice for challenging situations in remote locations'

– San Francisco Examiner

Arabic (Egyptian) • Arabic (Moroccan) • Australian *(Australian English, Aboriginal and Torres Strait languages)* • Baltic States *(Estonian, Latvian, Lithuanian)* • Bengali • Brazilian • Burmese • British *(English, dialects, Scottish Gaelic, Welsh)* • Cantonese • Central Asia *(Kazakh, Kyrgyz, Pashto, Tajik, Tashkorghani, Turkmen, Uyghur, Uzbek & others)* • Central Europe *(Czech, German, Hungarian, Polish, Slovak, Slovene)* • Costa Rica Spanish • Czech • Eastern Europe *(Albanian, Bulgarian, Croatian, Czech, Hungarian, Macedonian, Polish, Romanian, Serbian, Slovak, Slovene)* • East Timor *(Tetun, Portuguese)* • Egyptian Arabic • Ethiopian (Amharic) • Europe *(Basque, Catalan, Dutch, French, German, Greek, Irish, Italian, Maltese, Portuguese, Scottish Gaelic, Spanish, Turkish, Welsh)* • Farsi (Persian) • Fijian • French • German • Greek • Hebrew • Hill Tribes *(Lahu, Akha, Lisu, Mong, Mien & others)* • Hindi/Urdu • Indonesian • Italian • Japanese • Korean • Lao • Latin American Spanish • Malay • Mandarin • Mongolian • Moroccan Arabic • Nepali • Papua New Guinea • Pidgin • Pilipino (Tagalog) • Polish • Portuguese • Quechua • Russian • Scandinavian *(Danish, Faroese, Finnish, Icelandic, Norwegian, Swedish)* • South-East Asia *(Burmese, Indonesian, Khmer, Lao, Malay, Tagalog Pilipino, Thai, Vietnamese)* • South Pacific *(Fijian, Hawaiian, Kanak languages, Maori, Niuean, Rapanui, Rarotongan Maori, Samoan, Tahitian, Tongan & others)* • Spanish *(Castilian, also includes Catalan, Galician & Basque)* • Sri Lanka • Swahili • Thai • Tibetan • Turkish • Ukrainian • USA *(US English, vernacular, Native American, Hawaiian)* • Vietnamese

COMPLETE LIST OF LONELY PLANET BOOKS

AFRICA Africa on a shoestring • Cairo • Cape Town • East Africa • Egypt • Ethiopia, Eritrea & Djibouti • The Gambia & Senegal • Healthy Travel Africa • Kenya • Malawi • Morocco • Mozambique • Read This First: Africa • South Africa, Lesotho & Swaziland • Southern Africa • Southern Africa Road Atlas • Tanzania, Zanzibar & Pemba • Trekking in East Africa • Tunisia • Watching Wildlife East Africa • Watching Wildlife Southern Africa • West Africa • World Food Morocco • Zimbabwe, Botswana & Namibia

AUSTRALIA & THE PACIFIC Aboriginal Australia & the Torres Strait Islands • Auckland • Australia • Australia Road Atlas • Bushwalking in Australia • Cycling Australia • Cycling New Zealand • Fiji • Healthy Travel Australia, NZ and the Pacific • Islands of Australia's Great Barrier Reef • Melbourne • Micronesia • New Caledonia • New South Wales & the ACT • New Zealand • Northern Territory • Outback Australia • Out to Eat – Melbourne • Out to Eat – Sydney • Papua New Guinea • Queensland • Rarotonga & the Cook Islands • Samoa • Solomon Islands • South Australia • South Pacific • Sydney • Sydney Condensed • Tahiti & French Polynesia • Tasmania • Tonga • Tramping in New Zealand • Vanuatu • Victoria • Walking in Australia • Watching Wildlife Australia • Western Australia

CENTRAL AMERICA & THE CARIBBEAN Bahamas, Turks & Caicos • Baja California • Bermuda • Central America on a shoestring • Costa Rica • Cuba • Dominican Republic & Haiti • Eastern Caribbean • Guatemala • Guatemala, Belize & Yucatán: La Ruta Maya • Havana • Healthy Travel Central & South America • Jamaica • Mexico • Mexico City • Panama • Puerto Rico • Read This First: Central & South America • World Food Mexico • Yucatán

EUROPE Amsterdam • Amsterdam Condensed • Andalucía • Austria • Barcelona • Belgium & Luxembourg • Berlin • Britain • Brussels, Bruges & Antwerp • Budapest • Canary Islands • Central Europe •Copenhagen • Corfu & the Ionians • Corsica • Crete • Crete Condensed • Croatia • Cycling Britain • Cycling France • Cyprus • Czech & Slovak Republics • Denmark • Dublin • Eastern Europe • Edinburgh • England • Estonia, Latvia & Lithuania • Europe on a shoestring • Finland • Florence • France • Frankfurt Condensed • Georgia, Armenia & Azerbaijan • Germany • Greece • Greek Islands • Hungary • Iceland, Greenland & the Faroe Islands • Ireland • Istanbul • Italy • Krakow • Lisbon • The Loire • London • London Condensed • Madrid • Malta • Mediterranean Europe • Milan, Turin & Genoa • Moscow • Mozambique • Munich • The Netherlands • Normandy • Norway • Out to Eat – London • Paris • Paris Condensed • Poland • Portugal • Prague • Provence & the Côte d'Azur • Read This First: Europe • Rhodes & the Dodecanese • Romania & Moldova • Rome • Rome Condensed • Russia, Ukraine & Belarus • Scandinavian & Baltic Europe • Scotland • Sicily • Slovenia • South-West France • Spain • St Petersburg • Sweden • Switzerland • Trekking in Spain • Tuscany • Venice • Vienna • Walking in Britain • Walking in France • Walking in Ireland • Walking in Italy • Walking in Spain • Walking in Switzerland • Western Europe • World Food France • World Food Ireland • World Food Italy • World Food Spain

INDIAN SUBCONTINENT Bangladesh • Bhutan • Delhi • Goa • Healthy Travel Asia & India • India • Indian Himalaya • Karakoram Highway • Kerala • Mumbai (Bombay) • Nepal • Pakistan • Rajasthan • Read This First: Asia & India • South India • Sri Lanka • Tibet • Trekking in the Indian Himalaya • Trekking in the Karakoram & Hindukush • Trekking in the Nepal Himalaya

ISLANDS OF THE INDIAN OCEAN Madagascar &Comoros • Maldives • Mauritius, Réunion & Seychelles

MIDDLE EAST & CENTRAL ASIA Bahrain, Kuwait & Qatar • Central Asia • Dubai • Iran • Israel & the Palestinian Territories • Istanbul • Istanbul to Cairo on a Shoestring • Istanbul to Kathmandu • Jerusalem • Jordan • Lebanon • Middle East • Oman & the United Arab Emirates • Syria • Turkey • World Food Turkey • Yemen

NORTH AMERICA Alaska • Boston • Boston Condensed • British Colombia • California & Nevada • California Condensed • Canada • ...o • Deep South • Florida • Great Lakes • Hawaii • Hiking in Alaska ...g in the USA • Honolulu • Las Vegas • Los Angeles • Louisiana & ...eep South • Miami • Montreal • New England • New Orleans • ...ork City • New York City Condensed • New York, New Jersey & ...ylvania • Oahu • Out to Eat • San Francisco • Pacific Northwest • ...o Rico • Rocky Mountains • San Francisco • San Francisco Map • ...• Southwest • Texas • Toronto • USA • Vancouver • Virginia & the ...l Region • Washington DC • World Food Deep South, USA • World ...New Orleans

...TH-EAST ASIA Beijing • China • Hiking in Japan • Hong Kong • ...Kong Condensed • Hong Kong, Macau & Guangzhou • Japan • ...• Kyoto • Mongolia • Seoul • Shanghai • South-West China • ...n • Tokyo • World Food – Hong Kong

...TH AMERICA Argentina, Uruguay & Paraguay • Bolivia • Brazil • ...s Aires • Chile & Easter Island • Colombia • Ecuador & the Galapagos ...s • Healthy Travel Central & South America • Peru • Read This First: ...al & South America • Rio de Janeiro • Santiago • South America on ...oestring • Santiago • Trekking in the Patagonian Andes • Venezuela

SOUTH-EAST ASIA Bali & Lombok • Bangkok • Cambodia • Hanoi • Healthy Travel Asia & India • Ho Chi Minh City • Indonesia • Indonesia's Eastern Islands • Jakarta • Java • Laos • Malaysia, Singapore & Brunei • Myanmar (Burma) • Philippines • Read This First: Asia & India • Singapore • South-East Asia on a shoestring • Thailand • Thailand's Islands & Beaches • Thailand, Vietnam, Laos & Cambodia Road Atlas • Vietnam • World Food Thailand • World Food Vietnam

Also available; Journeys travel literature, illustrated pictorials, calendars, diaries, Lonely Planet maps and videos. For more information on these series and for the complete range of Lonely Planet products and services, visit our website at **www.lonelyplanet.com**.